Learn Object Pascal
with Delphi

Learn Object Pascal with Delphi

Warren Rachele

Wordware Publishing, Inc.

Library of Congress Cataloging-in-Publication Data

Rachele, Warren
    Learn Object Pascal with Delphi / by Warren Rachele.
      p. cm.
    ISBN 1-55622-719-1 (pbk.)
    1. Object-oriented programming (Computer science).   2. Pascal (Computer
program language)   3. Delphi (Computer file)   I. Title.

    QA76.64.R33   2000
    005.13'3--dc21   00-060032
                                                   CIP

ISBN 1-55622-719-1
10 9 8 7 6 5 4 3 2 1
0009

All inquiries for volume purchases of this book should be addressed to Wordware Publishing, Inc., at the above address. Telephone inquiries may be made by calling:

(972) 423-0090

Dedication

To David Hunter Rachele

He swings and hits a long one ...

Run, my boy, run.

Contents

Contents

Contents

Preface

"Why are you making us do this?" came the frustrated cry. It was quickly followed by the sharp report of a Pascal textbook slamming shut echoing off the walls of my classroom. "Nobody programs in Pascal anymore. I should be learning to program in C++ or Java, not this language that nobody uses," he said, looking directly at me.

Making sure that the question had garnered everyone's interest, I smiled and said, "Pascal is a strong, well structured, and strongly typed language that is ideal both for teaching and for creating robust, full-featured programs." They were still with me, so I continued, "Powerful, top-selling Windows programs such as HomeSite are built in Delphi. This is a fun language and we can have a good time exploring and learning how to write code using this easy to understand language and," I moved my eyes back to the original questioner, "lots of people use it."

Well, honestly, this might be more of a re-creation of the actual events, but certainly I had heard similar statements a number of times over the years. Recently, however, the cry had taken a new turn: "How much will I need these coding skills in the new era of programming?"

I thought about this as I prepared for a new semester. In the era of Delphi and Visual Basic and Visual this and that, should we even bother teaching coding anymore? The question on the surface might be a little extreme; of course we should be teaching programmers how to program, but how many of them need to know the fundamental control and logical structures, given the current trend toward point-and click-programming? I pictured someone sitting down in front of the Delphi IDE for the first time and opening the documentation to produce their first application. Drop a button on a form, add some text for an Edit box, and compile. The new programmer would certainly be impressed by what he could accomplish with a couple of mouse clicks. Within a couple of weeks he would have added some additional property assignments or method calls to the template-formed procedures that Delphi generated. The question nags though: would he be programming?

The applications created from this practice would indeed be nice GUI Windows applications, but real programming requires that you know the basic structure and syntax of your programs. I come from the camp that continues to support the building of a strong basic coding skills foundation. By learning these basics, my student programmer will be able to build any kind of program he or she wants to without being limited by the GUI or anything else. Any of the fantastic programmers who work in the gaming industry, or those who produce all of the amazing things we see on the Internet, or the geniuses who write operating systems for Sun or Microsoft all know this kind of code by heart. They too would say that you must start learning these basics of coding and you must keep coming back to them until you too know them by heart.

The maturing of the Delphi book market is bringing changes to the material available to the beginning programmer. The VCL is so rich that 1,000-page tomes can be written just teaching how all of the components fit and work together. Often, however, the page count is at the expense of fundamental Object Pascal coding instruction. The skills necessary for developing the underpinnings of something like Delphi are going wanting based on the assumption in the book market that readers already come to the table with the prerequisite coding skills. This book serves that group of the Delphi population who wants to learn how to program from the bottom up.

No Sleep 'til the Final Chapter

This book is not structured around some arbitrary and capricious calendar of activities such as "Learning Object Pascal While Your Laundry Dries." It is organized around specific programming skills. One builds upon the other in the sequence of chapters so, to loosely paraphrase what the King said to Alice, "Begin at the beginning and go until you reach the end." Don't hesitate to type the code in as you read it. Though it is all available on the companion CD-ROM, I have always found it to be more beneficial to actually see the code taking shape in the editor. By doing this I get the chance to play with the code and learn where the pitfalls are as I do so.

This book was purposely designed to have a textbook look and feel with the review questions and the exercises at the end of the chapters. Take a couple of moments to review these to ensure that you have learned the information that was presented. The Quick Check questions should be innate knowledge to any Object Pascal programmer so your answers should be sure and swift. If they are not, plan to review the information until they are.

The Test Your Knowledge exercises at the end of each chapter are designed to provide you with an idea for a program that will exercise the skills you attained in that chapter. There is always an easily accomplished project as well as a more formidable challenge. If you don't feel up to the challenge at first, put it aside until you have garnered sufficient experience. The more you code, the easier it becomes. On the other hand, working under a client deadline and trying to learn as you go is no fun at all and will not produce the top quality code for which you will eventually become famous.

Acknowledgments

All humble thanks goes to Him, who is the light by which I write.

A huge thank you to my wife, who exhibited more than her usual patience when her web site did not get updated on a regular basis. I would never have accomplished half of what I have without her love, support, and understanding.

I owe a big debt of gratitude to my students, who teach me something new about human nature every day. I learn as much from them as I hope they do from me.

I don't know how Jim Hill at Wordware manages to have so much patience but for it I am thankful. Charles Calvert at Borland taught me how to correctly write a computer book.

Though critics may be many, you can always count on your parents and grandparents to have a positive outlook on your work. My love and thanks go to David and Sharon Rachele and Raymond and Ruby Fowles.

Chapter 1

Getting Started with Object Pascal

As you thumb through the pages of this book a strange feeling grips you, a hesitance that you can't quite describe. Referring back to the title on the cover to confirm that it did mention Delphi you can't help but notice that there seem to be an awful lot of words in here with very few pictures of forms and components. In fact, many of the pages appear to be filled with some kind of sets of instructions. Pausing for a moment to take a deep breath you rifle through the pages again; slower this time, more deliberate. What kind of a Delphi book is this? One that takes a different approach than the others on the bookseller's shelf, one that will teach you to be a programmer.

Introduction

There are mountains of books about Delphi that will explain in infinitesimal detail how to utilize the Visual Component Library to build applications. Along the way you will encounter a smattering of code, tossed in here and there, just enough to support the components but not enough for the Pascal novitiate to get his feet wet past the ankles. The programmer who selects Delphi as a development tool often finds himself immersed in the visual environment without the necessary understanding of what is going on behind the scenes. This is not an acceptable situation if the programmer is ever to move beyond simply plugging together prebuilt components and clicking in values for the properties as needed.

Few of the many outstanding books currently on the shelves offer any introduction and training on the tenets of the Object Pascal language, the underlying code base for Delphi. The components are covered in depth along with the manipulation of properties and methods, but little material prepares the developer for meaningful use of the language to expand the depth and breadth of her programming efforts. Certainly the documentation that ships with the product is not bereft of this knowledge but it no longer serves it up in a tutorial style. All of the Object Pascal language specific information captured in this book does exist in some fashion in the help files and shouldn't be considered a substitute for the point-by-point support found there. Unfortunately, what you will find once you get there is a terse explanation and a snippet of code that is supposed to be a substitute for a full explanation of the programming construct or reserved word. Workable for the experienced programmer but not for the beginning developer.

This book strives to fill this niche. You will see very few pictures of the forms or VCL components in this book; those are amply covered elsewhere. What you will find is in-depth coverage of the Object Pascal language. The material is intended for those who have never programmed before or whose entire programming experience has been in the creation of Windows programs using visual components, their properties and the simple manipulation of the methods.

Why Bother with Object Pascal?

The simple answer to that question is because you've chosen to bother with Delphi. The long and complicated response is that the advantages of Object Pascal are often not well enumerated, while the rumors of its demise swirl fiercely through programming circles. These combined factors often lead to false impressions and misguided decisions. Being a Pascal supporter in any environment, whether it be academic or developmental, is often akin to being the kid with the balloon-tired bike while all of the other boys rode Sting Rays. They exclaimed over and over how their rides were better but they could never explain why... and strangely, all of you reached the Seven-to-Eleven (that's 7-Eleven for those of you under 40) at the same time.

Apart from COBOL, Pascal has been one of the more disparaged languages ever created. From the start it has been a middle ground language, falling between the everyman's simplicity of BASIC and the complexity and austerity of C. Pascal was designed from the ground up to be a fail-safe language, strongly typed and heavily structured to keep the programmer out of trouble while, at the same time, not hindering her progress. Much like the goals of later object-oriented languages, the initial design allowed the developer to concentrate on the development of a solution rather than the picayune details of the language or the emulation of logical structures.

While a great number of applications can be developed in Delphi without much programming, there will come a point at which the developer's career progression is stalled. Without knowing the underlying language of the visual tool, he will be forever trapped into using the components and methods developed by others. This might be satisfactory until that one day the components alone can no longer solve the problem. At that point the skin has to be pulled back to expose the Pascal statements that make up the instructions for the VCL. There's no getting around it—to be an effective programmer in the Delphi environment you must learn the basics of Object Pascal. Fortunately, the language itself was designed from the start to be learned.

A Little Historical Perspective

The Pascal language was developed by Professor Niklaus Wirth in Zurich, Switzerland, during the late 1960s and early 1970s. He was working on the committee that was designing the ALGOL language at the time. As that language description became more and more complex, Professor Wirth grew frustrated and made the decision to develop a much simpler language. He and his colleagues designed Pascal to be a good first programming language for those learning to program without limiting its capabilities. In addition to having a small number of commands and structures to learn, making it less intimidating, it was also known for directly implementing nearly every logical structure a programmer would need. This makes it significantly different from other languages that require the programmer to emulate some logical constructs when they aren't directly supported.

The design of the Pascal language by its very nature facilitates the writing of programs in what is recognized as good programming practice. Fundamental to the language is the requirement that all variables and other data objects be declared prior to their use in a program. This declaration has two parts, the name of the variable and the type of data represented by the variable. The logical flow of the Pascal language is constrained through the use of BEGIN and END statements. Nearly all of the logical constructs in the language are bracketed with a BEGIN and END pair, minimizing the programmer's ability to write spaghetti code. Pascal is not limited to educational pursuits; it is a general purpose computer programming language that is suitable for the development of a wide variety of applications. Scientific applications, programs for general business data processing, and even compilers have been written using Pascal. In fact, Delphi itself is written in Pascal, discounting discussion of the supposed limitations of the language.

Object Pascal is an extension of the original Pascal language that brings it into the modern era of object-oriented programming, or OOP. Object-oriented programming is an outgrowth of structured programming that improves the programmer's ability to model code around the real-life objects. We will discuss OOP in greater detail later on in the book. At this point it is better to examine the long-running internecine battle between the Object Pascal and C++ camps over which is the better language.

First I must say that I don't believe that any one language can claim a general superiority over any other. That kind of separation within the development community has raged forever and will probably always be around, resulting in hotly divided camps; even more so with the surge in the popularity of Java. The problem with this situation is that a lot of the support for one language or another is fueled by hearsay and wild speculation and is not based on fact. For Object Pascal programmers there are always going to be two hurdles to be surmounted in their support for the language. The first is the long-running falsehood that Pascal is only good as a teaching language and that no real programmers continue to use it after graduation. Well, the truth is, many programmers use Pascal in one form or another and in the Windows world, there are not many users who could identify the source code of the software they are using from looking at the interface. Object Pascal is designed around ease of use and clarity in the resulting code. If you are the kind of programmer to which the assembler or C++ hair shirt is a badge of honor, then these facts will fall upon deaf ears.

The second fallacy often tossed about with regard to Object Pascal is that it is an artificially limiting language. C++ programmers often defend their position with this falsehood when discussing the superiority of their chosen tool. Again, the truth of the matter is that Object Pascal, and especially the dialect used in Delphi, is more object oriented than C++ and it offers a much friendlier approach to this avenue when compared to the terse, punctuation-filled minimalist syntax of C++. To end this discussion and answer the question "what is the best programming language?" I say, as I say to my students, it depends.

Your choice of tools should not be made on the basis of the testosterone needed to work in the environment but rather on the outcome you want to achieve. No language is perfect for every single development effort or project. Each has strengths and weaknesses that the experienced business programmer will learn to apply when choosing the appropriate tool for an assignment. In your position as a beginning programmer or someone new to Delphi, you will find that the wide variety of components combined with the ease of use of the underlying language will allow you to winnow out some of the extraneous tools in your toolbox.

What to Do, What to Do...

Since we have some tacit agreement between us that you would like to explore programming in Object Pascal, that greatly simplifies my task. The pages that follow will focus exclusively on writing code in the Object Pascal language, specifically, the dialect used in Delphi. The topics will cover programming practices right up to the use and development of the visual components and then stop, leaving those to any number of the other fine books already available. So that you can plan your upcoming days and weeks, the coverage will break down as follows.

Chapter 1—Getting Started with Object Pascal

This chapter explains the layout of the book and the process that we are going to follow in learning to code in Delphi. The very first project that is going to be created is the building block for almost all that follow. Essential reading (since you're already here and should probably finish it!).

Chapter 2—Object Pascal 101

In this chapter we're going to start out by discussing the fundamental structure of an Object Pascal program and what goes into it. The compiler is explained as well as the resulting executable program. Finally, we round out the material by covering tokens, symbols, and identifiers.

Chapter 1

Chapter 3—Variables, Simple Types, and Operators

In the third of the foundation chapters we add to your programming skills by introducing constants and variables into the mix. Many of the Object Pascal data types are discussed here including integer, real, character, and Boolean data types. Finally, we are going to learn how to output data from our program.

Chapter 4—More Core

This chapter discusses how to gather input into your programs. Also discussed is the use of string data types and the development of your first larger scale programs. The chapter rounds out with a brief discussion of pointer, procedural, and variant data types.

Chapter 5—Making Decisions

This material probably will not help you in life with your decision-making capabilities but at least you will know what tools Object Pascal provides for choosing between alternatives. The control structures for building two-way branching or multiple branch decisions is discussed and demonstrated.

Chapter 6—Looping

Round and round she goes, where she'll stop nobody knows! Many programs require that sets of instructions be repeated indefinitely or, more commonly, a specific number of times. Object Pascal has a number of different constructs to facilitate this repeating of processes. An experienced programmer will recognize the differences between the constructs and select the one most appropriate to the task at hand rather than forcing all tasks to match up to a single loop structure.

Chapter 7—Procedures and Functions

This chapter marks a major turn in the structure of programs. Procedures and functions break up the larger program and unit files into smaller discrete development units. A discussion of the scope of variables is included to set the table for getting rid of the global variables used in the examples to that point in the book. Parameter passing is outlined as an alternative to passing data through the use of global variables.

Chapter 8—Units and Abstract Data Types

Two topics that don't really belong together but don't stand on their own either are covered in this chapter. Units are the libraries of an Object Pascal programmer. Correctly structured, a unit will enclose the classes that a programmer wants to make available to many programs and other programmers. Object Pascal provides the ability to make more complex data types from the simple data types that are natively supported, and the second part of this chapter covers how this is done.

Chapter 9—Arrays

Arrays are nothing more than organized collections of data but they are often not well understood. This material will introduce the structure in its simplest form and demonstrate the Object Pascal tools for working with the array and its contents.

Do you recall the movie *The Matrix*? Well, it doesn't have anything to do with this chapter but we will use the word. A multidimensional array allows the programmer to create complex tables of data for a program to work with. We will use the same tools described in the single-dimensional array discussion to create a structure with more depth and usefulness.

Chapter 10—Records and Other Data Structures

Similar to an earlier mention of utilizing simple data types to create new, more complex data types, the record will take the topic even further. Often made up of disparate data types, understanding the record is important to the development of more complex and useful programs. The record will then be put to use to implement two fundamental logical constructs, the stack and the queue.

Chapter 11—Introduction to Object-Oriented Programming with Object Pascal

Once the basics of the language have been established, we'll begin to explore placing them into an object-oriented wrapper. We will discover what classes are and how they are used. Object Pascal has exceptional support for object-oriented programming and the discussions in this chapter will mark another turning point in the learning process.

Chapter 12—File Handling and Pointers in Object Pascal

All of the programs that are created in the book up to this chapter are a bit ephemeral; that is, their data vanishes when the program is terminated. This process has limited appeal to most users since they have learned to expect that their work will be there the next time they fire up a program. This chapter will cover the file handling capabilities of Object Pascal so that our programs can save data from one session to the next. In this chapter, another that pairs two disparate topics together just for fun, we will also discuss the concept of pointers and dynamic data structures at the end of the file handling material. Though much of the memory management in modern programs is handled by the code libraries used to build your software, the topic of pointers is still an important one. We will look at what a pointer is and where it is appropriately used. The pointers are put to use with the building of a linked list. Along with the stack and queue, this structure ranks as one of the fundamental data structures that should be known by any Object Pascal programmer.

You will find that each of these chapters is structured in the same fashion, making the transition from one to the next easier and more productive. Take the time to design and develop the programs that are listed in the Test Your Knowledge section in each of the chapters. I think that you will find, as I do, that nothing beats learning by doing when trying to assimilate a new computer language. The solutions will give you an opportunity to cement the concepts from the chapter by using them in concert with those previously covered. They might take some time to do, especially in the later chapters, but the effort will be well worth it when you discover that you are able to select and implement the structures of your choice. If you choose not to spend your time typing the code for these applications, at least load the sample programs from the CD-ROM so that you can see their output and how they are assembled.

Getting Started

Your choice of current Object Pascal tools is more than likely going to be limited to the use of the Delphi compiler. Delphi 5.0 Standard is included on the book's companion CD-ROM to facilitate your learning, but all of the examples and assignments will also work in Turbo Pascal 7.0 if you still have this compiler available to you. The use of a DOS compiler in these learning stages might make the process slightly simpler because there are fewer steps involved in the creation of the programs but these are not a major drawback. It is likely that your preference will be to use Delphi since that probably drove your decision to pick up this book in the first place. In light of this we are going to look at the creation of character-based applications in the Windows environment. In any case, unless otherwise noted, the examples will compile equally well in either environment.

CRT Applications with Delphi

Delphi recognizes the character based programs that we are going to experiment with as console applications and has a relatively straightforward method of creating them. A Delphi console application consists of a code file without the graphical elements. The steps that are detailed in the following paragraphs will set up a Delphi console program that can be saved as a template for use in the remainder of the exercises. It is not necessary that this be done, but you will simply have to repeat these steps for each of the sample programs as you work your way through the book. (In other words, you might want to give it serious consideration.)

The applications that you are going to create are programs that run from the DOS prompt within a DOS window. The programs will not use any of the Delphi components and they display only a text interface. When compiled, the programs are going to be told to use DOS input and output commands only, which will not work in the Windows GUI. By not involving any of the components at this point you are going to be free to concentrate on the code itself rather than the interface aspects of the program. Fortunately, making the jump from these programs to a Windows application will be at light speed because Delphi makes the development of the graphical portion of a program a snap.

NOTE: The following step-by-step instructions for creating the console application assume that you have installed Delphi onto your development system. If you have not done so yet, complete instructions are included at the back of the book. Refer to that section and complete the installation of the compiler before going any further.

The Object Repository

The Object Repository is a tool included within the Delphi IDE that makes it possible to not only share forms, dialog boxes, and data modules but also create templates for your projects to be reused again and again. We are going to take advantage of this ability and create a template for a console application that can become the starting point for all of the sample programs in this book. Once saved into the repository, accessing the template is a simple point-and-click operation. The repository itself is a text file named *DELPHI32.DRO* that exists in the BIN directory. This text file contains references to the items that appear in the Object Repository and New Items dialog boxes, a sample of which is shown in Figure 1-1.

Figure 1-1: The New Items dialog box

Building the Template

The template that we will add to the Object Repository is nothing more than an empty shell. For this reason, you will not find any commentary on the coding of the program or an explanation of the inner workings. That will come in the next chapter. For now our task is to create a template and successfully add it to the repository. To begin, start Delphi. You will find yourself faced with the default project as shown in Figure 1-2.

1. Close the form by clicking on the Close button (the X) in the upper right-hand corner of the form. This will expose the default *Unit1.pas* file shown in Figure 1-3.

2. Close this unit window by the same method; click on the Close button. A dialog will appear asking if you want to save the changes to *Unit1.pas*. Answer **No** to this. This will leave you with only the menu, the VCL, and the Object Inspector on the screen.

Figure 1-2

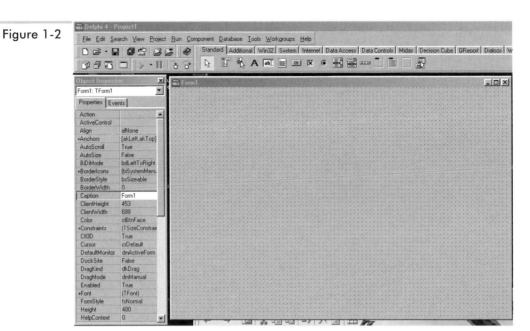

Figure 1-3

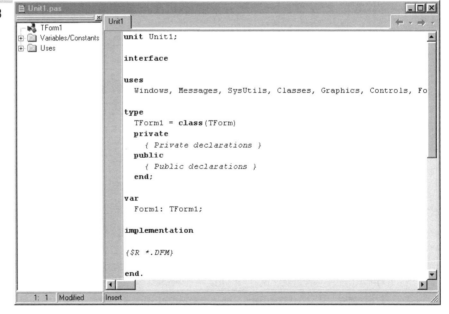

3. Select **Project -> View Source** from the menu. This will expose a window containing the main module for the program. The window is shown in Figure 1-4. The next few instructions are going to involve editing the contents of this file. Use your mouse to position the pointer within this window if the cursor is not already there.

Figure 1-4

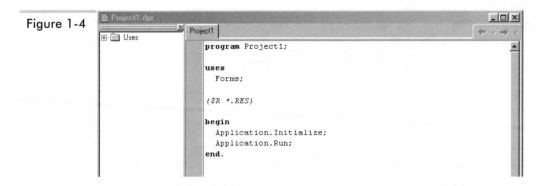

4. Move the cursor to the word Project1 and delete it. In its place, type the word **foo**.

5. Delete the lines that read

```
uses
   Forms;
{$R *.RES}
```

6. Delete the lines that read

```
Application.Initialize;
Application.Run;
```

7. The edited program file should match that shown in Figure 1-5. If not, go back over your work and locate the error.

Figure 1-5

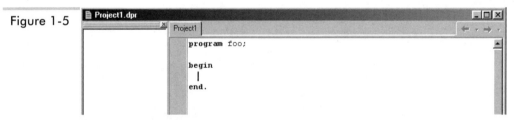

The details of the next step may differ slightly based upon the decisions you made when installing the Delphi compiler. By default, the Delphi installation program will place the program files in the C:\Program Files\Borland\Delphi4 folder. Within this folder, the executable files of the compiler are stored in the BIN subfolder and the files referred to by the Object Repository are maintained in a subfolder called Objrepos. If you installed the Delphi compiler in a location other than this default folder you will need to adjust your navigation accordingly when performing the file-save instructions.

8. Select **File->Save Project As** from the menu. The project files are going to be saved into a folder of their own called ConsApp within the Objrepos folder. The Save Project As dialog is shown in Figure 1-6. If your environment is Windows 98, you can use the Create New Folder button to simply add the ConsApp folder once you have navigated to Objrepos. Save the project and you will then be returned to the Delphi IDE. Once you are in the desired folder, change the name of the project

to *foo* from *Project1*. Leave the file type at Delphi Project (*.DPR) as shown and click on **Save**.

Figure 1-6

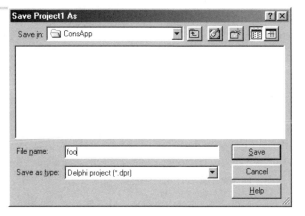

The next step in this process is especially critical to the success of the project. The applications produced by Delphi are normally GUI based and their input and output is directed through controls on the application's interface. With a console application we must use a different approach to collecting and disseminating data from the command line. The Delphi compiler must be told to recognize this fact during the compilation process and the next step will ensure that this occurs. Though this is only one way to inform the compiler of our intentions, it is the simplest and least intrusive into our learning process.

9. Select **Project->Options** from the menu. The Project Options dialog will be displayed. At this time we are only interested in one of the tabs shown, the Linker tab. Click on this tab and check the box that reads Generate Console Application as shown in Figure 1-7. Click **OK** to save this configuration information.

Figure 1-7

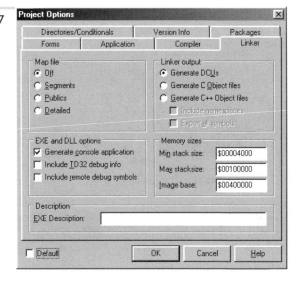

10. Save the project a second time.

You now have a template that will form the basis for development of the sample programs. Using this form you will be able to concentrate on learning the syntax rather than the mechanical process of building the application within Delphi. Now, we are going to add this project to the Object Repository.

Adding the Template to the Object Repository

The Delphi IDE puts templates for forms, projects, and other objects at your fingertips through the Object Repository. We are going to use this feature to our advantage by adding the Console Application template we just completed to the repository. By doing this you will be able to simply select the template from the Object Repository dialog when starting work on one of the sample programs.

1. If the *foo* project has been closed, reopen it. From the menu select **Project->Add to Repository....** The Add to Repository dialog shown in Figure 1-8 will appear. Add the values that follow to the dialog.

Title:	Console Application
Description:	Template for console application
Page:	Projects
Author:	Your name here!

The icon that you select is up to you. Two quick sources for icons within the Delphi folder structure start with the Objrepos folder itself. Another location that will provide icons is C:\Program Files\Borland\Borland Shared\Images\Icons, again based upon the assumption of a default installation. Click **OK** to save your addition to the repository.

Figure 1-8

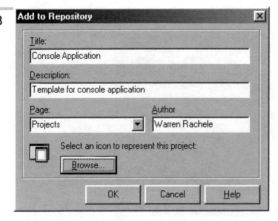

2. Let's confirm that all of the steps have been successful. Click on **File->Close All** from the menu to clear the current project. Select **File->New** from the menu to show the New Items dialog box. Click on the **Projects** tab where the Console Application item should be displayed. Figure 1-9 shows what you are looking for. Double-click on the icon for the console application or select it and click **OK**. You

will be asked for a new location to create the project in. Navigate to another directory and click **OK**.

Figure 1-9

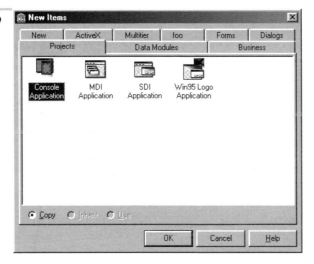

NOTE: If you type in the name and path of a new folder in the Select Directory dialog box, Delphi will create it for you if it does not exist.

If all of the previous steps have been successful, you should be staring at your application template, ready to work. Be sure that when you save the samples that you give them a new project name.

The Command Line Alternative

Creating programs within the IDE is not the only way to generate a Delphi application. An Object Pascal command line compiler is included with the product that allows you to create the source code files in a separate editor and then compile them without entering the Delphi IDE. You can use the DOS Edit text editor to create these files or use another programmers text editor such as Visual SlickEdit by MicroEdge, Inc. A programmers editor is designed to work apart from the visual environment when necessary and will speed the process of developing these programs by allowing you to link the program and the command line compiler into the same environment. You might find this a little less unwieldy when compared to firing up the Delphi IDE and following all of the above steps for a ten-line program. On the other hand, when the programs get a little longer the syntax checking and highlighting features in the Delphi editor pay big dividends to the programmer, so take that into consideration.

A major consideration in working from the command line is the path and how it is set from within the operating system. The default Delphi installation will point the path to the BIN folder where the compiler is located but if you have modified any of the settings during the installation process this may not be the case. A quick test will evaluate what your next step is. Go to the DOS prompt by selecting Start->Programs->MS-DOS Prompt or restarting in MS-DOS Mode. At the DOS prompt type DCC32. You should see the following output: "Borland Delphi Version 12.0 . . ." followed by a dizzying array of command line switches. If this is the case, your path is correctly set and you can ignore the rest of this section.

On the other hand if you receive a disturbing message along the lines of "Bad command or File Name" you have some further work to do. The first thing that you should examine is your typing. Be sure that you typed the command correctly. If you did and still get an error message, then we must examine your path statement. From the same command prompt type the word Path and press Enter. Examine the path statement that is returned to see if your Delphi\Bin directory is included. Figure 1-10 shows a non-standard installation of the Delphi compiler and the type of statement for which you are looking. No reference to the directory indicates a need for some additional work. Remember that the long filename support in Windows 95/98 will not exist in the DOS environment and your path could easily resemble something like "C:\Progra~1\ Borland\Delphi~1\bin," so look carefully.

Figure 1-10

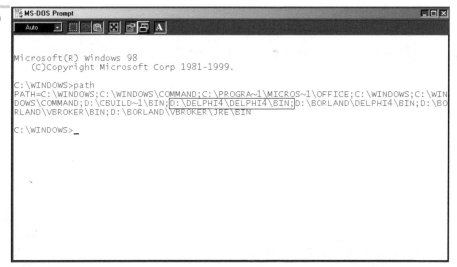

There are a couple of ways in which the path can be modified. The first approach involves editing the Autoexec.bat file for your system. This is easily accomplished in two steps.

1. If you are not there already, go to the DOS prompt. Change to the root directory of your computer by typing **CD C:** at the prompt and pressing **Enter**.

2. Type **edit autoexec.bat** at the prompt and press **Enter**. This will open the Autoexec.bat file in the DOS Editor. You will be looking for a line that begins with "SET PATH = ." If this line exists, you may append the path to your BIN folder to the end of this statement. Be sure to add a semicolon at the end, keeping in mind the limitations of the long filename mentioned above.

If for some reason your Autoexec.bat file does not contain a path statement, you may add one by typing the following line:

```
SET PATH = C:\progra~1\borland\delphi4\bin;
```

Remember, this path is dependent upon a default installation of the product. If you modified the installation directories your path should reflect these differences. Reboot your computer after making these changes.

NOTE: Note that this method of setting the path applies to Windows 95/98 based machines. Windows NT will require a different method altogether. The path in an NT environment can be examined and modified through the Environment tab of the System control panel applet. Your ability to change the values in this environment are controlled through your access security and you may need to approach a system administrator for help with this process.

One other alternative presents itself for handling the issue of the path, and that is the development of a batch file that can modify the path when necessary for development work. This uncomplicated batch could be run before starting your development sessions to temporarily set the path to accommodate the command line compiler. Building this batch file is as simple as the Autoexec.bat modifications discussed above.

1. Type **edit chgpath.bat** at the DOS prompt and press **Enter**. The DOS editor will start an empty file named chgpath.bat. The batch file will consist of a single line that reads:

```
set path=%PATH%;C:\progra~1\borland\delphi4\bin;
```

2. Select **File->Exit** from the menu and respond **Yes** when prompted to save the file.

The only drawback to using this batch file method is that you will need to be located in the same directory when you call the file or provide a fully qualified path and the batch filename to start it from a different directory. This alone might prompt you to reconsider the modification of the Autoexec.bat file.

Compiling from the Command Line

You may compile Object Pascal programs from the command line whether you have created them through an external editor and they have the .PAS extension or through the IDE and they carry an extension of .DPR. The method will be the same for either file. Once the path is established, the process is straightforward.

1. Go to the DOS prompt and change directories to the folder that contains your source file. (This is not a requirement but it will make for a cleaner command line. If you ignore this step, all references to your source code file must be fully qualified (i.e., path included)).

2. Type the following at the DOS prompt:

```
dcc32 -cc appname
```

Appname, of course, will be the name of your source file. The extension is not necessary as the compiler will reject any file type that it does not recognize.

The dcc32 command starts the Delphi command line compiler. It will create an executable file from your carefully crafted source code. The -cc option is a crucial part of this command line as it tells the compiler that you're creating an executable destined for use at the command prompt. The program will then know to expect input and output at the DOS prompt. If your source code contains no errors, your DOS window should appear similar to Figure 1-11. You could then execute the program by typing its name at the prompt. If any errors were encountered during the compilation process, they would be listed after the line that reads "Borland Delphi Version 12.0...." Each error would indicate the line on which it was found, making your debugging process much easier.

Figure 1-11

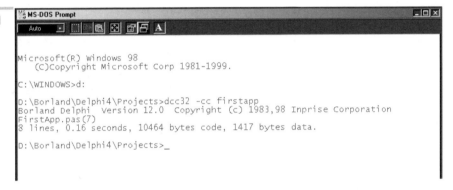

Each of the methods outlined on the previous pages has its pros and cons and each is appropriate in different circumstances. Consider these when selecting which route you want to take. The examples that follow in the book will work either way but the focus will be on development within the IDE environment using Delphi's editor and menus. The main reason for this will be the use of the debugger, a tool that will be discussed in detail in the coming chapters.

Compiler Options

A compiler often makes available a vast number of options for compiling the final executable product. In Delphi, these options are controlled through option settings in the IDE or through a program line called a *compiler directive*. Either way that these instructions are set, it is important to understand that these are directions for the compiler, not your program. They tell the Delphi compiler to treat your program statements a certain way or produce a specific type of output. There are three types of directives: switch directives, parameter directives, and conditional directives. Compiler directives can be inserted directly into your code in the form of a special comment. (Comments will be covered in more detail in the coming pages.) The comment takes the form:

```
{$A+}   or   (*$B+*)
```

A dollar sign ($) immediately after the opening brace or parenthesis-asterisk combination tells the compiler that this is a comment that needs to be interpreted. If you are going to use the command line method detailed above you can also specify the compiler directives on the command line in the form:

```
DCC /$A+ aprog
```

Many of the compiler directives can be set through a dialog box in the IDE. Figure 1-12 shows the dialog that is presented when you select Project->Options and then select the Compiler tab. Using this dialog, you can set the directives by checking or unchecking the boxes. Unless specifically directed in the pages of this guide it is unlikely that you will be modifying the values in this dialog or adding any directives on your own. Most of these are used in advanced programming situations beyond the scope of this book.

Figure 1-12

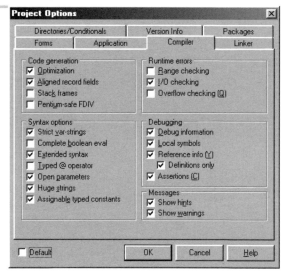

Moving Forward

Hopefully you're as ready as I am to get going. Remember that the title of this book is not *Learn Object Pascal in Thirty Minutes!* Take your time and work through the examples so that what you're reading has a chance to filter down to your fingertips. If my examples don't make any sense to you or you feel that additional input would help cement a point, don't hesitate to look up the topic in the help files or any other source you have at hand. Good luck.

Chapter 2

Object Pascal 101

Key Concepts

- The structure of an Object Pascal program
- Writing and compiling your first program
- Object Pascal tokens

Introduction

Welcome to Object Pascal 101—class is in session. The first couple of chapters in this book are going to introduce you, through words and examples, to the foundational concepts of writing programs in Delphi. Your work will cover small, manageable sections of the topic and the book will support you through examples and exercises. Though it might be tempting to bypass this basic information and utilize these initial chapters as references, I encourage you instead to learn this how and why material now. Doing so will benefit you later in the book when you will be able to avoid having to stop and research a fundamental concept in order to assimilate more difficult information. The groundwork is going to be built from these Object Pascal concepts:

- You will know and understand the structural requirements of a simple, structured Object Pascal program.
- You will learn how to build, compile, and execute an Object Pascal program from within the Delphi IDE.
- You'll understand what Object Pascal tokens are and how they fit into the structure of a program.

When you have finished reading and absorbing this chapter, test your knowledge by considering and answering the questions at the end of the chapter. This basic material serves to develop an important structural reference in your mind and you will want these topics to be automatic so that you can concentrate on the logical constructs discussed in the following chapters. This knowledge will also expose you to

19

the potential problems that could appear in your programs and save you from some of the frustration of trying to debug a mysterious problem during the learning process. If this is your first experience programming, take your time and have fun. Remember, nothing you will do with a program will hurt the machine so don't be afraid to experiment to see how something works. If you are moving to Delphi from another language, skim through the material and associate your knowledge base with the new requirements of Object Pascal.

Getting Started

In general, Pascal has a well-deserved reputation for being among the most highly structured of computer languages in use today. This fact is certainly not accidental. The strictly structured aspects of the language were a design decision based on fundamental tenets of the language: allow the user to learn computer programming within a protective environment that reinforces good programming practices while not limiting the capabilities of the resulting software. Pascal and its extended cousin Object Pascal have succeeded at all of these goals and remain true to them to this day. Delphi is the latest incarnation of this fun, vibrant, and growing language wrapped up in a fantastic development environment.

Object Pascal Program Structure

Pascal programming can be very, very simple.

```
program Howdy;

begin
  writeln( 'All Hail Manowar');
end.
```

These four lines of code represent a fully formed Object Pascal program. The results are not spectacularly useful but the program does serve to provide us with a framework for discussion. All Object Pascal programs will share this required structure so once it is established in your mind, though the number of statements will increase the complexity, you will easily be able to understand the logical flow of any set of statements. This said, our work begins by an examination of this basic syntax. The word "syntax" is used frequently in any discussion of programming and it deserves to be carefully defined. The syntax of a programming language describes the rules for writing and punctuating each statement within a computer program. This is the grammar of the language and it includes both the logical statement and the declaration of other objects.

The syntax of an Object Pascal program states that every program must start with a line called the *program heading*. In the case of our example above, the line

```
program howdy;
```

is an example of this type of statement. This line consists of the reserved word `program` followed by an identifier that provides the name of the program. The line is then punctuated with a semicolon. Punctuation in any programming language is very important to the proper operation of the compiler; in Object Pascal, the semicolon delineates one statement from the next. When the compiler reads, or parses, this statement it knows upon reaching the semicolon that it can now consider the collection of words logically to determine if they are meaningful in the context of the language.

Especially meaningful within a computer language are a collection of words that have special, specific meanings that can only be interpreted one way. These are known as *reserved words* because their use is controlled by the language. (See Appendix A for a list of reserved words in Object Pascal.) This means that they cannot be used for any other purpose in a program without being misconstrued. For example, we could not name this program *program* as shown in this line:

```
program program;
```

The compiler will read this line as having the reserved word `program` written twice and will generate an error message reminding us of this fact.

Building Your First Program

Rather than reading about a simple program, there is probably more benefit to building one as we talk. To begin, we are going to use the template that was constructed in Chapter 1. If you didn't follow through with that project, you need to go back and quickly build it. Don't worry; we'll wait. Start Delphi and follow along with the step-by-step instructions as we construct a very simple Object Pascal program, compile it, and execute it. Don't be concerned with the lack of explanation for the pieces of the language that we are utilizing in this example; they will all be fully explained in the coming pages. Our concentration here is with the structure of the program itself.

1. From the menu select **File->New**. The New Items dialog will be displayed. Select the **Projects** tab from within this dialog; you should see the Console Application icon that we added in the last chapter. Click on this item and then click on **OK**.

2. A dialog requesting the location for your new project is displayed. The book will follow a consistent structure in locating the files for each project. Under a general folder called BookProj, a folder for each chapter will be created. You might want to follow the same naming convention to keep your projects separate and easy to locate. If you select a different naming scheme, be sure that it is easy to remember so that you don't have to spend hours later searching for your projects or cleaning up.

    As shown in Figure 2-1, the name of the folder you want to use can be typed into this dialog box if it does not exist and you cannot navigate to it. If the folder you want to use does not exist, the dialog will create it for you. Once the loca-

Figure 2-1

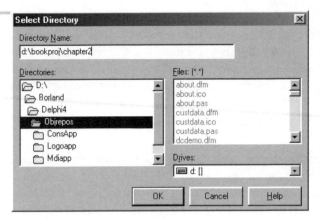

tion is decided upon, click OK to move to or create the directory. You must take one further step when working with the template—you must rename the copy you are going to use. The template process makes copies of all of the necessary files from the Object Repository to your new location but they all carry the template's original name. To create a new name for the files, select **File->Save Project As...** and give the project a new name. In this example, we will name it *Howdy*. Compare your screen to Figure 2-2 below.

Figure 2-2

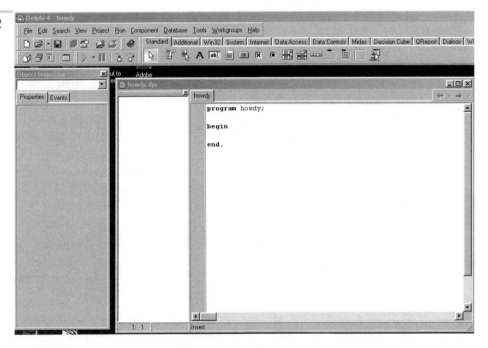

3. Add the line shown below to your program. The statement is shown in the format that this book will follow in the ensuing chapters. All programming statements will be offset and indented from the text and will appear in a different typeface.

```
writeln('All Hail Delphi on Mount Parnassus!');
```

Be sure that when you type this statement into your program that you observe all of the punctuation carefully. The quotation marks used must be single quotes and

Chapter 2

neglecting to add the semicolon at the end of the line will cause an error to be generated. Errors in the code will prevent the program from compiling and running.

4. Save the program by either clicking on the diskette icon on the toolbar or by selecting **File->Save** from the menu.

5. Now for the moment that you have been waiting for! Running the program from within the IDE is a matter of clicking a key or selecting a menu item. The program will be compiled and then executed automatically. From the menu select **Run->Run** and watch as your program executes.

If your program is correctly structured and runs, a DOS window containing the output of your program will be quickly displayed as shown in Figure 2-3. It will also just as quickly vanish and you will be returned to the IDE. This points to an anomaly of working on console applications within the IDE that needs to be mentioned. The design of the integrated development environment seeks to return you to your development tools upon reaching the end of an executing program. A program such as our example will run to completion, remove the window from the screen, and place you back at the editor as fast as you can snap your fingers. There are a couple of approaches to working around this.

Figure 2-3

The easiest way to accommodate your desire to watch the execution of this console application is to slightly modify the program. The change is going to be a simple modification to the code block, once we discuss what a code block is. A *block* is a statement or a compound statement enclosed within a BEGIN/END pair. Our block right now consists of the lines:

```
begin
   writeln('All Hail Delphi on Mount Parnassus!');
end.
```

The statement enclosed within the BEGIN/END pair is considered by the compiler to be one logical block. There can be numerous statements between the BEGIN and END delimiters but the compiler will still logically associate them together. Because these reserved words BEGIN and END delineate a program block, they must always be found in a program in pairs. In other words, there cannot be a BEGIN without a corresponding END or vice versa. A hint to remembering this is to notice that there is no punctuation after the BEGIN, only after the END telling the compiler that the two go together.

The program block that we are working with right now is unique within an Object Pascal program as it is only seen once throughout all of a program's code. What sets this block apart is the punctuation after the END keyword. A period after the END indicates to the compiler that this is the final statement in the program and is required in every program. All other BEGIN/END pairs within a program will be terminated with a semicolon. Using this block, there is a simple modification that will enable you to view the results of your program. To do this, modify the block to read as follows:

```
begin
  writeln('All Hail Delphi on Mount Parnassus!');
  readln;
end.
```

Adding the readln; statement creates a *compound statement*, a block that contains more than one individual program instruction.

Save your work and then run this version by pressing F9 (Run). This time you will have a chance to view your handiwork for as long as you like. Though we have not discussed writeln and readln yet, we can see that the former sends data to the screen. The readln statement is waiting for input from you in the form of a keystroke. In this case striking any key will return you to the IDE. We will be covering these statements and their usage in greater detail in the coming pages.

The Compiler

The word "compiler" has been mentioned numerous times in the past few pages of this book but it has not been explained yet. A *compiler* is a tool that translates a high-level language such as Object Pascal to a machine language that the CPU can understand. In order for the CPU to process an instruction such as adding two numbers together it needs to receive a set of instructions that resembles

```
0110 1001 1010 1111 0001
```

because the CPU only works in the realm of ones and zeroes. This binary notation doesn't make for a terribly productive programming environment. Because human beings (well, most of them anyway) don't work well by speaking in this numeric tongue, there is a language that is one step above this on the evolutionary scale, assembly language.

The equivalent assembly language statement to add our two numbers together would be similar to

```
ADD X Y C
```

which translates into "add the contents of memory location X to the contents of memory location Y and place the result in memory location C." This is a little closer to the comfort zone of most people but it is still very difficult to work with. Assembly language also requires that it ultimately be compiled, or assembled, into machine language that can be processed by the CPU. One important facet of both assembly and machine language that separates them immediately from high-level languages is that they are processor dependent. The instructions that a programmer knows for one processor will not necessarily work for any other processor.

A high-level language is one that is designed for the comfort of the human beings using them. Their syntax is designed to be read and written by people and then translated by a tool called a compiler into the machine language needed by the CPU. Our addition problem written in Object Pascal is much easier to comprehend:

```
C := X + Y;
```

The statement uses words and symbols that are meaningful to people and is much easier to write and read back than the previous examples. The output from the Delphi compiler takes the source program that we provide, as in the example that we have been building, and compiles it into an executable program. An executable program is one which the operating system recognizes as able to run on its own within the environment.

The Executable Program

The other way of seeing this program run is to execute it within its target environment, the operating system. The Run command that was used earlier to execute the program within the IDE also served to compile the code into an executable form. The file *howdy.exe* was placed by default in the working directory that you had stored your code in. Using the Windows Explorer, as shown in Figure 2-4, navigate to the folder in which your project is stored. The executable program can be started by double-clicking it or right-clicking and selecting Open from the context menu. Either way, the program will execute in a DOS box and then clear from the screen. Since this is a console application intended for execution at the command prompt we should try to run it from there.

Figure 2-4

Go to the DOS prompt by selecting MS-DOS Prompt from the Start menu. Depending on the configuration of your environment, this may open within a window as shown in Figure 2-5 or it may open to the full screen dimensions. Either way, the program will work the same way. Once again, you must make your project folder the current directory in order to execute the program. Type the name of the program at the command prompt, as shown in the example. It will execute and return you to the prompt as shown in Figure 2-5. This last example gives you a number of options for running the sample projects in this book. It is likely that you will want to simply run them within the IDE so that you can quickly get back to working on the project but it is good to know your options.

Figure 2-5

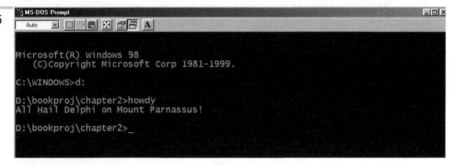

Program Crashes

The preceding pages have all operated on the assumption that everything worked perfectly; positive thinking at its best. Even within the confines of a one-line program many errors can crop up. The most common errors encountered at this stage of programming are either misspellings or missing punctuation. In Figure 2-6 on the following page, notice that the `writeln` statement has been intentionally misspelled. In attempting to compile the program, Delphi was unable to identify the meaning of this new word and therefore could not finish its task. The compiler returned an error message which is displayed at the bottom of the code window. Notice that it also gives you the line number on which the error was encountered. In attempting to help the programmer correct errors, Delphi has placed the cursor in the code window on the spot at which it located the first error.

Figure 2-7 displays the same program with a more extensive error list. This is an example of how a single mistake can generate multiple messages. In the program the single quotes were exchanged with double quotes, a very common error for beginning programmers coming from other languages. Clearing either of the types of errors we have encountered here is a matter of going back to the identified error and modifying your code to meet the compiler's requirements. Though we are focusing on simple syntactical errors here we will cover logical errors as the topics advance throughout the book.

Figure 2-6

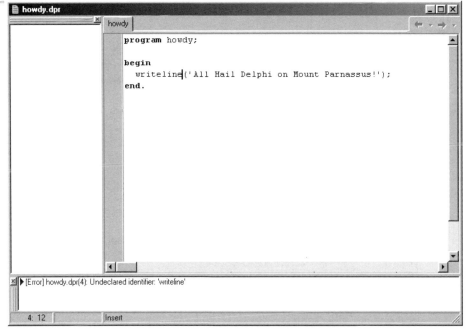

Figure 2-7

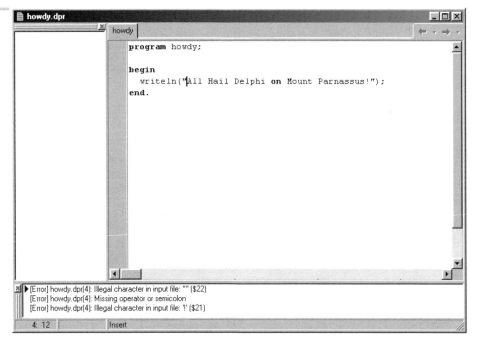

Tokens and Separators

Now that you have had an opportunity to write your first program we'll further our exploration with an examination of some additional core knowledge. Object Pascal programs are composed of only two things—tokens and separators. The separators are easy to understand; they are either blank spaces or comments, leaving everything else to be considered a token. The token is the smallest meaningful unit in an Object Pascal program and they fall into the following categories:

- Symbols
- Identifiers
- Labels
- Numbers
- Character strings

Is it necessary to start our exploration of the language at such a low level? A survey of this basic information will prove to be beneficial because the structure and rules of Object Pascal are easily demonstrated and understood on this micro level. By implanting these facts early, the programmer in training will develop a much greater sense for what works and what doesn't. We will examine each category to understand how it is described and where it fits within the context of a program, starting with the symbols.

Symbols

All of the text that you will enter in the process of creating your Object Pascal programs will utilize the characters described below. Each of the groups is composed of a subset of the ASCII character set. Symbols that are not identifiable to the Object Pascal compiler will be flagged as being in error.

Letters

All of the letters from A to Z, both upper- and lowercase, are valid for use in forming key words or identifiers. Object Pascal is not case sensitive, so a lowercase "a" or an uppercase "A" will be considered to be the same letter in the view of the compiler.

```
COMPILE
Compile
compile
```

are all the same word when compiled as a part of a program.

Digits

Numbers are represented by using the digits 0 through 9 and combinations of them as appropriate.

Hex Digits

Hexadecimal digits in the base 16 counting system are represented using both letters and digits to form the number. To explain hexadecimal numbering, look at the similarities and differences with the base 10 numbering system, the one that we are most familiar with. This is a positional numbering system with each column representing multiples of the previous column. Put another way, the number 837 represents 7 ones, 3 tens, and 8 hundreds. The counting digits count from zero to nine before incrementing the column to the left.

Hexadecimal numbers work in a similar fashion but they have 16 counting digits in each column. The characters that represent the hexadecimal digits are 0, 1, 2, 3, 4, 5, 6, 7, 8, 9, A, B, C, D, E, and F. Decimal 28 would then equal 1C hex meaning one sixteen and 12 ones. Hexadecimal is used in computing quite often because it can quickly be translated to and from binary, the base 2 number system that the machine understands.

Blanks

Blank spaces can include more than just the true ASCII blank character, ASCII 32. Also considered to be a blank space are all of the ASCII control characters, ASCII 0 to ASCII 31. These control characters include the carriage return (ASCII 10) and newline (ASCII 13) characters.

Certain ASCII characters have special meaning within an Object Pascal program. Table 2-1 shows these symbols and identifies their use. In addition to single characters, you can see from the table that certain pairs of characters also hold special meaning within the context of your code. We will discuss these characters again with an explanation when we get to the point of putting them to use.

Table 2-1: Symbols that have special meaning in Object Pascal

Symbol	Meaning
+	This operator serves two purposes; it concatenates two strings or serves as the addition operator with two numerals
–	As an arithmetic operator it serves to subtract one numeral from another. It also performs pointer subtraction and acts as the difference operator between two sets.
*	The asterisk is the multiplication operator.
/	The slash is the real type division operator.
=	The equals sign alone tests for equality.
<	The less than symbol tests to determine if one operand is less than another operand.
>	The greater than symbol tests to determine if one operand is greater than another operand.
.	The period (dot) is used as a decimal position within numerals and separates qualifiers when used with identifiers.
,	The comma is used to separate items within a list.
( )	The parentheses are used mathematically to group statements and also indicate the beginning and the end of parameter lists.

Table 2-1 (cont.): Symbols that have special meaning in Object Pascal

Symbol	Meaning
:	The colon is also a separator. It separates identifiers from types in a number of different contexts.
;	The semicolon serves to terminate a statement.
^	The caret is the pointer dereference operator.
@	The "at" symbol returns the address of a variable.
{}	Comments are enclosed between left and right braces.
$	The dollar sign prefix used with a numeral tells the compiler that this is a hexadecimal number. This symbol is also used to indicate compiler directives.
#	The pound symbol within a string tells the compiler to translate the integer immediately following it as a control character.
<=	This relation operator represents a test for less than or equal to.
>=	This combination represents greater than or equal to.
:=	The colon / equal sign combination is the assignment operator.
..	The symbol created by two consecutive periods is used when defining membership in sets. It is shorthand to indicate all of the ordinals between operand A and operand B.
(* *)	Comments are enclosed between left and right parentheses-asterisk combinations.
//	Text following the double slash to the end of the line is considered a comment.
[]	Square brackets are used in a couple different contexts. When defining a string variable, the length of the string is set between two brackets. In the context of an array, the index is defined between the brackets.
(. .)	The parenthesis-period combination is the same as the square brackets.

Identifiers

Identifiers are the names that the programmer gives to things in an Object Pascal program. These include storage locations, subroutines, and separate files that are compiled together to create the executable program. The primary requirement of an identifier is that it be unique within its range of usage. While we will discuss the concept of scope fully on later pages, for the time being, the rule that we will operate by will be that two identifiers cannot share a name. All identifiers must be unique.

When you create an Object Pascal identifier, it must start with either a letter or an underscore. After the first character, the identifier can be composed of letters, digits, or underscores. No other punctuation characters or spaces can be included within an identifier. The identifiers can be as brief as a single character or as long as you care to make them. Be aware, however, that Object Pascal considers only the first 255 characters significant in differentiating identifiers from one another.

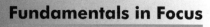

Fundamentals in Focus

Object Pascal is pretty picky about how you form your identifiers. Fortunately, the rules are fairly simple: 1. Start identifiers with only an underscore or a letter. 2. Only letters, digits, or underscores can be used to compose the identifier. Look at these examples.

```
X          TotalSales        _START        end_of_year
```

These are all valid identifiers. What about some that don't make the cut?

```
1x         Total Sales       START.PROG       %ofSales
file       sub-total
```

Hey, what's wrong with `file`? Another requirement of the identifier is that you cannot use a keyword, an identifier that is reserved by Object Pascal. There is a complete list of keywords in Appendix A at the back of this book. Can you identify the problems with the others?

Labels

Labels, as a token, not a component or property, are used in conjunction with the GOTO statement to redirect the flow of your code. While this practice has its place, it is generally a frowned upon programming structure when there are a number of other ways to accomplish the same logical flow. A label can be any valid identifier or four-digit number that is in a range between 0 and 9999.

Numbers

Object Pascal supports a wide range of numeric formats from short simple integers to huge numbers described in complex scientific notation. The following Fundamentals in Focus section lists the two most common numeric formats that you will find your programs working with, integer and real. Real and integer constants are represented by ordinary decimal notation. Hexadecimal values are written in alphanumeric notation and prefaced with a dollar sign ($). Scientific notation, a.k.a. key notation, represents times 10 to the power of in real types.

Why are there so many numeric formats? The easy answer is that there are differing needs for precision and magnitude in representing numerical data. The same can be said for the difference between integer and real data. The magnitude of each type of integer or real number type is driven by the physical amount of memory used to store the number. This is described by the number of bits that are available in the numeric format from which to create values. What are bits then?

The numbers that we utilize in our daily lives are more often than not decimal numbers, or numbers based upon the base 10 numbering system. The internal representation of a number within the computer does not have the luxury of a base 10 system as it only has two digits to work with, 0 and 1. This is due to the binary nature of the machine itself. A computer is built around two discrete states: on or off. To encode data within the computer, these binary digits (0 being off and 1 being on), or bits, are combined into units known as bytes. We will work with 8-bit bytes as the basis for our discussion.

The base 2 number system works on the principle of powers of 2. In Figure 2-8 we see an example of a byte. Just as with decimal numbers, the byte values grow from right to left. Using this single byte we can count from 0 to 255 by using each column to represent an increasing power of two. For example, to represent the number 241, we add columns as follows:

```
128 + 64 + 32 + 16 + 1 = 241
2^7 + 2^6 + 2^5 + 2^4 + 2^0 = 241
```

The bit representation, following the columns shown above, would be:

```
1 1 1 1 0 0 0 1
```

The minimum and maximum values of this byte are then determined by the number of bits available. With all of the bits turned off, or set to zero, the byte will equate to zero:

```
0 0 0 0 0 0 0 0 = 0
```

Figure 2-8: The byte storage unit

128	64	32	16	8	4	2	1
0	0	0	1	0	0	0	1
2^7	2^6	2^5	2^4	2^3	2^2	2^1	2^0

17 decimal = 0001 0001 in base 2

Counting in decimal and base 2

Base 10	Base 2
0	0000
1	0001
2	0010
3	0011
4	0100
5	0101
6	0110
7	0111
8	1000
9	1001
10	1010
11	1011
12	1100
13	1101
14	1110
15	1111

Likewise, setting all of the bits to one will add up to 255:

```
1 1 1 1 1 1 1 1 = 255
```

The shortint integer type shown in the chart appears to have a considerably smaller magnitude than we just described for an 8-bit number. The reason for this is that it can represent both positive and negative numbers. This is known as a signed integer. In order to accommodate the sign in any size of a signed number, one bit must be devoted to representing the sign, leaving n–1 bits available for representing the number. In the case of the shortint, one bit is utilized for the sign, leaving seven bits that determine the magnitude of the number. Referring back to the byte shown in Figure 2-8 it is easy to see why the maximum positive magnitude is 127. The leftmost bit is used to store the sign, with a 0 being positive and a 1 being coded as negative. This leaves the remaining seven bits to represent the number $(n - 1)$:

```
0   1 1 1 1 1 1 1
```

equates to

```
+   64 + 32 + 16 + 8 + 4 + 2 + 1 = 127
```

The negative numbers are derived through a rather non-intuitive process that utilizes two's complement notation. To explain this concept we need to establish one point of fact to begin. The byte

```
1 0 0 0   0 0 0 0
```

equals –128 and this value is utilized in every equation that determines a negative number. If a signed byte has a 1 in the sign bit, then you calculate the value of the integer by reading the remaining seven bits as normal for a positive number and then subtracting 128 from that number. For example, to represent the value –1 the byte would appear like this:

```
1 1 1 1   1 1 1 1
```

The bit sign equals 1 so the remaining seven bits are computed to equal +127. The equation used to derive the answer would be $(64+32+16+8+4+2+1)-128$. This also explains why the negative side of a signed data element is always one higher than the positive side. The byte

```
1 0 0 0   0 0 0 0
```

is the equivalent of saying $0 - 128 = -128$.

Fundamentals in Focus

How high can they go? Different forms of numbers and types have different ranges, or magnitudes, that they are capable of representing. This is due to their storage formats, or the number of bytes used to hold the data element, and whether or not the number is signed.

Integer Type	Range
shortint	–128 .. 127
smallint	–32768 .. 32767
longint	–2147483648 – 2147483647
byte	0 .. 255
word	0 .. 65535

Real Type	Range
real	2.9×10^{-39} .. 1.7×10^{38}
single	1.5×10^{-45} .. 3.4×10^{38}
double	5.0×10^{-324} .. 1.7×10^{308}
extended	3.4×10^{-4932} .. 1.1×10^{4932}
comp	$-2^{63}+1$ .. $2^{63}-1$
currency	–922337203686477.5808 .. 922337203685477.5807

Examples of the usage of these data types will be seen in the coming pages.

Character Strings

The character string in Object Pascal is a collection of zero or more characters surrounded by single quotes. The quotes encapsulate the ASCII characters so they are not interpreted by the compiler keeping combinations of letters, digits, and other characters from generating errors. The character string is measured in terms of the number of characters it contains, the measure being known as its length. Object Pascal also allows these character strings to contain embedded inline control characters from the ASCII control set. These control characters, carriage return and line feed for instance, are interpreted when they are sent to the output device, not by the compiler.

The character string with nothing between the quotes is known as the null string. Object Pascal uses the single quotes as delimiters for the compiler, serving much the same purpose as the semicolon; they tell the compiler not to worry about the contents and to consider the string as one object. This makes the compiler picky about where it finds the single quote character. A common problem in an Object Pascal program is a programmer's attempt to include a single quote within a character string such as seen here in the word *programmer's*. In order to do this, the programmer must actually place two sequential single quotes within the string. The last example in Table 2-2 demonstrates what is needed to overcome this.

Table 2-2: Character strings

String	Notes
''	Null string.
'Character String'	Regular character string.
'EOL#10#13NewLine'	Character string with embedded control characters.
'You''ll See'	The two consecutive embedded single quotes results in an output string of You'll See.

Comments

Earlier in this chapter we established that an Object Pascal program was composed of tokens and separators. The separators were segmented into two groups, spaces and comments. Spaces are easy enough to understand; they are all the white space between all of the other characters. Comments perform a different task; they are intended to provide annotation to a program. You will add these to your programs to provide explanation and clarification, and in general to make your programs easier to understand. Object Pascal supports three different sets of characters to tell the compiler that the text that follows the comment marks or is enclosed within the comment marks represents a comment and is not to be compiled. Any comment that is prefaced by a dollar sign ($) immediately after the opening brace is viewed as a compiler directive. These instructions are specific to the compiler that you are using.

Fundamentals in Focus

Comments

Programmers add comments to their programs to document the code. This documentation benefits the coder when her memory fails or when she gets promoted and leaves the program to her replacement.

Object Pascal supports a number of different formats for comments.

```
{ This is a comment within curly braces. This type of
comment can span numerous lines.}

// This type of comment only goes to the end of the line

(* This is the same as the curly braces *)
```

Summary

We have taken the first steps in our exploration of programming in Delphi, just enough to get a taste of what is involved in building an Object Pascal program. The fundamental structure of an Object Pascal program was examined in both the theory and application by building and then examining a short sample program. By learning the most basic aspects of program construction in this chapter we will be free to concentrate on the new syntactical elements introduced in each chapter. You also learned what tokens are and how they fit into the overall structure of your program. To review and test your knowledge of these concepts, why not take a few minutes and check your comprehension of the following questions before moving on to the next chapter.

TEST YOUR KNOWLEDGE

1. Which of the following are valid identifiers?

X_1	ABC123z8	Big Bonus	%change
Data-Good	Y	z.555	1Volume

2. What are tokens? What is represented by the following Object Pascal tokens?

    Symbols
    Identifiers
    Labels
    Numbers
    String constants

3. Write out the basic structure of an Object Pascal program. You may want to use pseudocode (English-like statements that describe the logic of a program). Be sure that you place the appropriate punctuation at the end of each line.

Variables, Simple Types, and Operators

Key Concepts

- Understanding constants and variables
- Understanding the differences and usage of the integer, real, character, and Boolean data types
- Outputting statements using write and writeln

Introduction

You will spend a good amount of time working through the text and exercises in this chapter and when you're done, you will have developed a comfortable facility with the following Object Pascal concepts:

- Your programs will put `integer`, `real`, `character`, and `Boolean` data types to work in Object Pascal programs.

- You will recognize the difference between the basic data types. Using this information you will be able to select the most appropriate data type to use when solving a problem.

- You will gain experience in using both `write` and `writeln` for output and understand the fundamental differences between the two.

- Through examples and practice you will develop your skills in formatting output statements.

As we saw in the last chapter, each of these topics will be introduced and reinforced through the use of examples, supporting tables, and the sparkling text that accompanies each concept. Even if this is not your first time working with Delphi or the Object Pascal language, take the time to work through the code so that these simple tasks become automatic. Remember that these code building exercises are second nature to truly advanced programmers and they have become a natural part of their vocabulary. Building and retaining this knowledge level lets you concentrate on solving problems rather than on the implementation of the code.

Variables and Constants

Variables and constants are the two Object Pascal data structures that you will probably use more than any other. These objects are used to hold values during the execution of your program. The distinction that must be drawn between the two is that values in the variable can change during the execution of the program, while the value in a constant is fixed and cannot be modified. We will start by looking at the more stable of the pair, the constant.

The Constant

A *constant* is used in your program to hold an unchanging value that is used throughout your program. The constant data object is used rather than repeatedly entering a value that is used by the code. As an example, consider a reporting program that produces management reports for a company on a daily basis. One of the requirements for the banner heading at the top of each of the hundred or so reports is that it include the name of the company, as in:

ENORMO CORPORATION DATA PROCESSING

DAILY PRODUCTIVITY REPORT

....

The name of the report will be different in each case but the corporate name should remain consistent. If the reporting program produces 100 or more reports, that would mean that the corporate name would be used 100 or more times within the program. The programmer might elect to type the name into the code as a part of the program. The pseudocode—pseudocode is a way of writing programming statements in plain English so that the focus is on the logic of the program rather than the particular syntax of a computer language—for this solution might appear as follows:

```
START Productivity Report
New Page
Set PageNumber to 1
Set LineCount to 0
PRINT "ENORMO CORPORATION DATA PROCESSING"
PRINT "DAILY PRODUCTIVITY REPORT"
....
END Productivity Report
START Management Wish List Report
New Page
Set PageNumber to 1
Set LineCount to 0
```

```
PRINT "ENORMO CORPORATION DATA PROCESSING"
PRINT "MANAGEMENT WISH LIST REPORT"
....
END Management Wish List Report
......
```

Following this pattern, the programmer will have to type the same group of words more than 100 times. This leads to the possibility that he will produce some inconsistencies within the program. The first ten times he will produce the correct corporate title, "ENORMO CORPORATION DATA PROCESSING," without problem. But if he begins to code the eleventh program at 4:55 in the afternoon he might easily substitute "ENORMO CORP DP" in the heading in order to be out of the parking lot at 5:01. The recipient of this particular report might take umbrage at this slight.

The value of a constant is set once in a program and then remains unchanged throughout the execution of the program. Once set, the value of the constant can be used to produce consistent results or output. In the case of the reporting program, the use of a constant, CORP_HEADING, would produce consistent headings on each report.

```
CORP_HEADING = "ENORMO CORPORATION DATA PROCESSING"
START Productivity Report
New Page
Set PageNumber to 1
Set LineCount to 0
PRINT CORP_HEADING
PRINT "DAILY PRODUCTIVITY REPORT"
....
END Productivity Report
START Management Wish List Report
New Page
Set PageNumber to 1
Set LineCount to 0
PRINT CORP_HEADING
PRINT "MANAGEMENT WISH LIST REPORT"
....
END Management Wish List Report
......
```

Though the example uses an alphabetic constant, it works equally well for numeric values such as tax or pay rates, cost of items, etc.

As we see from the pseudocode example, when a constant is defined within a program the identifier can be used in place of the value anywhere throughout the program. Defining the constant is simple.

```
program constant;
const
```

```
CORP_HEADING = 'ENORMO CORPORATION DATA PROCESSING';

var
  ...
```

The `const` keyword tells the compiler that the statements that follow are constant definitions. This block is placed at the top of the program, prior to any variable declarations. The identifier is followed by an equal sign and the value that you want to assign. The value can be either a fixed value, as shown in the example, or an expression that can be computed by the compiler prior to executing the rest of the program. Once this constant is defined, anywhere the identifier `CORP_HEADING` is used throughout the program, the value ENORMO CORPORATION DATA PROCESSING will be substituted.

A quick program will demonstrate this facility. It is composed of just a few lines but it will give you the opportunity to work with the constant object.

1. Create a new project by select **File->New** from the menu. Click on the **Projects** tab of the New Items dialog and select **Console Application** from the panel.

2. When prompted for the project directory, modify the folder name to reflect Chapter 3. If you are following the convention that we established in Chapter 2, the folder will be D:\bookproj\chapter3.

3. Save the project as *constant.dpr* by selecting **File->Save Project As**.

4. Type the program exactly as shown in Figure 3-1.

Figure 3-1

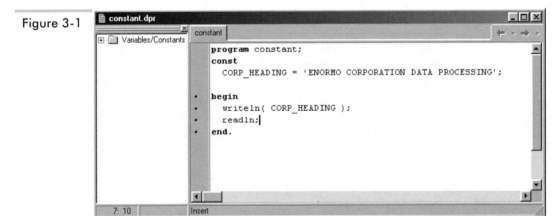

When you execute the program, be prepared for the fireworks! The program will provide the value assigned to the constant anywhere in the program that the constant is used, whether once or a hundred times.

The real payoff from the use of constants occurs when a modification needs to be made to the value in `CORP_HEADING`. Rather than having to search and replace every instance of ENORMO CORPORATION DATA PROCESSING in the program, the programmer simply modifies the value bound to the constant. Once that change is made and the program is compiled again, the change is instantly propagated throughout the program.

The Variable

Variables take an entirely different approach to data handling. Rather than having their value fixed throughout the program, they allow the program's statements to modify their values as needed. A *variable* is a named spot in memory into which our programs can store values during the execution of a program. The value in the bucket can be used alone or in combination with other values while the program is running but it is erased once the program terminates. Though this usage sounds a lot like the constant that we just discussed, the names of these two data objects do reveal their intended task; the constant contains a value that cannot be changed during the execution of the program while the variable expects to be modified as the program runs. So what do variables look like to the computer?

A variable is composed of two parts, an identifier and a data type. The *identifier* is the name by which the variable will be known within the program and it must follow all of the rules we outlined in the previous chapter. The *data type* tells the compiler what types of values are allowed to be placed into the variable bucket. Object Pascal is extremely picky about this subject due to its design as a strongly typed language. This means that when you define a data type for a variable the compiler is going to enforce that choice and not allow you, or anyone else, to place any other kind of data into that variable. Simply put, the data type tells the compiler that either numeric, alphanumeric, logical, or some other type of recognized data items are going to be allowed in that variable. We are going to explore data types in great detail in the coming pages.

A variable declaration is converted by the compiler to a named location in memory. Every time the program is executed, a new space in memory is identified and named. When the variable is used, the value is stored in this memory location. The size of this memory location is determined by the data type assigned to the variable. We will start exploring the variable with a short program.

1. Create a new project by selecting **File->New** from the menu. Click on the Projects tab of the New Items dialog and select **Console Application** from the panel.

2. When prompted for the project directory you are going to continue to use the folder named Chapter3. You will receive a confirmation dialog this time out because the files from the template (*foo.dpr*) already exist in this folder. Go ahead and replace the files since you are going to rename the project.

3. Save the project as *variable.dpr*.

The code for this sample program is shown in Figure 3-2. Type the program and save your work and then let's discuss some of the new things we see in this program.

Figure 3-2

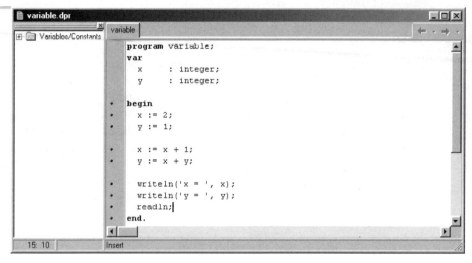

```
program variable;
var
   x       : integer;
   y       : integer;

begin
   x := 2;
   y := 1;

   x := x + 1;
   y := x + y;

   writeln('x = ', x);
   writeln('y = ', y);
   readln;
end.
```

The first thing that we need to address is the addition of a new block of statements:

```
program variable;
var
   x    : integer;
   y    : integer;
....
```

Immediately following the program header statement is the reserved word `var`. This statement tells the compiler that all lines that follow until the `begin` reserved word are going to be variable declarations. All variables used within this program must be defined in this block or the compiler will not recognize them. In the coming chapters we are going to see how it is possible and even desirable to declare variables in multiple places but for now we are going to only declare them once. Following the `var` statement are the declarations used in this program:

```
x    : integer;
y    : integer;
```

Each of these statements is composed of three required parts and all of your variable declarations will follow this same template. The first part is the identifier, or name of the variable. In our examples we use the simple x and y as the names of our variables. Once established, these are the names by which the program will refer to the variable's memory space. The second part is the required punctuation, a colon. Finally, following the colon is the data type. We have declared both of these variables to be of the type `integer`.

An integer is a whole number, one with no decimal portion. More important than what we have selected in this example is how the Object Pascal compiler treats this declaration. By telling it that we wish to use x and y as integer variables the compiler has reserved a very specific amount of memory for each of them. Once this has been established, the compiler will hold us to our word and only allow us to assign integer values of a specific range to these variables. This means that the variable buckets will hold the values 1, 10, or 100 but will reject the values of 11.56 and 34.99 as these do not meet the requirements of an integer value. Once again, this is the design of the compiler in being strongly typed. Not all computer languages have this requirement. Once the variables have been declared we can utilize them in the body of the program.

The body of the sample program is very simple but it effectively demonstrates the basic usage of the variable. The first two lines in the body

```
x := 2;
y := 1;
```

are called assignment statements. The combination of the colon and the equal sign (:=) is called the assignment operator. It assigns the value on the right side of the statement to the variable on the left side of the statement. In the case of the two lines shown the assignment statements read "take the value 2 and place it into the variable x" and "take the value 1 and place it into the variable y." If we could peek into memory and see the variables, they would appear as shown in Figure 3-3.

```
x := 2;
y := 1;
```

X
2

Y
1

Figure 3-3: The x and y variables in memory after assignment

In the next pair of lines the program makes use of the variable's ability to accept new values to replace the current residents during execution of the code. The lines

```
x := x + 1;
y := x + y;
```

are going to perform both retrieval and replacement of the values in the variables. Though an expression is involved, both lines remain simple assignment statements. The Object Pascal compiler will always resolve the expression to the right of the assignment statement before making the actual assignment. In the case of the first line, the expression x := x + 1 will be processed by retrieving the value in the x variable, 2, and then adding 1 to that value. The sum of the expression, 3, will then be assigned into the x variable, replacing the original value. This sequence is shown graphically in Figure 3-4.

```
x := 2;
```

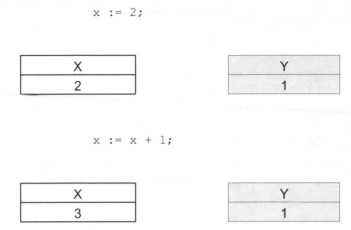

```
x := x + 1;
```

Figure 3-4: Processing the expression x + 1

The next two lines of the program body

```
writeln('x = ', x);
writeln('y = ', y);
```

display the final contents of both of the variables after all of the processing is complete. The output is shown here in Figure 3-5.

Figure 3-5

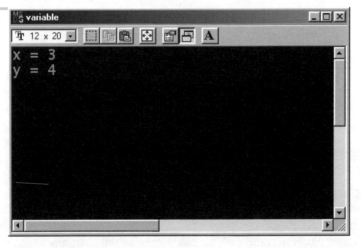

Is the result what you expected? The values contained in each variable remain in memory even though it appears that we have pulled them out for display. This means that they are available for use in any further computations necessary in the program. The fact that the variables shown retain their value requires that you as the programmer keep track of the values and their state as you write the program. Since the variable is not going to be reset on its own, the requirement lies with you to manage it. Keeping track of the state of your variables is a crucial skill for the programmer, one that is necessary to ensure that undesirable results don't creep into your software.

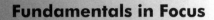

Fundamentals in Focus

Initializing Variables

Until your program places a value into a variable, it has no value. This statement on its face seems to make sense, but computers can make fools of us all. When a program is executed, it places its imprint on the shared memory locations in RAM. When you close the program, those memory locations are simply released to be used by another program; they are not cleaned up in any way. When you start another program and that software assigns its variables to those old memory locations, the values that were already in memory will suddenly come seeping back into your current program. If you don't initialize your variables, setting their values to zero, or a blank in the case of character data, you might be surprised at what they contain the first time they are used.

Some languages automatically initialize variables when they are declared but Object Pascal is not one of them. Even if the variables are not initialized in the examples in this book, you should develop the habit of initializing all of your variables. (Do as I say, not as I do?)

Variables and constants are workhorse objects in any Object Pascal program, and we will use them extensively throughout the coming pages of the book. Remember that the object's job is precisely parallel to its name, and vice versa. The value of a constant will remain unchanged through the execution of a program, while the variable can be modified an infinite number of times as the program runs. We will see both of these objects in numerous new situations as the complexity of the programs increases, but their fundamental jobs remain the same. As this chapter continues we are going to look at the basic data types that are assigned to the variables and constants.

Getting the Message Out

The Write and Writeln Statements

In order for your message to be conveyed to the world, one of the primary requirements of any program is that it contain some type of output statement. This exercise doesn't always have to take the form of a screen display. Output can take the form of displaying characters on the screen, paging your screen to a printer, saving your name list to a file, or sending weather data to a serial port. Since most of the software that you are going to write in Delphi is going to have a graphical interface, your output statements will direct their data to components on your interface forms or some other output mechanism such as a file or communication port. In order to focus on the code without the hindrance of the interface, all of our output is going to be sent directly to the screen using the `write` or `writeln` procedure. We have used this procedure in all of the sample programs developed so far and the time has come to explain its usage.

The syntax for the `write` procedure is as follows:

```
procedure write([var F:Text;], P1 [, P2,...,Pn)
```

If you have not worked with a syntax diagram previously, and even if you have, the procedure description as shown can be somewhat confusing. This type of syntax definition is what you will find in the help files and in Borland's documentation and it presents all of the possible options that can be used with the function or procedure. The punctuation used in the description adds to the clutter in the name of clarification. In the syntax description the use of square brackets `[]` indicates an optional parameter. Consistent with the examples that we have used thus far, a single parameter is all that is required to use the `write()` procedure as indicated by the `P1` parameter. When an appropriately formatted parameter is left out of the optional `F`, or `File` parameter, as in the line

```
write('Output');
```

the output is directed to the default `Output` variable. Object Pascal has two default system variables called `Input` and `Output` that represent the standard I/O files for the environment. In this case, the `File` parameter is pointing to the screen for the output of the `P1`, `P2`, ... , `Pn` parameters.

The `Px` parameters represent the values, constants, or expressions that represent the desired output. You can output a simple character or a string of characters as in

```
program ase;
begin
  write('A');
  write(' string example');
end.
```

that will result in the output shown in Figure 3-6.

Figure 3-6

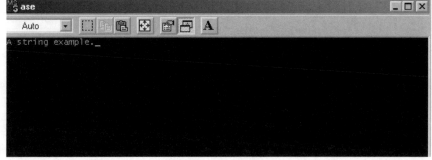

In either case, whether `character` or `string`, the write statement simply forwards the constant value provided to the screen. The actions of the statement are no different when a variable is used. In the following example, a value is assigned to the variable x, followed by the variable x being passed as the parameter to the write statement.

```
program ase2;
var
  x     : string;
begin
  x := 'American Spectator';
  write( x );
end.
```

outputs what is shown in Figure 3-7.

Figure 3-7

Another Form—The Writeln Statement

An extended form of the Object Pascal `write` statement is the `writeln` procedure (the suffix "ln" is pronounced "line"). The extended form serves the purpose of adding a carriage return/line feed pair of characters to the end of the output. To modify our earlier example, we are going to change the `write` statements to `writeln` statements:

```
program ase;
begin
  writeln('A');
        writeln('string example');
end.
```

The output from this version of the program, shown in Figure 3-8, demonstrates the change in the output when `write` is changed to `writeln`. A carriage return/line feed pair is composed of two characters, ASCII character 13 and ASCII character 10(0D0Ah).

Figure 3-8

It is appended to the end of the values that are output when the `writeln` procedure is used. The CRLF (carriage return/line feed) characters are ASCII control
characters that will not appear on the screen. The control characters used in this
context provide formatting instructions to the display subsystem of the operating
system. Notice that the cursor is moved to the next line after the words "string
example" are written, setting up the position for the start of your next output statements. When you are trying to determine which of the two forms of `write` to use
in your program, take the time to examine the planned output from your program
so that your code generates the layout you are looking for. (You do have a plan,
don't you?)

Another subtle property of the `writeln` procedure is that it can be used in a program without specifying any output parameters. When issued without parameters
the result is a blank line being written to the output device. For example, the following snippet adds a blank `writeln` to the mix:

```
writeln('A');
writeln;
writeln('string example');
```

This additional statement modifies the output to appear as follows:

```
A

string example

_
```

The empty `writeln` statement places the blank line between "A" and "string
example."

QUICK CHECK

Using either `write` or `writeln` to output the following data elements, what
would the resulting output look like? Use one output procedure for each element.

a)   'A' 'B' 'C' 'D'

b)   'A' 'Simple Plan'

c) 'The' 'total = :'

d) 'MountainHomeGuide.com' 'PO Box 3682' 'Evergreen,CO'

Data Types

Object Pascal is known as a "strongly typed" language. This means that each data object, such as the variables we have seen, must have its data type defined prior to use. With the exception of one specific data type (`variant`) this type cannot be dynamically modified during the execution of the program. Once a variable has been declared as an integer, for example, this variable cannot be modified as the program runs to accept real or character values. Programmers have debated this approach since day one, some arguing for more flexibility while the other camp supports this rigid structure as necessary to quality programming. Whichever direction you lean in, this strong-typing requirement usually turns out to be a positive aspect of the language. Because of this design decision, the compiler can do a much more effective job of validating your code and preventing logical errors that would pop up at run time.

A data type describes the contents of a data object, defining what it will hold. The type determines the values that are acceptable for that container and the operations that work upon that data. Data types fall into two broad designations, fundamental and generic. Fundamental data types do not change across all of the implementations of Object Pascal. They are independent of the CPU and operating system on which the code is compiled. Generic data types are affected, in terms of their range and format, by the underlying CPU and operating system. When designing software for a specific platform, the best performance will be generated through the use of generic data types. Carefully consider compatibility issues when your data will be used in cross-platform situations.

Data types in Object Pascal are classified into six categories: simple, string, structured, pointer, procedural, and variant. We are going to focus on the simple types in this chapter with the remainder seen in the coming chapters of the book.

Simple Data Types

Simple data types are so called because they are ordered collections of discrete values. This class of data types is further sub-divided into two categories, ordinal and real.

Ordinal Data

Ordinal data is that in which each value in the data collection has a fixed and predetermined position in the set. Each value within the set, except for the first, has a specific predecessor and all items except for the last have a unique successor. An integer is a good example of an ordinal data type. The value "9" is always preceded by the value "8" and succeeded by the value "10." You can see that given an ordinal value, it is easy to deduce the predecessor and successor from your understanding of the data set. For example, if you are given the statement x = 'D', you can determine that x - 1 will result in 'C' based only on your knowledge of the alphabet. This ordering is determined by the properties of the character set on which the list is based. Ordinal data in Object Pascal includes `integer`, `character`, and `Boolean` data types.

Integers

The integer is a predefined data type in Object Pascal. An integer is a whole number, a number without a decimal point in it.

   1   100   863   32,101   −9

are all integers. The following numbers:

   .55   −999.87

are not. An integer in Delphi is stored as an exact number, and the range of values is dependent upon the number of bytes used to store the data. Fundamental integer representations that are supported in Delphi include `shortint`, `smallint`, `longint`, `byte`, and `word` with the generic integer types being `integer` and `cardinal`. The latter pair will offer the best performance for the underlying CPU and operating system. Refer to Table 3-1 to see the range of possible values for each of these representations.

Table 3-1: The range of values for real and integer data types

Integer Type	Range
shortint	−128 .. 127
smallint	−32768 .. 32767
longint	−2147483648 .. 2147483647
byte	0 .. 255
word	0 .. 65535

Real Type	Range
real	2.9 x 10-39 .. 1.7 x 1038
single	1.5 x 10-45 .. 3.4 x 1038
double	5.0 x 10-324 .. 1.7 x 10308
extended	3.4 x 10-4932 .. 1.1 x 104932
comp	−263+1 .. 263-1
currency	−922337203686477.5808 .. 922337203685477.5807

Let's put the integer to work in a sample program. Start by creating a new project called *learnint*. Add the following code to the project and then save your work:

```
program learnint;
var
        i        : integer;
        s        : shortint;
        w        : word;
begin

     i := 32767;
  s := 32;
  w := 32767;

     writeln('integer     : ', i);
     writeln('shortint    : ', s);
     writeln('word        : ', w);
end.
```

The program simply displays the contents of the variables after values have been assigned to them through the use of the assignment operator. Attempting to assign a value outside of the recognized range for the variable type will result in an error as shown in Figure 3-9.

Figure 3-9

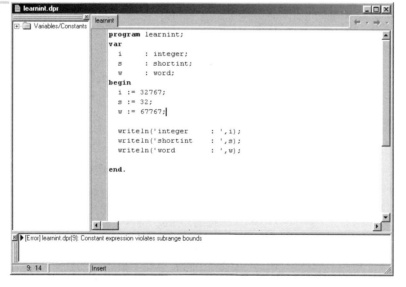

An interesting occurrence is seen when an equation modifies an integer variable so that the value exceeds the range of the variable. Modify the *learnint.dpr* project to appear as it does in the following listing:

```
program learnint;
var
     i        : integer;
     s        : shortint;
     w        : word;
```

Chapter 3

```
begin

    i := 32767;
    s := 32;
    w := 65535;

    writeln('integer    : ', i);
    writeln('shortint   : ', s);
    writeln('word       : ', w);

    w := w + 3;
    writeln('New word val : ', w);
    readln;
end.
```

Note that the maximum upper range value of the word variable is 65535. This is determined by the number of bytes (2) used to store the variable, making it a 16-bit variable. The word type is an unsigned integer with a range of positive values from 0 to 65535. The assignment statement that was added sums 3 and 65535; as a programmer you would expect an error to be generated from the value 65538. Run the program to see if this is the case. What you will find in fact is the assignment statement will result in the value 2 being displayed. The variable has looped around itself and moved three spots up in the ordinal listing of numbers. If you are not aware of this peculiarity, debugging programs that display this behavior could become very tricky.

Character

Character data includes the letters, numerals, punctuation marks, and graphics characters of the character set being utilized by the operating system. Character data in Object Pascal is only stored in variables of type char. A char variable holds a single character which could include the characters

A   c   ?   9   £

but not

And   987   ...

Using character data in an Object Pascal program is nearly the same as the integers previously discussed. Build the following example program called *learnchr.dpr* to experiment with the character data type:

```
program learnchr;
var
    ch      : char;

begin
    ch := 'A';
    writeln( ch );
```

```
    readln;
end.
```

Notice that the assignment of the character requires the use of single quotes around the character value. Character data is also categorized into fundamental and generic types. The fundamental character types in Object Pascal are `AnsiChar` and `WideChar`. `AnsiChar` data is byte sized and follows the ANSI character set while `WideChar` data is word sized. The generic character type is `char` and it corresponds in size to the `AnsiChar`.

When a numeral is assigned to a variable of type `char`, it retains only its ordinal representation. As a character, it has no numerical value and cannot be used in a computation without typecasting. For example, modify the *learnchr.dpr* program as shown, substituting the character 9 for the character A:

```
program learnchr;
var
   ch      : char;
   x     : integer;

begin
   ch := '9';
   writeln( ch );

   x := ch + 2;
   writeln( x );
   readln;
end.
```

Compiling this program will generate an "incompatible types" error message because you are attempting to sum the character and the integer. If you are going to be performing numerical computations with your variables, the safest route would be to declare them as numeric types right from the start. Sometimes, however, it is useful to treat one data type as though it were another type. In this situation Object Pascal offers the ability to *typecast* one variable as another data type. For example, a statement from the *learnchr.dpr* project can be modified to read

```
x := integer(ch) + 2;
```

This typecast (integer(ch)) temporarily changes the data type of the variable ch to an integer and then uses the integer representation in the expression. Modify the program and run it. Do the results match your expectations? If not, where does the sum being displayed come from? (The answer is at the end of this chapter.)

Boolean

Boolean data types hold one of two possible values, True or False. In general usage its ordinal reference places false before true so that false < true. Object Pascal supports a variety of Boolean representations including `Boolean`, `ByteBool`, `WordBool`, and `LongBool`. Simple `Boolean` data types are preferred as they utilize the least amount of memory. The other representations are included in the language for compatibility with other languages and the Windows environment. Boolean variables are easy to use in a program as shown here in *lernbool.dpr*.

```
program lernbool;
var
   ans      : Boolean;
begin
   ans := false;
   writeln( ans );

   readln;
end.
```

In the storage of a Boolean value, 0 is used to represent false and any non-zero value will be interpreted as true.

Peripheral to the use of Boolean variables is a brief discussion of the differences between the colon-equal operator (:=) and the equals operator (=). The := operator is used for assignment only. Values on the right-hand side of the := operator are assigned to the variable on the left-hand side of the operator. This is a common action that we have used in nearly every example so far. The = operator tests the equality between two operands (the variables on either side of the operator) and returns a true or false result. If we test a statement such as 3 = 3 we can determine that this statement is true and the operator would return that response. If the test changes to 3 = 99 then the operator would give us the false response we need. In the upcoming chapters we are going to explore the use of the = operator in greater depth. To see what happens when the colon-equal and equals operators are confused, type in the following program and attempt to compile it.

```
program op_test;
var
   b      : integer;
begin

   b = 3;
end.
```

A compile-time error will be generated, reminding you that this use of the equality operator is inappropriate.

Real

`Real` data types are not ordinal in nature. There are an infinite number of possible values in between value x and value y. With an `integer`, an ordinal, we know that "4" will be followed by "5." When looking at a `real` data type, sometimes called floating-point or decimal values, we cannot make the same assertion. Real variables represent not only the whole portion of the number but also can contain the decimal portion of a number. The `real` data types are not ordinal because if, for example, "4" is assigned to a variable there could be any number of values such as 4.10 or 4.8765333321 between it and the value "5." Real data utilizes floating-point notation within a fixed number of digits and can be written in either scientific or fixed-point notation. The following values are acceptable as `real` data:

   4.10   7.77   10   .09887

Wait a minute; 10 is an `integer` value. Well, yes, but it can also be a `real` data value. The decimal portion of a `real` is not required so `integers` can be `reals` but `reals` cannot be `integers`.

The use of `real` variables follows the same pattern as the variable types we have seen thus far. The following program, *lernreal.dpr*, demonstrates the simple usage.

```
program lernreal;
var
   r      : real;
begin
   r := 7.77;
   writeln( r );

   readln;
end.
```

When this program is executed, you might be surprised at the output. By default, the value is displayed in scientific notation. A real value written in scientific notation has two parts, the *mantissa* and the *exponent*. The mantissa is everything to the left of the letter E and the exponent is everything to the right. In the value 7.000E+02, the 7.000 represents the mantissa which indicates the number of significant digits. The exponent, or the power of ten that determines the placement of the decimal point, is the +02, which is the same as saying 10^2. Later in this chapter we will see how best to format the output to guarantee maximum readability for the user.

Object Pascal supports six types of `real` data as shown back in Table 3-1. They differ in their range of values and precision and the number of bytes used to store the variable. `Real` data is used mainly for computational purposes and other numeric applications where an ordinal type is not appropriate. This statement is made with one caveat—while `integer` data is considered precise because there is no variability to the numbers, the precision of `real` data is wholly dependent upon the number of digits used to represent the decimal portion of the number.

Chapter 3

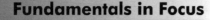

Fundamentals in Focus

A Note about Style

The greatest thing about programming is that it is both an art and a craft. Because it is an art, most developers will style their programs a certain way that they are comfortable with. My style, demonstrated throughout this book, need not be your style. For example, I never declare more than one variable per line, even though I could. This habit was formed by an early programming instructor who insisted that a comment follow each variable declaration to describe the variable and its usage. Another item you will notice is that my logical indentations are only two spaces. This amount of space works for me but you might find that more spaces work better for you. Feel free to modify the programs and write your own code in any fashion that you like so long as it remains readable.

QUICK CHECK

Which of the following data elements can be placed into the data types listed below them?

| A | 10 | 11.77 | 0 | false | z | 1 | .00776 |

a) integer

b) character

c) Boolean

d) real

Operators

Operators are symbols that give the statements in your programs the ability to create and perform logical, arithmetic, and other operations. Operators require one or more *operands*, or values, to operate upon. *Unary* operators require one operand; *binary* operators require two. As an example, let's consider the + operator first. When we create a statement that is composed of a pair of integers and the + operator, as in

```
z := x + y
```

the + operator is operating on the x and y variables. What the result of this operation will be is not always intuitive and is dependent upon the data type of the operands. If the x and y operands are integers, for instance, the result will be the sum of the two numbers. On the other hand, if x and y are character variables, the result will be the concatenation of those values. The combination of operators and operands is called an *expression*. All of the operators supported by Object Pascal are detailed in Table 3-2.

Table 3-2: The Object Pascal operators

Operator	Category	Meaning
@	Addressing	Returns the address of its operand
not	Logical	Negates the current logical result
*	Arithmetic / Set	Multiplication or intersection set logic
/	Arithmetic	Division
div	Arithmetic	Integer division (quotient)
mod	Arithmetic	Integer division (remainder)
and	Logical	Logical evaluation of operands on both sides of the operator
shl	Logical	Shift bit operation left
shr	Logical	Shift bit operation right
as	Class	Dynamic type checking
+	Arithmetic / String / Set	Addition or union set logic. When used with characters or strings it is the concatenation operator.
−	Arithmetic / Set	Subtraction or difference set logic
or	Logical	Logical evaluation of operands on either side of the operator
xor	Logical	Logical evaluation of operands on either side of the operator
=	Relational	Tests for equality
<>	Relational	Not equal
<	Relational	Less than
>	Relational	Greater than
<=	Relational	Less than or equal to
>=	Relational	Greater than or equal to
in	Relational	Tests for membership in a set
is	Class	Performs checked typecasts

When the expression becomes more complex, containing multiple combinations of operators and operands, rules of precedence specify the order in which the operations are performed. The precedence table is shown in Table 3-3 with the first order of precedence having the highest priority and the fourth order the lowest. This priority determines which parts of a complex expression are evaluated before the others.

Table 3-3: Order of precedence

Operators	Precedence	Categories
@, not	first (high)	unary operators
*, /, div, mod, and, shl, shr, as	second	multiplying operators

Table 3-3: Order of precedence

Operators	Precedence	Categories
+, −, or, xor	third	adding operators
=, <>, >, <=, >=, in, is	fourth (low)	relational operators

The rules of precedence are as follows:

1. An operand between two operators of different precedence is bound to the operator with higher precedence. In the following expression

   ```
   x * a + b
   ```

   the multiplication operator (*) will bind the x and a operands. This means that the value in x will be multiplied by the value in a and then the product will be summed with the value in b. The compiler will interpret this expression as

   ```
   ( x * a ) + b
   ```

   sometimes giving unexpected results.

2. When the operators surrounding an operand are of equal precedence, the operator is bound to the one on the left. The expression

   ```
   a + b - c
   ```

   will be evaluated from left to right. Operands a and b will be added before c is subtracted from the sum.

3. The parentheses is used to control the order of evaluation in expressions containing mixed precedence. Consider the expression

   ```
   x * a + b
   ```

   If the programmer's desire is to add a to b and then multiply the sum by x, a set of parentheses can be used to cause this. The expression is modified to read

   ```
   x * ( a + b )
   ```

   ensuring that the operands bound to the + operator are evaluated first.

Our discussion of the use of the various operators will be spread throughout the book. In this chapter we will examine the use of the arithmetic operators.

Arithmetic Operations

We are going to first explore the mathematical operators: the plus, minus, division, and multiplication signs. As we explore expressions composed of operands and operators, there are two general concepts that should be kept in mind. The first consideration is the range of values that is recognized for the variable type. If the program statement performs a mathematical operation and then assigns the result to a variable, will the variable have sufficient storage space to contain it accurately? Second, the combination of two different types of numeric values, namely `real` and `integer` data types, can create a result in a different data type than the programmer might expect. Will the target variable for the results of an operation accept the value? Becoming familiar with the answers to these questions will help to prevent possible design-time or run-time errors.

Integer and Real Expressions

Variables and constants of the data types `integer` and `real` are easily combined to form complex mathematical expressions. These expressions make use of the +, −, *, and / operators to create the equations and the parentheses to override the order of precedence for these operators. The following program demonstrates some simple equations. To create this program, create a new project and save it with the appropriate name.

```
program learnops;
var
   a       : real;
   b       : real;
   c       : real;
   x       : real;
   y       : real;
   z       : real;
begin
  a := 5;
  b := 10;
  c := 15;
  x := 3;

  // addition
  z := a + b + c;

  // subtraction
  z := a + b - c;

  // multiplication
  y := c * b;

  // division
  y := c / x;

  // combination plate
  z := c * x + b - a;

end.
```

Assignment Compatibility

The assignment compatibility of variables is an issue that must be addressed when designing expressions. This potential problem area only arises when variables of different data types are combined in an expression and the result of the operation is assigned to yet another variable. An expression is considered assignment-compatible if the result of the expression can be assigned to the target variable without error. Simple expressions containing a single value of type `real` or `integer` on the right-hand side of the assignment operator are compatible with a `real` variable on the left-hand side. The inverse is not true; a `real` value cannot be assigned to an `integer` variable. When two values are combined in an expression, one being `real` and the other being an `integer`, the result is always a `real`. When two `integer` types are combined in an expression, the result is always an `integer`. Finally, when two data elements are combined with the / operator, the result will always be a `real`. Remember that the resulting type is a product of the operands and operators involved in the expression, not the value of result. Even if it results in a whole number, the value of a division expression will be a `real`.

QUICK CHECK

What is the result of the following expressions when the Object Pascal order of evaluation is applied?

1. 3 + 5 * 10
2. 10 * 10 / 5 + 6
3. 27 − 4 + 7

Modify the statements so that the answers are

1. 80
2. 9.09
3. 16

Div and Mod

You might have noticed a couple (well, probably more than a couple) of oddly named operators in the second level of the precedence chart called mod and div. These mathematical operators serve the unique purpose of allowing you to perform division on integers and have the result also be an `integer` type. (Division using the / operator will result in a real number.) These operators work by splitting the quotient into its two components, essentially the dividend and the remainder. The div operator returns the number of times one variable goes into another. In this equation

```
17 div 5 = 3
```

you see that 5 goes into 17 three times. The remainder is ignored and discarded in a `div` operation. `Mod` does just the opposite, returning the remainder and discarding the dividend. If we take the same equation

```
17 mod 5 = 2
```

we say that after 17 is divided by 5 there is a remainder of 2.

Output Redux

Formatting Output

Object Pascal includes a feature within the `write/writeln` procedure with the ability to specify the number of spaces to be allocated in displaying each value. For example, if you want to evenly space a series of values when they are output, the following statement will accomplish the task.

```
Write('Student1':15, 10:5, 12:5, 14:5, 16:5, 18:5);
Write('Student2':15, 20:5, 22:5, 24:5, 26:5, 28:5);
```

Appended to each value that is going to be output, we have added a colon and a number that is called the *field width*. In the case of the constant value `'Student1'`, the number of display spaces has been defined as 15. Because the value itself is only eight characters in length, the remaining space up to the defined total allocated will be filled with the space character. The output from the statements will appear as follows (without the periods that represent the leading spaces):

```
.......Student1    10    12    14    16    18
.......Student2    20    22    24    26    28
```

One item of note is that the additional spaces will be placed before the value. This allows for the growth and contraction of the values displayed by your program. What about the situation in which the space allocated is insufficient? If the space specified in the `write` statement is not large enough for the value to be displayed correctly, the Object Pascal compiler will come to the rescue. The computer will override the space allocated by the compiled program using code included within your program by the compiler to ensure that the value is not truncated or otherwise displayed incorrectly. You should remain aware of this possible behavior so you can prevent any issues that might arise from the alignment of your screens being shifted due to a size change in the expected output.

A second format specifier is used when you want to format decimal, or `real`, numbers. You probably noticed that the *learnops.dpr* program did not output anything when you ran it. This is because the native output from a `real` number is displayed in scientific notation. Try this modified version of the program:

```
program learnops;
var
  a      : real;
  b      : real;
```

```
        c       : real;
        x       : real;
        y       : real;
        z       : real;
     begin
        a := 5;
        b := 10;
        c := 15;
        x := 3;

        // addition
        z := a + b + c;
        writeln('z = ', z );

        // subtraction
        z := a + b - c;
        writeln('z = ', z );

        // multiplication
        y := c * b;
        writeln('y = ', y );

        // division
        y := c / x;
        writeln('y = ', y );

        // combination plate
        z := c * x + b - a;
        writeln('Combo platter = ', z );

     end.
```

When you run this version of the program, the output will appear similar to that shown in Figure 3-10. This does not lend itself to easy interpretation by the user. The write/writeln procedures provide the proper formatting capabilities for displaying these numbers. Modify the output statements from the program above so that they have their format specifiers written as:

```
        writeln('z = ', z:0:2);
```

Figure 3-10

As we saw above, the first colon-numeral combination defines the number of spaces to be reserved for the display of the data. The second colon-numeral combination that we have added here defines the number of decimal positions to accommodate in the displayed number. In the case of our example statement, it is two. When all of the output lines have been modified in this fashion the output will appear in the more readable form shown in Figure 3-11.

Figure 3-11

Outputting Expressions

Output with one of the `write` statements is not limited to variables or constant values. The `write` or `writeln` statements can be used to directly output the results of expressions as well. As an example, the following snippet will combine statements into a single string:

```
x := 3;
y := 5;
write('Equation : ', x + y);
```

This line results in the expected output

```
Equation : 5
```

QUICK CHECK

1. Write the output lines necessary to produce the following output:

```
Tomes of Delphi Win32 Database Developer's Guide
------------------------------------------------
Wordware Publishing, Inc.
ISBN 1-55622-663-2

AUS $79.99   CDN $54.55   US$ 49.95
```

Chapter 3

Summary

The programs that you are ready to write now are a little more meaningful even though they are still simple output generators. The use of either the `write` or `writeln` statements for output is an easy decision to make—the choice comes down to the formatting decisions you make for the design of your interface. Planning ahead for the effect that you want to achieve from your user interface makes these decisions much easier. We've also taken a closer look at using some of the variety of data types supported by Object Pascal. Utilizing `integer`, `real`, `character`, and `Boolean` data types in your Object Pascal programs is key to effectively modeling the real-life situation that you are re-creating with your software.

TEST YOUR KNOWLEDGE

To develop your programming skills, try your hand at writing one or more of the following programs. Programming is all about problem solving and experience comes from exposing yourself to as many different types of problems as you can.

1. Write a program that evaluates two `integer` variables using each of the arithmetic operators (+, −, *, div, mod).

2. Write a program that mixes `real` and `integer` values in equations similar to those used in program #1 above. Be sure that the variables you are going to use to receive the results are of the correct data type.

3. Typecast two character variables (i.e., "9", "3") to sum them together into an `integer` or `real` variable. Is the answer what you expected?

Answer from page 53: The numeric value in this computation comes from the ASCII value of the character, its position within the set. Refer to an ASCII chart for verification of this fact.

Chapter 4

More Core

Key Concepts

8—⚿ Writing input statements using the read and readln procedures

8—⚿ Understanding the usage of the string data type

8—⚿ Putting all of the concepts together into a program

8—⚿ Understanding the usage of the pointer, procedural, and variant data types

Introduction

This chapter rounds out the introductory material needed to establish your foundation in the Object Pascal language. The logical structures needed to build more complex Delphi programs will follow in the coming chapters but in this chapter we will continue exploring the basics.

- We will add the read and readln procedures to your programs so that we can begin experimenting with inputting values into your programs.

- We're going to add the string data type to your collection to broaden the types of data that your programs can handle.

- Through examples and practice you will prepare yourself for the more complex programs to be developed in the coming chapters.

- The chapter will close with a discussion of more advanced data types such as the pointer, procedural, and variant types.

The examples and explanation style that you have become accustomed to in the previous pages will continue. Remember, these four chapters consist of core concepts that will not be discussed again in the logical structure sections of the book.

It is important, as we discussed before, that these concepts be studied in such a way that they can take hold.

Input—Read and Readln

Computer programs do not operate in a vacuum; they usually accept variable input from the user to perform their tasks upon. As we saw in the previous chapter, your Object Pascal program is quite good at outputting the results and constants from within a program and it is equally adept at accepting variable input from the user. The `read` and `readln` statements are provided for this purpose and are similar in structure to the `write` and `writeln` statements we examined earlier. The syntax for the `read` statement is

```
procedure Read( [ var F: Text; ] V1 [, V2,...,Vn ] );
```

`V1` through `Vn` must be variables of data types that can be keyed, such as `reals`, `integers`, `characters`, or `strings`. Similar to the `write` and `writeln` procedures, if the `F` parameter is empty the `read` procedure will default to the standard I/O variables. In the case of the `read` or `readln` statements, that I/O variable points to the default input device, your keyboard, and your program will expect input to be typed by the user.

Read

When the `read` procedure is processed, input values are read from the input source and assigned to the variables in the parameter list in the order in which they are received. Look at the following program in which a single variable is read from the command line:

```
program readtest;
var
  n1     : integer;

begin
        writeln('Enter an integer value');
  Read( n1 );

  Writeln('The number entered was ', n1 );
end.
```

(Be sure that when you start to build the programs for this chapter that you segregate them into a new folder called Chapter4.) When this program is run, the resulting output should match that shown in Figure 4-1. You will notice that when the program reaches the `read` procedure, the processing will pause and await input from the user. It will wait indefinitely for the user's input, ignoring the number of times the user presses the Enter key without typing any values.

Figure 4-1

Remember that the compiler verified any value assignments that we made inside of our program. For example, if we attempted to assign a character to an integer variable an error message was generated and the program was not compiled until this was corrected. These were referred to as *compile-time errors*. Object Pascal does not give up its strong typing at run time either. If the user attempts to provide an incompatible value for assignment to a variable when the program is running, a *run-time error* is generated. In Figure 4-2 the user has attempted to assign a character value to the integer variable. The *readtest.exe* program crashed, providing the error message shown. The error is identified by its number, 106, and can be referenced through the Delphi documentation. In this case, runtime error 106 indicates that our program has generated an operating system error. The error description is "Invalid numeric format" and the detail of the message states that it is "Reported by Read or Readln if a numeric value read from a text file does not conform to the proper numeric format."

Figure 4-2

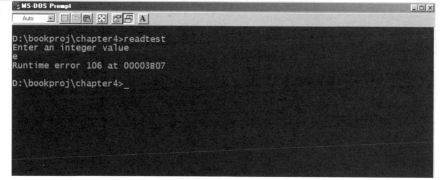

One of the properties of the `read` procedure is that it will continue to wait for input until all of the variables have received a value. In Figure 4-3, it appears that the user was unsure of what to type and pressed the Enter key a number of times in order to bypass the input field. Delphi's patience will always win out in that race.

Figure 4-3

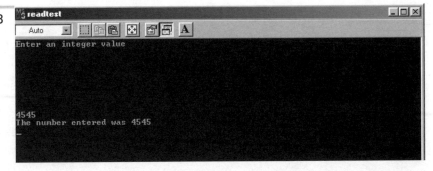

Often, this action on the part of the user is caused by a lack of instructions being provided to them but there is another feature of the Object Pascal read procedure that can create this confusion. The read procedure has the ability to accept a number of values through a single call to the procedure as shown in the following program:

```
program read2;
var
  n1 : integer;
  n2 : integer;
  n3 : integer;

begin
  writeln('Enter your three lucky numbers');
  read( n1, n2, n3 );
  write('Lucky numbers : ', n1, n2, n3 );
end.
```

When the program is run, the read procedure will wait patiently for the user to enter all three required integers. Until it receives these values, the execution of the program will not move on to the next statement. Because a familiar user knew what was expected by the program, at execution the interaction appears as shown in Figure 4-4. It could just as easily have been entered as shown in Figure 4-5 due to the user's natural tendency to push the Enter key after typing a single value. Either way, the program will not continue its processing until the correct number of valid values have been entered.

Figure 4-4

Figure 4-5

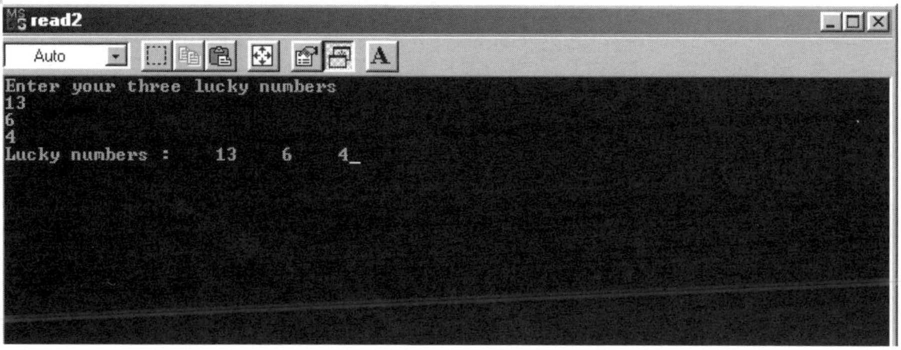

Let's modify the program to add some variety to the input values. The variables listed in the read procedure's parameter list do not have to be of the same data type. Consider this new version of the program:

```
program read3;
var
  n1 : integer;
  r1 : real;
  c1 : char;

begin
  writeln('Enter your age, income, and first initial');
  read( n1, r1, c1 );
  write('Ultra personal information : ', n1, r1, c1 );
end.
```

When the program is executed, we get the output shown in Figure 4-6.

Figure 4-6

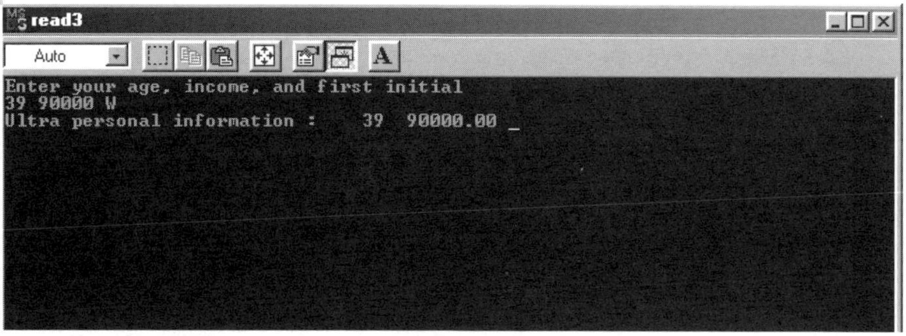

There seems to be something missing, however; what happened to the "W" that was entered? It was never stored in the variable c1 because the space that was typed after the income information was stored instead. The space is considered to be a valid character value so the variable accepted it. The user could continue to enter values all day long, but as soon as the variables have received the values they are looking for, any further input is simply ignored. The user must be made aware

Chapter 4

of this proclivity as well as the requirement that the data be entered in a specific order. If the user mistakenly enters data values in the incorrect sequence, a run-time error as we saw in the previous example will occur.

Readln

The `readln` variant of the `read` statement tells the program to go to the next line after reading the values for all of the variables, ignoring the rest of the line. There is a difference in this behavior for numeric data and character data, so let's have a look. Modifying the previous example as follows we can test the actions of the `readln` statement:

```
program read4;
var
   n1      : integer;
   n2      : integer;
   n3      : integer;

begin
  readln( n1, n2 );
  read( n3 );
  writeln( n1 );
  writeln( n2 );
  writeln( n3 );
end.
```

If the following data values are input:

```
4  6  8
10
```

the output will show that some data has been ignored, as shown in Figure 4-7.

Figure 4-7

The `readln` statement instructed the program to move on to the next line after it received appropriate values for the variables `n1` and `n2`. This caused it to ignore the 8 on the first input line, rather than assign it to `n3` as you might have expected. While it will discard additional input if it has more than it needs on one line, the `readln` statement will search the next line if it does not have enough values to fulfill its variables.

A little more caution is required when utilizing `readln` with character or string data. With character input, `readln` will discard any extraneous data that it finds once its variable needs are satisfied but it takes a different approach when there are not enough. Be sure that your users are required to enter sufficient data on each line to satisfy the needs of your string requirements. If the data is too short, the results might not be what you expected.

The String Data Type

String data is a sequence of character data strung together and referred to as a single unit using a single identifier. The string can contain letters, spaces, punctuation, numerals, and other symbols and can vary in length from a single byte to many thousands of bytes. These are strings:

```
Jets to Brazil        Arizona        XXX        Borland
```

and these can also be strings if declared correctly:

```
9999.99        A        The whole of the part of the .....
```

String data is among the most flexible of the data types. There are a couple of different ways to represent a string in Object Pascal using the three predefined string types: `ShortString`, `AnsiString`, and `WideString`. The traditional byte-length string is a fixed-length set of characters that begins with a hidden byte containing the length of the string. The memory map of this string is displayed in Figure 4-8.

| 10 | W | a | r | r | e | n | | R | a | c |

Figure 4-8: The byte-length string in memory

The 0 byte that contains the length of the string is not displayed when the value is seen by the user. These variables are defined at design time using the form shown in the following program.

```
program learnstr;
var
  FirstName    : string[10];

begin
  FirstName := 'Warren Rachele';
  writeln('First Name: ', FirstName );
end.
```

This defines a string with a fixed length of ten characters. The program can fill this with a set of zero to ten characters. As seen in Figure 4-8, this poses a bit of a problem for the program, as it will truncate the value being stored in it. The output is shown in Figure 4-9. Once truncated, there is no way to recover the lost data.

Figure 4-9

Figure 4-9

You will notice that the generic `string` identifier is used rather than the more specific identifiers. In the default state of the Delphi compiler, it interprets `string` as the type `AnsiString` when it appears without a bracketed number after it. If backward compatibility is needed, a compiler directive {$H-} can be used to turn `string` into `ShortString`. `ShortString` strings can be declared without the length being declared. When used in the following fashion, the string variable will take up the amount of space needed for the value being assigned. The *learnstr.dpr* program is shown in a revised version below:

```
program learnstr;
var
  FirstName    : string;

begin
  FirstName := 'Warren Rachele';
  writeln('First Name: ', FirstName );
end.
```

This has repaired the truncation problem as seen in Figure 4-10.

Figure 4-10

Figure 4-10

Modern software built with a current compiler such as Delphi will utilize null-terminated strings rather than byte-length strings. These string types do not use the length byte to determine how long the string is; instead, each variable is terminated with a null. The program can read the string character by character until it reaches the null telling it that the string has ended. While the `ShortString` has a maximum capacity of 255 characters, the `AnsiString` and `WideString` can support strings that measure up to 2 gigabytes in length. The `AnsiString` is the preferred string type for most uses in Delphi programming. The `WideString` is included for use with Unicode characters and in COM servers and interfaces. String types can be mixed in assignment statements and expressions and the compiler will automatically generate the code necessary to handle the conversions.

The compatibility between a variable of type `char` and type `string` is much less flexible. A `char` variable can be assigned to a `string` variable but not vice versa; a `string` variable cannot be assigned to a `char` variable. This is the case even if the `string` variable is declared as `string[1]`.

```
program lernstr2;
var
  character    : char;
  string1      : string[1];
begin
  character := 'z';
  string1 := 'y';

 // this statement will work
  string1 := character;
 // this one will not
  character := string1;

  end.
```

The program will generate an incompatible types compiler error when it reaches the `string` to `char` assignment statement. The reason for this is that the `char` variable is stored as a single byte while the `string` has characters appended/prefixed to it that cannot be seen. Even if the `string` is defined to have a length of 1, additional housekeeping bytes are attached that would exceed the byte allocated for the `char`.

Fundamentals in Focus

String Types

As the Object Pascal language has progressed through the years, many fundamental changes have occurred. One of those that you should pay particular attention to is what type of string is assumed by the compiler when the plain vanilla `string` data type is used. This choice is driven by the implementation that you use and it is important to refer to the documentation before you base your algorithm on the wrong data type.

Chapter 4

Quotes

As you have seen in the code samples displayed up to this point, a string constant is created by surrounding a set of characters with single quotes. This is the standard delimiter for strings in Object Pascal. Inconveniently, this poses a minor problem for strings that contain a representation of an apostrophe such as "You're not listening to me." The following assignment statement will generate a compiler error:

```
scold := 'You're not listening to me';
```

This occurs because the compiler performs a matching exercise with the quotes to determine the beginning and ending of the string. When it parses the right-hand side of the expression, it identifies a string of "You" and then the trouble starts. In this statement the compiler would immediately look for an operator or the terminating semicolon, neither of which it finds in this case. This is easy to solve. Object Pascal accepts two single quotes enclosed within a string constant to represent the apostrophe character. Modifying the statement to

```
scold := 'You''re not listening to me';
```

solves the problem.

String Operators

The selection of operators used with string data is much more limited than that used for the numeric data types. The plus sign operator (+) serves to concatenate multiple strings into a single unit as seen in the following program:

```
program lernstr3;
var
  playlist : string;
begin
  playlist := 'MXPX'+' '+'Under Lock and Key';
  writeln( playlist );
end.
```

The output from this simple code is shown in Figure 4-11.

Figure 4-11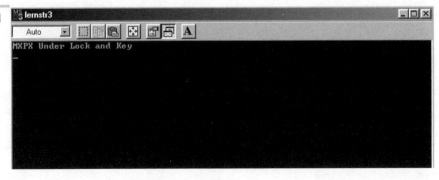

The three separate data values—MXPX, the space, and Under Lock and Key—have been combined into a single value contained in the variable `playlist`. The string resulting from this operation takes the type of the variable to which it is assigned. The concatenation does not require string constants; a mixture of `string`, `char`, and `constant` data can also be used. None of the other mathematical operators (−, /, *) accept `string` or `char` operands. Modify the *lernstr3.dpr* program as shown below to see the effects of concatenation of character and string data into a string variable:

```
program lernstr3;
var
  playlist  : string;
  numberone : string;
  x         : char;

begin
  playlist := 'MXPX'+' '+'Under Lock and Key';
  writeln( playlist );

  x := '1';
  playlist := 'Rollins Band' + ' ' + 'Get Some Go Again';

  numberone := x + playlist;
  writeln( numberone );
end.
```

The results of this modified program are shown in Figure 4-12. The mixed types were assigned and output using a single variable.

Figure 4-12

When the logical operators (<, <>, =, >, <=, >=) are used with `char` or `string` data, the results are sometimes not what the programmer expected. Remember that the characters in the variable have no meaning other than their position within the ordinal set. The letter "a," for instance, has a value of 97. It is this value that is used in the logical argument. The line

```
'A' < 'a'
```

evaluates to true since the value of "A" is 65. We will be putting this to the test in an upcoming chapter after we have discussed some new logical structures.

Projects

The two projects on the coming pages will give you an opportunity to stretch out and use most of the things that we have discussed up to this point. Each project is presented in full and is much longer than the samples that have been presented. Take the time to code the projects and experiment with them to increase your familiarity with the core Object Pascal concepts. The practice will serve you well as our discussion shifts to logical structures in the chapters that follow. If you don't want to type these, the full code for each is included on the CD-ROM.

Project 1

A simple question and answer program demonstrates the usage of the input and output statements in Object Pascal. The program doesn't really do anything useful; it just gets the fingers going on the keyboard to begin our exploration of the language. Don't bypass the opportunity to bang out a program from the book, no matter how trivial it is. Just as you swing your sticks to learn the groove of your golf swing, typing the code shown in the book teaches your muscles to quickly build programs.

```
program QandA;
{ --------------------------------------- }
{ Simple Q & A program to demonstrate the  }
{ input and output statements              }
{ --------------------------------------- }
var
  first       : string[10];
  last        : string[10];
  age         : integer;

begin

  writeln('20 Questions':34);

  write('Your first name is: ');
  readln(first);

  write('Your last name is: ');
  readln(last);

  write('Your age is : ');

  read(age);

  writeln('Welcome to Object Pascal programming, ',first,' ',last);
  writeln('You''re a spring chicken at the age of ',age);

end.
```

If you've typed in the code exactly as shown or loaded it from the CD-ROM, the program should generate output that looks something similar to that in Figure 4-13. There are a couple of lines in the program that bear a quick explanation to reinforce the point. The first line to look at is the one that reads:

```
writeln('20 Questions:34);
```

Figure 4-13

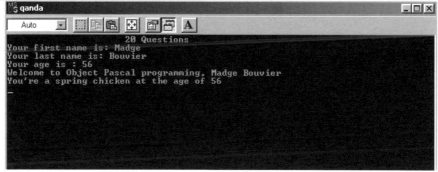

The output is being formatted through the use of the space specifier. Knowing that the string '20 Questions' will be right-justified in the space allotted we took advantage of this to center the heading. We used the old typewriter (what's that?) trick of dividing the number of characters across the page by two and then subtracting half of the number of characters in the heading to find my starting point.

Project 2

Let's add the mathematical skills that we've gained here to the input and output knowledge practiced earlier. The code shown here builds a simple program to determine the cost of your daily commute and uses `real` and `integer` values to compute the answer.

```
program Commute;
{ --------------------------------------- }
{ Simple computation program that computes }
{ the cost of a daily commute              }
{ --------------------------------------- }

var
   miles       : real;
   gas_cost    : real;
   mpg         : real;
   total_cost  : real;
   days        : integer;
   passengers  : integer;

begin
   { -- get the information from user -- }
```

```
writeln('How many miles do you travel? ');
readln(miles);

writeln('How many miles per gallon does your car get? ');
readln(mpg);

writeln('What is the cost of gasoline? ');
readln(gas_cost);

total_cost := gas_cost * ( miles / mpg );
writeln('The total cost of your commute is
',total_cost:6:2);

writeln('How many days per week do you commute? ');
readln(days);
writeln('How people do you carry in the car? ');
readln(passengers);

writeln('The weekly cost is ', days * total_cost:6:2);
writeln('The weekly cost per passenger is ', (days *
total_cost) / passengers:6:2);
end.
```

The user questioning design used in this program is really no different from what we encountered in the previous code examples. The write and writeln procedures are used to prompt the user with pointed questions and then a follow-up readln procedure is used to gather the answer. The mix of write and writeln procedures was driven by the layout that we wanted to achieve shown in Figure 4-14. By utilizing a write, the readln statement will appear to be on the same line, immediately following the punctuation. When we have a need to simply output a line of information without a trailing query, the writeln statement ensures that the next statement starts on a new line.

Figure 4-14

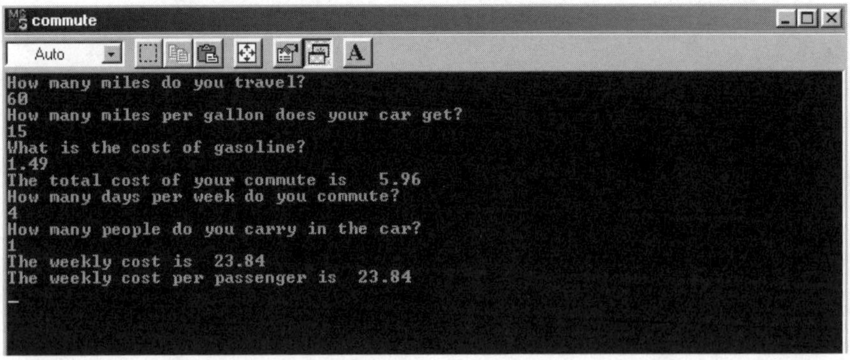

The first assignment statement is made up of all `real` data elements so the result will be a `real` as well.

```
Total_cost := gas_cost * ( miles / mpg );
```

Because the multiplication and division operators are used in the same statement and these are of equal precedence, parentheses were added in order to control the order of evaluation. If we allow the default left to right computation to occur, our total cost will be much different than we expect. Notice that on the very next line when the total cost is output, we use a format specifier to determine how the `real` data will be output.

```
Writeln('The total cost of your commute is ',
total_cost:6:2);
```

The specification used is for `real` data only. The first number after the colon indicates the total amount of space to be allotted for this output as previously discussed. In this statement a second colon and digit are used to indicate the number of decimal positions to be displayed; in the case of this statement we used 2 to represent the cents portion of the cost.

TIP:

Silly Format Specifier Tricks

There is another specifier trick that can be used very effectively in certain situations that forces the computer to figure out how many spaces to use by specifying 0 spaces, as in

```
total_cost:0:2
```

The computer will supply exactly the number of spaces needed by the output for it to display correctly and no more. We can use this effect to prepend symbols to an output. If the output line being discussed were changed to

```
Writeln('The total cost of your commute is $',
total_cost:0:2);
```

the answer would come out with the dollar sign aligned with it.

In the last two lines of the program there are also a couple of new things going on. First, notice that the expressions are mixing `real` and `integer` data without any detrimental effect. What is the output type from these expressions? The second change made to the style of the program is that the expressions are embedded within the output statement rather than simply used in an assignment statement. When the expression is a part of another statement the compiler takes an approach much like that of applying parentheses to an expression; it will resolve all of the expressions contained within the parentheses of the `writeln` statement before outputting the line.

Chapter 4

Fundamentals in Focus

The Algorithm

Computer programming is problem solving via electronic means using a logical sequence of instructions that lead to a resolution. A single word that embodies this description is algorithm. The algorithm is a finite set of instructions that leads to the result you are trying to achieve with your program. The word itself has an interesting history. Webster's dictionary indicates that the word is a corruption of the word *algorism* which is defined as the Arabic system of doing arithmetic using Arabic numerals. This word is attributed to a famous Persian textbook author in the ninth century Al-Khowarizmi who wrote *Kitab al jabr w'al-muqabala* ("Rules of restoration and reduction"); the word algebra is derived from this title.

There are specific rules that differentiate an algorithm from the random and meandering thoughts of a brainstorm. The characteristics are easily enumerated:

1. FINITE. An algorithm must always terminate after a specified number of steps. The terminator may be triggered by some external input but it must have the ability to halt.

2. DEFINITE. Each step of the algorithm must be clearly defined and not be ambiguous as to its purpose. Computer languages are written to provide this type of definite syntax; they mean exactly what they say. Human languages are full of nuance that can cause words to mean different things based upon factors such as context and inflection.

3. INPUT. An algorithm has zero or more input values. These are the values that the algorithm has available for use when the problem solving steps begin.

4. OUTPUT. An algorithm has one or more outputs. These results are the product of the algorithm and are related to the inputs.

5. EFFECTIVENESS. This seems sort of obvious but the algorithm must be effective. This simply means that the steps solve the problem to which they are being applied.

Complex Data Types

In addition to the simple data types that we have discussed in the previous pages, Delphi supports a number of more specialized data types. The more complex data types are not as commonly used or have a more esoteric function than the simple data types. In order to discuss them fully and provide meaningful support for your learning, the types that follow are going to be introduced here but much of the detail of their implementation is found later in the book. By delaying their full explanation, the book will have a chance to provide some further building blocks that support the comprehension of these advanced topics.

Structured Data Types

The structured data types cover a wide variety of programming needs and include the `array`, `record`, `class`, `class reference`, `set`, and `file` types. Structured types are composed of numbers of instances of simple and/or string data types. For example, an `array` data type can be defined as containing ten integers or ten reals. As Figure 4-15 shows, the array in this example, known as *ArrayOfIntegers*, is a collection of integer values. Within the structure, each of the elements has its own unique address. The advantage in using the structured type is that all of these elements can now be addressed and referenced as a single, combined unit while retaining the ability to reference an individual element within it. With the exception of the `class` and `class reference` data types, all of the other structured types fall under this definition. These, on their own, form the basis for all object programming and can contain far more than simple data types. The structured types are better explained when we have developed some more programming skills so we will leave these for now.

1	2	3	4	5	Element Number
99	2	34	7	56	Value

Figure 4-15: The ArrayOfIntegers data structure

Pointer Data Types

A *pointer* is a unique data element that holds the memory address of another variable. The variable pointed to can be of the data types discussed already or of an undefined type. The pointer then indirectly refers to a value; this relationship is shown in Figure 4-16. The declaration for the pointer variable `PtrCharacter` would be

```
type
    PtrCharacter = ^char;
```

Figure 4-16: The pointer type

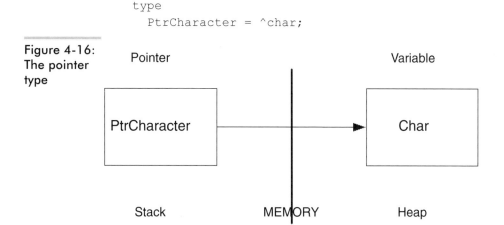

In addition to using a new character, the carat (^), the definition falls under a section of the program that we have not discussed yet. We will examine the type section in an upcoming chapter but for now, understand that it is where user-defined types are defined. The carat is the pointer dereference operator.

The pointer does not need to have a value. If this is the case it can be assigned the value of nil. Using the pointer variable you can assign it the address of any variable of the same type using the @ operator. The pointer supports the dynamic allocation and deallocation of memory that is necessary for dynamic data structures that grow and contract with the needs of the program. We will see this in use later with the development of a linked list. The data types that we have reviewed so far are static; their size has been defined during the development stage and their contents cannot exceed these predefined boundaries. One of the great features of the Delphi environment is much of the pointer handling is done for you, allowing you to concentrate on your program's design. Still, this doesn't remove the necessity of understanding the object.

Procedural Data Types

Procedural data types are included as a part of Object Pascal so that procedures and functions can be assigned to variables or passed as parameters. This is truly an advanced programming topic, made especially difficult by the fact that we have yet to even discuss what a procedure or function is. It is covered here to keep the discussion topically organized. To understand this type we will set the stage by defining a function that accepts a couple of parameters and returns an integer:

```
function square( i: integer; j: integer ): integer;
```

The definition for this type is going to be syntactically similar to a standard function or procedure header except that you will leave off the identifier:

```
type
   SquareFunc = function ( i: integer; j: integer ): integer;
var
   x      : SquareFunc;
```

When assigned to a variable identifier, the parameter calling list will determine what can and cannot be assigned to the variable. In the case of the example we have built, the program could make the assignment statement

```
x := square;
```

The variable of this type will contain a pointer to the procedure or function. Closer to the ideal of Object Pascal is the Method pointer. This procedural type references the procedure or function method of an object. The Method pointer is a little more complicated in what it stores; it is encoded as two pointers. The first pointer references the memory address of the method identified while the second pointer stores a reference to the object that owns the method. As we get further into this book, examples of both of these will be presented in a better contextual setting. It is recommended that you continue on with the text and then return to this topic later on in your programming career.

Variant Data Types

Going against all that the designers of Pascal held important are the `variant` data types. `Variants` are used only in situations in which it is not possible to determine the data type to be used at compile time. The `variant` data type was introduced into Delphi in order to accommodate the use of the variant in Visual Basic to implement COM. Microsoft allowed Visual Basic syntax to be adopted by a wide range of applications such as Word and Excel. It is strongly recommended by Borland that you utilize `variants` only when doing COM programming and for no other reason. A `variant` is capable of dynamically accommodating a wide variety of scalar and structured data elements during the execution of the program. A short program can demonstrate this facility.

```
program lrnvarnt;
var
   v     : variant;
begin
  v := 1;
  v := 0.08888;
  v := false;
  v := 'Without batting an eye';
end.
```

The `variant` is type-checked and computed at run time. While this goes against the strongly typed design of Object Pascal, the `variant` does offer significantly more flexibility to the programmer. The flexibility does not come without a cost; `variant` types take up much more memory than their static counterparts and operations on these variables are significantly slower. In addition, illegal operations on this data type often result in run-time errors of the type that would have been caught at compile time using static data types. Consider the design and usage carefully before committing your program to a `variant` data type. Better yet, unless COM is in your plans, don't use it at all.

Summary

This chapter ends the first part of the book. The foundational aspects of the Object Pascal language as it is implemented in Delphi have been covered. In this chapter we discovered how to use the `read` or `readln` procedures to gather input values for our programs to use. As we mentioned in an earlier chapter in regard to the `write` or `writeln` procedures, most Delphi based software will gather input and dispense output through the use of components on a form rather than at the command line. You have also added the `string` to your collection of data types, increasing the flexibility of your programs. In addition to the `string` the final pages of the chapter discussed some more advanced types supported in Delphi. Watch for these in upcoming topics.

The two, more extensive projects presented in this chapter stretched your programming muscles a little bit. Be sure that you have a good understanding of everything that is going on within the two code sets. You will not want to be wondering about these basic topics when we start using these foundation concepts to build more extensive logical structures. If there is anything that is still giving you trouble, take a few minutes to go back to those pages in the previous chapters and review it before moving on. In addition to this book, Object Pascal information can be had by referring to one of the help files included with Delphi, *del4op.hlp*. This can be accessed through the Start menu under the Borland Delphi selection in the help files where it is referenced as Object Pascal Reference.

TEST YOUR KNOWLEDGE

Ty Cobb didn't become the toughest man in baseball by reading about it. He learned the game and then went out and practiced, practiced, practiced until he became one of the best. Programming has the same apprenticeship requirements. You should practice as much as possible so that your skills become automatic. Try to write one or more of the following programs to help hone your skills.

1. Write a program that will read in two integers and then output their sum, difference, and product.

2. Students will be given four quizzes during their programming course. Write a program for the instructor to accept the four quiz scores as integers and output the average score.

3. You are going to be taking your car on vacation in Europe. Convert the program written for project 2 so that it can be used to keep track of your travel costs while there. Two conversion factors will be needed to make this work, miles to kilometers and gallons to liters. One kilometer equals 0.62137 mile. One liter equals 0.264179 gallons. Use constants for both the liter and kilometer values.

Chapter 5

Making Decisions

Introduction

Computers excel at making certain kinds of Boolean decisions. Though people are not always as logical in their decision making they will generally follow a selected path once the decision has been made between two or more alternatives. Since many computer programs are designed to emulate and model real-life situations, it's going to be expected that the software that we produce can branch onto a new logical course when a decision prompts it to do so. To this end, this chapter will focus on the tools that Object Pascal uses for making decisions.

- We will learn more about the logical operators used in Object Pascal.
- You will put the IF .. THEN .. ELSE structure to work in your programs, adding the capability to branch in different directions.
- Using nested IF .. THEN .. ELSE structures allows Object Pascal programs to examine a number of options and branching paths in a series.
- Nesting IF .. THEN .. ELSE structures can complicate a program when they are several layers deep. When the purpose of the structure is to test for membership, sometimes a set is a better choice. We'll examine this structured data type and the Boolean `in` operator.
- You'll put the power of the CASE structure to work in your programs.

We will be making extensive use of the data elements and structures that have been discussed in previous chapters, so be sure that you understand that material before moving forward. Don't be overly concerned about the number of different structures that will be covered here. Simply remember that they all share the common trait of creating a branching mechanism for our programs.

Making Choices

Every day, you and I have to make a choice between two or more alternatives: waffles or bran flakes for breakfast, nine or eighteen holes of golf this afternoon. Why should our computer programs be any different? By their very nature, the binary patterns of execution within the computer processor lend themselves neatly to choosing between divergent paths, and this is one of the most common tasks that programs are asked to perform. Programs make a choice of one of two or more alternative execution paths based upon a condition, the condition being evaluated in the Boolean terms of being true or false. The decision tools allow one and only one path to be followed if the result is true and one of the alternatives if false. Let's look at an example.

In order to complete this book on time, I must write about 5000 words per week. Every Friday afternoon, I review my progress for the week and if I have met my goals for the week (the 5000 words), then I can play golf on Saturday. If I come up short, I need to continue to work on the project through the weekend. My performance review breaks out logically like this:

```
If I wrote 5000 words or more
then I can play golf
otherwise
I have to work.
```

Figure 5-1 shows the logic at work in a flowchart.

Figure 5-1

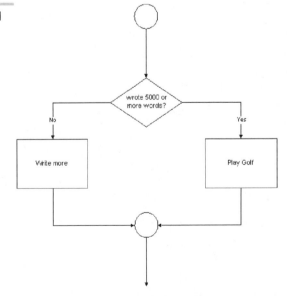

The logical branch is represented by the diamond in the chart. The logical flow comes into the top of the diamond in which a choice is made. Based upon the outcome of the choice, one of two branches is taken. It is important to note that this branching operation ignores the other path once a decision is made; the actions in that path will not be taken.

Boolean Expressions

Notice that the condition that I base my decision has only two answers, yes or no. I can't answer this question with a maybe; either I wrote 5000 words or I didn't. In computing, this type of a statement is referred to as a *Boolean* expression. These logical expressions are often composed of two operands and a logical operator. The operator compares the value of the left operand to the value of the operand on the right to determine if the expression evaluates to true or false. The relational operators are shown in Table 5-1. If we translate the production needed to play golf into an expression it would look like

```
production > 5000
```

Table 5-1: The Object Pascal relational operators

Operator	Description	Usage Example
=	Equality	X = 3
<>	Inequality	X <> 5
<	Less than	Y < 22
<=	Less than or equal to	Z <= 25
>	Greater than	Z > A
>=	Greater than or equal to	Y >= Z

where `production` is a variable containing the words output for the week. If I met or exceeded my goal, then the statement will evaluate to true. Examining that statement closer there appears to be a difference between the requirements and the expression. If we use the expression as is and I produced 5000 words exactly that week, I would be denied golf. We must be careful to match the operator to the logical requirement. A better design for the problem would use the greater-than-or-equal-to operator:

```
production >= 5000
```

Chapter 5

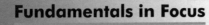

Fundamentals in Focus

Type Boolean

Like the battle between good and evil, the study of true and false dates back to antiquity. This might lead you to believe that the term Boolean has an ancient and colorful source similar to that of the word algorithm. Actually, the source of the word is a much more modern character by the name of George Boole, a nineteenth century mathematician. Bertrand Russell identified Boole as the father of symbolic logic by Boole's book ***The Laws of Thought***.

The computer programming data type Boolean is derived from the use of true and false in mathematics. George Boole was the scholar who developed a formal calculus for these types of expressions.

Complex Boolean Expressions

Often, real life dictates a choice that is not so clear cut. Many times it is necessary to consider a couple of equal or opposing conditions when making a decision. The golf question discussed above was not entirely accurate. It really looks something like

```
If I wrote 5000 words or more AND my wife doesn't have other
plans
     then I can play golf
otherwise
     I have to work.
```

In order to play golf on Saturday, I not only need to meet my writing goals but I must also make sure that my wife doesn't have other plans. In order for the whole condition to be true, both of the sub-conditions must be true as indicated by the addition of the AND operator to the statement.

To create the complex Boolean expression we used the logical operator AND. All of the Object Pascal Boolean operators are shown in Table 5-2. These operators are easily explained by a tool called a truth table. Table 5-3 is the truth table for the AND statement. It takes the two operands, expressions that can be evaluated to true or false, and states all of the possible combinations and their result. In the case of the AND operator, both sides of the expression must evaluate to true in order for the entire statement to evaluate to true. Modifying the logical statement into pseudocode, it becomes

```
( production >= 5000 ) AND ( spousal_approval = true )
```

Table 5-2: The Object Pascal Boolean operators

Operator	Description	Usage Example
NOT	Negation	Not (name in ['Warren', David'])
AND	Conjunction	(x=1) AND (y<10)
OR	Disjunction	(X<3) OR (y>10)
XOR	Exclusive disjunction	(Z<=25) XOR (Y>=25)

Table 5-3: The AND operator truth table

Expression A	Expression B	Result
True	True	True
True	False	False
False	True	False
False	False	False

Table 5-4 contains the truth tables for the other three Boolean operators.

Table 5-4: The OR, XOR, and NOT truth tables

OR

Expression A	Expression B	Result
True	True	True
True	False	True
False	True	True
False	False	False

XOR

Expression A	Expression B	Result
True	True	False
True	False	True
False	True	True
False	False	False

NOT

Expression A	Result
True	False
False	True

The rule for the OR operator states that either expression or both of them can evaluate to true to make the entire statement evaluate to true. XOR (Exclusive OR) modifies that rule to say that either expression may be true but in the case both of them are true, the statement evaluates to false. Finally, consider the unary NOT operator. This may be the toughest of all to understand. NOT true is false; NOT false is true. See what I mean?

The Boolean operators are not limited to the evaluation of only two expressions. When numerous conditions need to be tested, we put the parentheses to work again. For example, let's add parentheses and a new condition to our ongoing statement

```
If ( I wrote 5000 words or more AND there are no family
commitments) AND
( The sun is shining)
     then I can play golf
otherwise
     I have to work.
```

First, the production and spousal approval expressions are evaluated to see if both of them are true because they are enclosed within parentheses that control the order of evaluation. If that pair of expressions evaluates to true, the statement as a whole is ANDed with the Sun is Shining statement. Production, spousal approval, and sunshine mean tee it up and swing. Production, spousal approval, and the first snow of autumn means back to work.

QUICK CHECK

1. Determine if the following expressions evaluate to true or false.
    a. 'A' = 'a'
    b. (0 < 1) AND (3 < 2)
    c. ((1 > 0) AND (2 > 1)) OR ('z' > 'x')
    d. not (3 > 4)
2. Write Object Pascal statements that represent the following expressions:
    a. The letter X is not equal to the first two letters of the alphabet
    b. The variable Y is not evenly divisible by 4
    c. 3 multiplied by 3 equals 9
    d. i plus 8 is less than 50 or it is greater than 200

The IF .. THEN .. ELSE Control Structure

The Object Pascal IF .. THEN .. ELSE structure is the most common logical structure that you will use to enable your programs to branch in different directions. Using the relational and Boolean operators we have just discussed, the IF .. THEN .. ELSE structure tests conditions and directs the logical flow to one of two alternatives based upon the result of the evaluation. The logical template for this control structure is

```
if expression1 operator expression2 then
    statement1
else
    statement2;
(Next statement)
```

Object Pascal considers this entire structure to be one complete statement. Note the placement of the semicolon that terminates the statement, as this is an important key to understanding how the execution will flow. Execution of this statement will compare expression1 to expression2 and evaluate the result. If the expression (exp1 compared to exp2) evaluates to true, then statement1 will be executed; if it evaluates to false, then statement2 is executed. After either of the two statements is executed (one of them will always be executed) the next statement following the semicolon will run. When working with a branching statement you must remember that both of the statements will never be processed, only one of the two will.

Let's convert the golf problem into Object Pascal so that we can build a project around it. We will start by testing the action of the IF .. THEN .. ELSE statement first with a simple production equation:

```
program golf0;
var
  production    : integer;
begin

  production := 3256;

  if production >= 5000 then
    Writeln('You may play golf')
  else
    Writeln('Back to work boy!');

end.
```

The program will compare the value contained in the variable production to the constant 5000 to determine if it is greater than or equal to it. If it is, then the line writeln('You may play golf') is executed and printed to the screen. Otherwise, if I have come up short on my goals, I will be ordered back to work. In the case of the example as it is written we know that I will be typing away come Saturday morning. Modify the production value to 7000 so that you can see the other branch in action.

Fundamentals in Focus

Watch Out!

A very common programming error when using the IF .. THEN .. ELSE structure is placing the semicolon in the wrong position. Often, programmers will be tempted to place a semicolon at the end of statement 1:

```
if production >= 5000 then
    Writeln('..');
else
    Writeln('..');
```

This will generate a compiler error that states "; not allowed before ELSE" as seen in Figure 5-2. (A DOS compiler such as Turbo Pascal 7 will flag this as an "error in statement".) This is because the compiler interprets the semicolon as the end of the IF statement, making the ELSE stand on its own. Since the keyword ELSE must be a part of an IF .. THEN structure rather than standing alone, the error is generated.

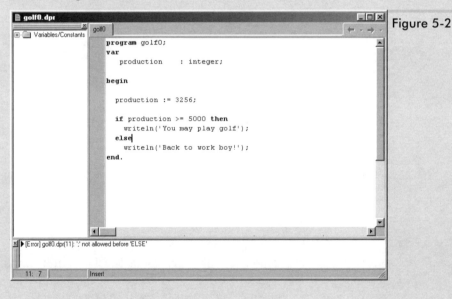

Figure 5-2

Project 1

Enough theory for now; let's create a program that interactively determines if we are going to get to spank whitey on Saturday. The program combines all of the tools that we have worked with up to this point and includes the use of the Boolean variable type. As always, you can build this program from these pages or copy it from the CD-ROM. See Figure 5-3 for an example of the output for this program.

```pascal
program Golf1;
{ ---------------------------------------- }
{ Program uses an IF . THEN . ELSE control  }
{ structure to determine if the user can    }
{ play golf or needs to work                }
{ ---------------------------------------- }

const
  {--Set up a constant to hold the minimum number of words--}
  WORDS = 5000;

var
  production : integer; {production = number of words from user}
  play       : Boolean; {play = Boolean if play allowed}

begin

  { -- Initialize the variables -- }
  production := 0;
  play := false;

  { -- Get the input from the user -- }
  write('How many words did you write: ');
  readln(production);

  { -- compare variable to constant --}
  if production >= WORDS then
    play := true;

  { -- if play = true then send PLAY message -- }
  if play then
    writeln('You may play golf.')
  else
    writeln('Back to work boy!');

end.
```

Figure 5-3

In the *Golf1* program, the first thing we did was set up a constant named WORDS. This constant holds the number of words that I need to generate each week to gain my reward. Remember, by using a constant I can use this identifier in place of the hard-coded value throughout my program. This way, if my deadline looms and I haven't finished my project, I can change the value to 7500 words in one place rather than having to seek it throughout the program to modify multiple instances. Constants are usually written in all capitals so that they are easily picked out in the program code.

What happened to the else in the first IF .. THEN .. ELSE structure? It reads

```
if production >= WORDS then
   Play := true;
```

The else is an optional part of the structure and is only required if you need to control the program when the expression evaluates to false. In the case of the *Golf1* program, I had already initialized the value of the variable play to false. If the production expression had evaluated to false then the value of play would remain false; adding the else clause to this structure would have been redundant. However, if the program is designed to repeat this set of instructions numerous times, the else would have been necessary to ensure that the correct value is always assigned to play.

Finally, the full IF .. THEN .. ELSE structure is used to output the correct line. The first line of the structure reads

```
if play then
```

How does this work without an operator or a second expression? The IF instruction is evaluating the expression as a whole to determine if it evaluates to true or false. Because the variable play is of type Boolean it evaluates by itself to true or false, so it is not necessary to write out the whole expression as

```
if play = true then
```

Expanding Project 1

The *Golf1* project can be expanded to handle multiple specified requirements. To do this we're going to approach it in two different ways. The first, seen in *Golf2*, will add another IF .. THEN .. ELSE structure to the program to handle the third requirement:

```
program Golf2;
{ ---------------------------------------- }
{ Program uses an IF . THEN . ELSE control  }
{ structure to determine if the user can    }
{ play golf or needs to work                }
{ Golf2 adds spousal approval and weather   }
{ ---------------------------------------- }
const
   { -- Set up a constant to hold the minimum number of words --}
   WORDS = 5000;
```

```
var
  production : integer; {production = number of words from user}
  play       : Boolean; {play = Boolean if play allowed}
  honeydo    : integer; {honeydo = number of items on list to do}
  response   : char;    {response = input from question}
  sunny      : Boolean; {sunny = sun shining?}

begin

  { -- Initialize the variables -- }
  production := 0;
  honeydo    := 0;
  play       := false;
  sunny      := false;
  response   := ' ';

  { -- Get the input from the user -- }
  write('How many words did you write: ');
  readln(production);

  write('How many items are on the Honey-Do list: ');
  readln(honeydo);

  write('Is the sun shining Y/N');
  readln(response);

  { -- Handle the response variable -- }
  if (response = 'y') or (response = 'Y') then
    sunny := true;

  { -- compare variable to constant --}
  if (production >= WORDS) and (honeydo < 1) and (sunny = true) then
    play := true;

  { -- if play = true then send PLAY message -- }
  if play then
    writeln('You may play golf.')
  else
    writeln('Back to work boy!');

end.
```

This is certainly not the most elegant programming solution but it accomplishes the task handily. The data needed for all three of the requirements is gathered from the user. Notice that the weather input requirement has to be handled in two parts.

The user cannot directly input a Boolean value from the keyboard so the program accepts a character as input and then tests it for equality. If the user inputs a Yes response in the form of a "y" then the value of true is assigned to the Boolean variable sunny. Why does the program test for both upper- and lowercase Y? You must always keep in mind when accepting character input into your programs that the user can type both upper- and lowercase characters. If the variable will be used as an operand in a comparison with another value your program needs to be able to accommodate both types of character. Another aspect of this input statement to keep in mind is the character on which your statement focuses. If the user types a Y in either upper- or lowercase the value of true will be assigned to sunny. If the user types <u>any other character</u> then the value will be false; it is not limited to a response of n or N. This characteristic becomes an important factor in the development of your user prompts. Users must be able to easily interpret your instructions so that the correct input is received. For example, the golf-wannabe might believe that T and F are adequate replacements for the Y and N asked for. Inputting these values will provide him with consistently disappointing results. Later on in the book, as your skills increase, we will add supporting code to our programs to prevent the user from entering inappropriate values such as this.

Fundamentals in Focus

Short-Circuit Evaluation

Implementations of Object Pascal can take two different approaches to the evaluation of Boolean statements and it's very important to your success in programming to know which is used. For the AND and OR operators the two forms of evaluation are complete and short-circuit, or partial, evaluation. Complete evaluation means that the expressions on both sides of the operator (and, or) will be fully evaluated even if the first expression determines the outcome of the statement. For example, in the statement (5 < 2) AND (3 < 6), the first expression immediately determines that the entire compound statement is going to be evaluated as false. Using short-circuit evaluation, the program would not bother to consider the second expression since the true or false result of the entire expression had already been determined.

Complete evaluation is just the opposite of this; both sides of the statement will be evaluated regardless of the determination of the first statement. This makes the code a little slower and a little fatter. Depending on your Object Pascal implementation there are usually a couple of ways to turn this feature on and off. With Delphi, you will use the $B compiler directive to control the evaluation mode. The default state is {$B-} which enables short-circuit evaluation. Delphi also enables your evaluation choice through the Compiler options dialog. The menu choice is Project->Options, which will take you to the dialog shown in Figure 5-4. Select the Compiler tab; we're going to focus on the Syntax Options quadrant. Check the Complete Boolean Eval box to force complete evaluation. Click on OK to complete the settings. Remember that these settings are for your current project only; you will have to reset this for each new project.

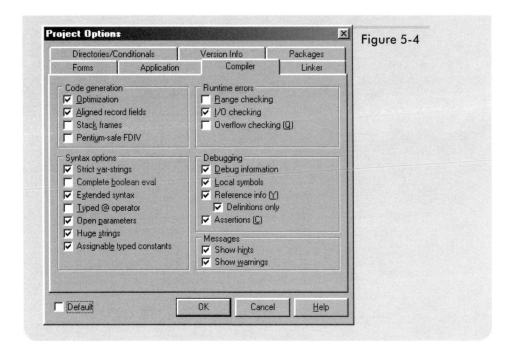

Figure 5-4

Nested IF Statements

The programs that we have seen up to this point have had the ability to make choices between just two alternatives. Programs that model reality must have the ability to choose between a greater number of options. Object Pascal offers two control structures for performing this task, the nested IF .. THEN .. ELSE statement and the CASE structure. We'll look at the concept of nesting first.

The IF .. THEN .. ELSE structures that have been presented to this point were strictly one-trick ponies; each alternative consisted of but a single statement. Object Pascal considers code blocks—sets of statements enclosed within a BEGIN .. END block—as though they were a single statement. The IF .. THEN .. ELSE construct supports blocks of statements as easily as it does single statements. For example, the following structure processes additional input statements based on the values of the user's initial input:

```
program lernnest;
var
  country      : string[5];
  outside_US   : Boolean;
  zip_code     : string[10];
        postal_code  : string[9];
begin
  outside_US := false;

  writeln('What country are you mailing from ?');
```

Chapter 5

```
          readln( country );

                if (country <> 'US') and (country <> 'us') then
begin
  outside_US := true;
  writeln('Enter Postal Code');
  readln(postal_code);
end
else
begin
  writeln('Enter Zip code');
  readln( zip_code );
end;

if not outside_US then
  writeln('Zip Code : ', zip_code )
else
  writeln('Postal Code : ', postal_code );

end.
```

Figure 5-5

A sample session is shown in Figure 5-5.

The same rules with regard to placement of the semicolons apply when code blocks are used. Note that the end immediately prior to the else has no semicolon. This tells the compiler to continue the IF .. THEN .. ELSE statement with the else and the code that follows it. Within the code blocks the punctuation rules still apply; each statement must end with a semicolon with the exception of the last statement immediately prior to the end. Since the IF .. THEN .. ELSE structure can contain blocks of code, it can also contain other IF .. THEN .. ELSE structures. This is called *nesting*.

The code block in Listing 5-1 demonstrates the nesting concept.

Listing 5-1: **A deeply nested structure**

```
if (UpCase(card) = 'K') OR (UpCase(card) = 'Q')
  OR (UpCase(card) = 'J') OR ( card = '1' ) then
    value := 10
else
  if card = '9' then
    value := 9
  else
    if card = '8' then
      value := 8
    else
      if card = '7' then
        value := 7
      else
        if card = '6' then
          value := 6
        else
          if card = '5' then
            value := 5
          else
            if card = '4' then
              value := 4
            else
              if card = '3' then
                value := 3
              else
                if card = '2' then
                  value := 2;
```

This construct is used when you have more than two conditions that need to be checked before an action is taken. Suppose that you wrote a program to simulate a blackjack game. Some cards will share the same numeric value while others will be considered on an individual basis. Regardless of the card, the ultimate goal of the code block is to apply a numeric value to the variable face based on the character input received from the user. To enable this function the program should keep the code trapped in the nested IF .. THENs until each possible card has been examined for equality. When the correct value has been matched and assigned to the variable, the logic should allow escape through the else clause. Nesting IF .. THENs can continue indefinitely but you should consider other alternatives if the code becomes unwieldy and difficult to understand.

Chapter 5

Fundamentals in Focus

UpCase

You probably noticed that the code in Listing 5-1 contained a new addition, the UpCase function. We are going to discuss functions and procedures in the coming pages so we won't go into depth about their inner workings here. UpCase serves the purpose of converting the case of a character that the user types in to an uppercase representation of the character. This prevents the program from having to check for both lowercase "k" and uppercase "K," shortening the code in the example. Its usage as a modifier is simple

```
ch := 'k'
        UpCase( ch )
        writeln( ch );
```

This results in the output of ch being capitalized. The function can be used inline or within an output statement to modify that variable.

Project 3

The *taxes.pas* project will build a program with a fair number of nested IF .. THEN .. ELSE statements. Within the program, the user is asked to enter his or her annual income, which is then compared against a series of declining tax brackets. Using the IF .. THEN .. ELSE structure to test each bracket, it can be safely assumed that if it does not meet the requirements of the higher tax bracket that it must fall into one of the lower brackets. The descent continues until the lowest tax rate is applied. The number of processing statements was kept low so that the structure of the multi-way branching could be examined. A structure such as this could become much more difficult to decipher if there were a greater number of processing lines between each testing statement.

```
program taxes;
{ ----------------------------------- }
{ Program that demonstrates multi-way }
{ branching using the if .. then ..   }
{ else structure. This program        }
{ continues to branch and test each   }
{ income group before it assigns the  }
{ tax rate.                           }
{ ----------------------------------- }

var
   income      : real;

begin
```

```
write('Enter your annual income : ');
readln(income);
writeln('----------------------------------');
writeln('            Tax Report');
writeln;

if income > 100000 then
begin
  writeln('Your income bracket is taxed at %43');
  writeln('Your taxes will be $',(income * 0.43):0:2);
end
else
  if income > 70000 then
  begin
    writeln('Your income bracket is taxed at %38');
    writeln('Your taxes will be $',(income * 0.38):0:2);
  end
  else
    if income > 50000 then
    begin
      writeln('Your income bracket is taxed at %29');
      writeln('Your taxes will be $',(income * 0.29):0:2);
    end
    else
      if income > 35000 then
      begin
        writeln('Your income bracket is taxed at %22');
        writeln('Your taxes will be $',(income * 0.22):0:2);
      end
      else
      begin
        writeln('Your income bracket is taxed at %15');
        writeln('Your taxes will be $',(income * 0.15):0:2);
      end;

end.
```

The output from this program is shown in Figure 5-6.

Figure 5-6

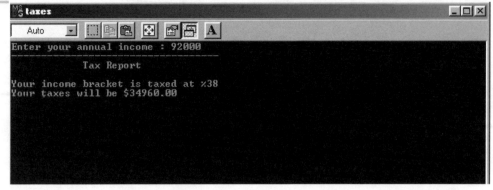

Be sure that you plan any testing of your programs to include all of the possible branches. Never take for granted that a specific branch will work just because all of the others like it do.

The Type Declaration

Not all of the data types supported by Object Pascal are native to the compiler itself. Structured data types and user-defined types can be created by the user of their own design and be declared and recognized by the compiler. The declaration of the types is carried out in the type section of a program file. A simple type declaration takes the form shown here:

```
program lerntdec;

type
  counter = integer;

var
  c : counter;

begin
  c := 10;
end.
```

Following the reserved word `type` we have declared a new data type with the name of `counter`. In this declaration we have assigned the properties of the predefined data type `integer` to a new type `counter`. This means that we can use the data type `counter` anywhere that an `integer` data type can be used. In the main body of the program you see that we have used it in an assignment statement.

Why would we perform such a seemingly redundant action? Mainly for clarification. As programs grow larger and larger it is easy to lose track of the meaning of variables, that is, what they are intended to be representing. If a variable is typed as `counter` instead of `integer` it is easy for the programmer to glance at the declaration and understand the intended purpose. In addition to making the program easier to understand, we will see the type declaration section used to define much more involved abstract data types in later pages of this book. One of the types that is declared in this section of the program is our next topic, sets.

Fundamentals in Focus

Ordering of Declarations

We've added a lot of items to the top end of our programs and there are more to come. Object Pascal is very particular about the order in which the compiler encounters these sections. The ordering makes good sense when you consider that one has to occur before another, for example, data types must be declared before we can declare variables of that type. The order of declarations in a program is:

1. Constant declarations

2. Type declarations

3. Variable declarations

4. Procedure and function declarations

Sets

If we go back and reexamine the code in Listing 5-1, a subtle problem makes itself known to us. What happens if a clever user enters an "X" or a "0"? Neither one of these values is acceptable to the nested IF .. THEN structure and could result in an aberrant value finding its way into the output. One way of preventing this type of GIGO (Garbage In Garbage Out) error from occurring is to verify the input values before they can enter the processing structures. The easiest way to accomplish this is to determine if the input value is a member of a predetermined group of elements.

Object Pascal supports a data object called a set that can be used to accommodate this requirement. A *set* is a structured data type composed of an unordered collection of up to 256 elements, each of the same specific data type. The Object Pascal set supports `char`, `integer`, and `Boolean` data types. Sets can be defined as a type or inline, as we will do here. The set is a comma-separated list of constants, as in:

```
[1,3,5,7,9]
```

which is surrounded by square brackets. Though the set can be composed of any of the ordinal data types, it is rarely used to support `Boolean` data because of the limited number of members. Character members in the list must be surrounded by quotes, as in:

```
['A','a','B','b']
```

The in operator is commonly used with Object Pascal sets. This Boolean set operator determines membership within a set and returns a true or false value. For example, test the following program.

```
program lernset1;
begin
  if 'Y' in ['Y','y','N','n'] then
    writeln('In Set')
  else
    writeln('Not In Set');
end.
```

You will receive the "In Set" message because the in operator will return a true value as the uppercase "Y" is a member of the set. After you run it in this form, change the test value to "q" or some other letter. The in operator will then return a false value.

Where would this fit into the problem posed in the first paragraph of this section? The program would want to only allow the entry of the face cards and specific numbers as input, disposing of all others. A fine solution to this would be to require membership in a set prior to the logic entering the long series of nested IF .. THENs. Let's test out this idea with a program.

```
program lernset2;
var
  card   : char;

begin

  write('Enter a face card (K,Q,J,A) : ');
  readln( card );

  if card in ['K','k','Q','q','J','j','A','a'] then
  begin
    if (UpCase(card) = 'K') then
      writeln('King');
    if (UpCase(card) = 'Q') then
      writeln('Queen');
    if (UpCase( card ) = 'J' ) then
      writeln( 'Jack' );

    if (UpCase( card ) = 'A' ) then
      writeln( 'Ace' );
  end
  else
  begin
    writeln('This is not a face card')
  end;
```

```
end.
```

Now the handling of the cards becomes simpler since we do not have to perform the repeated verification; the statement containing the Boolean set operation will have already filtered them out. Rather than validating the cards, the individual IF .. THEN .. ELSE statements can be put to better use.

Sets can be created at the point of use, as we did in the example listing above, or they can be declared as a variable. There are two methods that can be used in Object Pascal to declare a set as a variable type, both involving the SET OF construction. The first method of performing this task is to declare the set directly within the var statement, as in

```
var
   Lowercase    : set of 'a'..'z';
```

The segment 'a'..'z' uses a special shorthand; the two dots indicate that the set contains all of the members of the enumerated type that fall between the upper and lower delimiters (the a and the z). We are going to explore the enumerated type in much greater depth in a later chapter but for the time being we will establish a short definition. An enumerated type defines an ordered set of values by simply listing identifiers that denote these values. The members of the set only have value in their order; the individual elements have no value of their own. In the example set we recognize these characters as members of the ASCII set and it is easy to identify what letters will fill in the rest of the set. One note of caution in using the SET OF construct: it is not supported by all Object Pascal implementations so be sure that your compiler supports it before trying to implement it.

The preferred method for utilizing predefined sets is to declare the data type in the type section of your program. This sample program creates an enumerated type and then declares a set from it:

```
program lernset3;
type
  DaysOfWeek = (Mon, Tue, Wed, Thu, Fri, Sat, Sun);
  Week = SET OF DaysOfWeek;

var
  alldays    : week;
  weekend    : week;

begin
  weekend := [Sat, Sun];
  if Tue in Weekend then
    writeln('Days off')
  else
    writeln('Work day');
end.
```

The membership operator (in) is not the only one that applies to sets. As you see in Table 5-5, an entire range of operators is available for use with sets. These operations will be familiar to you from your mathematics studies back in high school.

Table 5-5: The set operators

Operator	Description	Example
+	Union	U3 = Set1 + Set2
*	Intersection	I3 = Set1 + Set2
−	Difference	D3 = Set1 − Set2

Union

The union operation results in a new set that contains all of the members of Set A and Set B. If Set A consists of [Elephant, Giraffe, Monkey] and Set B consists of [Horse, Tiger, Lion], the union of these two sets results in the set Circus [Elephant, Giraffe, Monkey, Horse Tiger, Lion]. The program *uniontst.dpr* demonstrates the union of two sets and then verifies inclusion of members from both subsets:

```
program uniontst;
type
   charset = set of char;
var
  setA   : charset;
  setB   : charset;
  setU   : charset;

begin
  setA := ['A','B','C'];
  setB := ['D','E','F'];

  setU := setA + setB;
  if ('A' in setU) and ('F' in setU) then
    writeln('Union Success');
end.
```

Intersection

An intersection of two sets consists of the members that are common to both sets. We start the process with two sets. Set 1 contains the names [Joe, David, Hunter] and Set 2 is composed of [Hunter, Lee, Jared]. When an intersection operation is performed on these sets, the result set will contain [Hunter]. The program *unionint.dpr* demonstrates the intersection of the two test sets:

```
program unionint;
type
   charset = set of char;
var
```

```
    setA   : charset;
    setB   : charset;
    setI   : charset;

  begin
    setA := ['A','B','C'];
    setB := ['Z','X','B'];

    setU := setA * setB;
    if 'B' in setI then
       writeln('Intersection Success');
  end.
```

Difference

A difference operation on Set A and Set B will result in Set C, which contains those members that are in Set A but not in Set B. If Set A contains [Portland, Salem, Medford] and Set B contains the members [Arlington, Salem, Richmond] the result of the set operation

```
    SetC := SetA - SetB;
```

is the set [Portland, Medford]. Again, test the Delphi code to see the operator at work.

```
    program uniondif;
    type
      charset = set of char;
    var
      setA   : charset;
      setB   : charset;
      setD   : charset;

    begin
      setA := ['A','B','C'];
      setB := ['Z','X','B'];

      setD := setA - setB;
      if ('A' in setD) and ('C' in setD) then
         writeln('Difference Success');
    end.
```

There is also a subset of the relational operators that we examined earlier that can be used with sets. Table 5-6 shows these operators. The results of the operations, Boolean values, are much as expected. The table shows examples of expressions that will result in a true outcome.

Chapter 5

Table 5-6: The relational operators used with sets

Operator	Description	Example of True Result
=	The sets are equal	[A,B,C] = [A,B,C]
≠	The sets are not identical	[A,B,C] ≠ [C,D,E]
<=	All of the elements in Set1 are in Set2	[A,B,C] <= [A,B,C,D,E,F]
>=	All of the elements in Set2 are in Set1	[A,E,I,O,U] >= [A,E]

The Case Statement

Using nested IF .. THEN .. ELSE statements more than a few levels deep can create a very complicated structure in your program. While it certainly may be understandable for you, the original programmer, the poor soul who follows behind you may pull her hair out trying to understand your logic. Fortunately, Object Pascal provides an alternative to these statements, the CASE structure. This construct enables your program to evaluate an expression and compare the result against a range of items from which it will match one or none. If a match is found, a block of statements can be executed and the structure exited, all within an easy to understand code block. The CASE structure also allows you to define an `else` option to be processed if no match is located. The logical format for a case structure is:

```
case expression of
  Choice1 :
    Choice1 code block
  Choice2 :
    Choice2 code block
  ...
else
  Otherwise code block
end;
```

The expression that follows the keyword `case` is known as the controlling expression and it must evaluate to an ordinal response. It is this result that is compared for equality against the list of constants that follows, called the Label list. There is no `begin` for the `end`; it matches up to the `case` keyword.

The controlling expression can either be a variable or a statement that evaluates to the required ordinal value. The Label list has similar requirements in that each label must be an ordinal value; no `real` or `string` data types are allowed. In the following structure the user is asked to input a menu choice which is then evaluated and processed through the CASE structure:

```
program menu;
var
  choice    : char;

begin
  writeln('(O)pen a file');
  writeln('(S)ave a file');
  writeln('(Q)uit the program');
  writeln;
  Write('Enter your choice from the menu: ');
  readln(choice);

  case upcase(choice) of
    'O':
        begin
  writeln('switching to file open');
      end;
    'S':
begin
  writeln('saving file, please wait...');
end;
    'Q':
begin
  writeln('quitting application, please wait...');
end;
    else
      writeln('invalid menu choice ...');
    end;    { end case }

end.
```

If the user enters "Q" in response to the prompt, the value is assigned to the variable `choice`. The value will be compared against the labels "O" and "S" in turn and each will result in a false result. When the variable is compared to label "Q" and a match is indicated, the statements that follow the colon are processed to either a block terminator (end) or the next label. When the `end` keyword for the block is processed, the logic transfers to the `end` statement at the bottom of the case structure. Processing continues with the first line after the semicolon, where the comment {end case} appears. The output that is generated by this program is shown in Figure 5-7.

Figure 5-7

If the user were to enter a code of "X," which has no match in the Label list, each label would be tested in order. When none were found to match, the execution would shift to the `else` clause in the CASE construct. The line `writeln('invalid ...')` would be processed and execution shifted again to the `end` at the bottom of the CASE structure. Under no circumstances will a second block of statements be processed within the CASE structure as it is structured. If your program requires that a range of user options trigger a single action, *case lists* can be used to enable this feature. The following example shows this concept in action. When the CASE structure is entered, the control expression will be evaluated against all of the labels that precede a colon before moving on.

```
program many2one;
var
   choice   : integer;
begin
   writeln('Select a value between 1 and 7');
   readln( choice );

   case choice of
     1, 2, 3 :
writeln('In the first group');
     4..7:
writeln('In the second group');
   end;
end.
```

Remember the use of the .. notation. This shorthand means all of the members between the bounding elements shown. In other words, if we write 4 .. 7 then the set includes 4, 5, 6, and 7.

QUICK CHECK

1. What is the output of the following code block (if it were written in the context of a complete program)?

```
x := 'Y';
if 2 <= 3 then
  if x in ['A'..'Z'] then
    if x < 'c' then
       writeln('First Writeln')
    else

       writeln('Second Writeln')
  else
     writeln('Third Writeln')
```

2. What is the output of the following code block (if it were written in the context of a complete program)?

```
x := 10;
case ( x - 1 ) of
  1, 5, 10 :
writeln('Audi');
  2, 6, 8 :
writeln('Fiat');
  3, 7    :
writeln('Puegot');
else
  writeln('Japanese brand?')
end;
```

Project 4

As always, the best way to reinforce a new concept is to immediately build something that uses it. The *cardshark* program shown below puts two nested CASE structures to work.

```
program cardshark;
{ ----------------------------------- }
{ prog will accept a two character val }
{ that is meant to be shorthand for a  }
{ playing card. It will then use a case}
{ structure to reply with the full card}
{ description. If either piece of data }
{ is bad, the nesting will kick the    }
{ card out.                            }
{ ----------------------------------- }
```

```
var
   incard        : char;
   insuit        : char;
   outcard       : string[8];
   outsuit       : string[8];

begin

   { -- Be sure to give the user a help prompt if necessary --}
   write('Enter a card value and a suit (ex: 3H for Three of Hearts):');
   readln(incard,insuit);

   { -- check the card value first -- }
   if UpCase(incard)
      in ['1','2','3','4','5','6','7','8','9','A','K','Q','J']
then
   begin
     case incard of
       'A','a' :
         outcard := 'Ace';

       'K','k' :
         outcard := 'King';

       'Q','q' :
         outcard := 'Queen';

       'J','j' :
         outcard := 'Jack';

       '1'     :
         outcard := 'Ten';

       '2'     :
         outcard := 'Two';

       '3'     :
         outcard := 'Three';

       '4'     :
         outcard := 'Four';
```

```
      '5'      :
        outcard := 'Five';

      '6'      :
        outcard := 'Six';

      '7'      :
        outcard := 'Seven';

      '8'      :
        outcard := 'Eight';
      '9'      :
        outcard := 'Nine';
    end;

    { -- good card, check the suit -- }
    if UpCase(insuit) in ['H','S','D','C'] then
    begin
      case insuit of
        'H','h'  :
          outsuit := 'Hearts';

        'S','s'  :
          outsuit := 'Spades';

        'D','d'  :
          outsuit := 'Diamonds';

        'C','c'  :
          outsuit := 'Clubs';
      end;

      {Only if we have a good card and suit will it get here}
      writeln('The card is the ',outcard,' of ',outsuit);
      writeln('Thanks for playing.');

    end
    else
      writeln('I don''t recognize that suit.');
  end
  else {incard}
    writeln('That is an invalid card, sorry.');
end.
```

Summary

This chapter has added a bevy of logical decision-making tools to your quiver. Your programs are not going to be forced into a linear processing path anymore as you are able to include logical structures that enable the program to select alternative paths. Before we could discuss the structures themselves we came face to face with the logical operators and took a look at how they evaluate operands to come to a true or false conclusion. These led us directly to the IF .. THEN .. ELSE structure, the fundamental building block of all decision making in Object Pascal. This control structure enables a program to test a condition and, based on the true or false result that it generates, point the program in one of two directions. If the program needed to go in more than two directions, which is a common requirement, then this simple structure could be nested to create a more complex set of testing conditions.

The set data structure simplified things for us again. If the purpose of a complex IF .. THEN .. ELSE structure was simply to test for membership in an ordinal set we found how it could be simplified by the use of a set and the in operator. Confirming membership took a lot of the bulk out of the structures that were starting to develop. Another tool that Object Pascal offers to simplify decision making is the CASE structure. Even though the structure only allowed the programs to select one choice from many, it certainly was simpler than a long set of IF .. THEN .. ELSE statements that would lead to the same result. Decision making is a common and very basic task in nearly all programming situations and it pays to be familiar with all of the available options of your selected programming environment.

TEST YOUR KNOWLEDGE

Try putting some of this newfound knowledge to work by writing one or more of the following programs. Remember that the skills tested at the end of each chapter are meant to reinforce what was discussed in the chapter. For that reason, the projects are going to seem somewhat pointed and might be missing a lot of features or requirements that a production program would have.

1. Convert the multi-way branching to a CASE structure to simplify the *taxes* program from project 3.

2. Write a program that accepts a birthday in the form of three integers:

   ```
   11 15 60
   ```

   and then outputs a message in the form of a birthday greeting that says:

   ```
   Happy Birthday on November 15. You are XX years old!
   ```

   Store the current year as a constant.

3. Long-distance rates are very confusing to most people, so you are going to write a program to simplify the explanation. The O.P. long distance company charges according to the following rate schedule:

A. Any call started between 8 AM and 6 PM Monday through Friday is billed at 50 cents per minute.

B. Any call starting before 8 AM or after 6 PM Monday through Friday is billed at 40 cents per minute.

C. Any call started Saturday or Sunday is 24 cents per minute.

The input to the program will consist of the day of the week, the time the call started including the AM/PM designation, and the length of the call in minutes. The time will consist of two integer values and one character, for example, 1 27 p for 1:27 pm. You should read the day of the week as one of the following pairs of character values: SU MO TU WE TH FR SA. The output will consist of the total cost of the call in dollars and cents.

Looping

Introduction

One of the noted advantages that machines have over human beings is that they do not mind engaging in repetitive activities. Once instructed on how to perform a certain task, the machine will gleefully repeat the process over and over until told to stop or the bushings seize, whichever comes first. Computer programs, which are composed of a series of instructions, can be written to execute statements repeatedly until told to stop or until some sentinel event occurs that causes the process to halt. This action is known to programmers as *looping*, and enabling that action within your programs is the subject of this chapter. On the following pages we will examine the Object Pascal looping mechanisms and learn how to put them to work. We'll cover a range of subjects including:

- The design decisions that need to be considered before any of the looping control structures can be selected and implemented within your program.

- The `while` statement, a basic logic controlled loop that can allow your program to loop indefinitely.

- The `for` statement counter controlled loop structure, used to build loops that run a specific number of times.

- How the `repeat` statement is different from the other loop structures.

By this point in the book you should have a pretty good familiarity with the fundamental structure of a Delphi program so we will no longer spend our time reviewing the basics of the language. Be sure that you are comfortable with the structures and data types that have been discussed up to this point, as you will find that they again come to be used when discussing the looping mechanisms. This chapter especially will drive home one of the less-discussed benefits of the Object Pascal language and that is that it directly implements a wider variety of fundamental logical constructs. There are three loop structures available within the language that correspond to the basic logical tools used by algorithm designers, the `for`, `while`, and `repeat` loops. This is much different from other languages that offer one type of loop and force the programmer to *emulate* the logical structures that they want to include in their program. Keep this in mind as you read the book and wonder why there seems to be duplication within the structures.

Repeating Statements

Looping is the programming process of repeating an instruction or set of instructions a specific number of times. The number of times, or *iterations*, that the loop completes can be fixed and initialized by the program prior to entering the loop. It can also be a variable figure, determined to be zero or more iterations by decisions that occur inside or outside of the loop *body*. The body of a loop is that statement or set of statements that is enclosed within the control structure.

Consider a practical example, a program that is designed for recording the results of an exam taken by the members of your Introduction to Programming class. The program must record the individual scores in a file and then present the average score for all of the students to the instructor. Both of these processes require a fixed set of instructions:

Step 1 — Get the test score from the user.

Step 2 — Write the test score to a file.

Step 3 — Add the test score to a running subtotal of all of the scores.

The programmer can approach this in a couple of ways. The first would be to simply type these commands into her program the number of times that they need to be processed. In other words, if there are 22 students in the class, these lines will be added to the program 22 times. This jumps out immediately as an unwieldy choice for two reasons. Number one, the program would have to be rewritten every time a student is absent and misses a test or simply drops the class. If it is not, then the divisor of 22 for the average would give an incorrect result. The second reason that this is not a practical choice is that the redundant lines would be a maintenance nightmare for the programmer. Any changes to the code would require 22 or more separate modifications to the program, leading to the possibility of errors corrupting the program.

A better approach to solving this programming problem is to build the code that needs to be repeated—getting the score, writing the file, and running the subtotal—into a loop control structure. The loop can then be told to execute 22 times, repeating the instructions contained within the body until the loop terminates. This is a much more satisfactory solution than the initial approach. If the class size changes, the loop only needs to be told the new number of exam scores it will be gathering. Better yet, the program can count the number of scores entered during processing rather than requiring upfront information. Either of these ideas will ensure that there is always an accurate number for the divisor in the averaging equation. From the maintenance perspective, any modification to the program will be limited to a single area of the code, making it less likely that errors will be made.

The topic of looping is best begun with a brief discussion of the design considerations necessary when a loop is planned as a part of the program's design. Three key elements of every loop require careful examination before the appropriate structure and control elements are implemented in code. Once the common theoretical aspects of looping have been reviewed, we will look at the Object Pascal control structures that are used to implement a loop structure in a program: the `while`, `for`, and `repeat` statements.

Designing a Loop

Before we enter into a discussion of the specific Object Pascal looping structures, some time should be spent learning to appropriately design the structures. This will ensure that they will work the way that we expect them to and help us avoid the dreaded "infinite loop." There are three segments to a loop that require consideration prior to implementation:

1.   The body of the loop

2.   The initialization statements

3.   The conditions for exit

Figure 6-1 shows the flowchart for a simple counter controlled loop. This design will add together six numbers using the following instructions:

```
Start
SUBTOTAL = 0
COUNTER = 0
DOWHILE COUNTER < 6
    Read DATA
    SUBTOTAL = SUBTOTAL
      + DATA
    COUNTER = COUNTER +
      1
ENDDO
Stop
```

All of these steps are needed in a computer program to emulate a simple daily activity such as entering these same six numbers into a

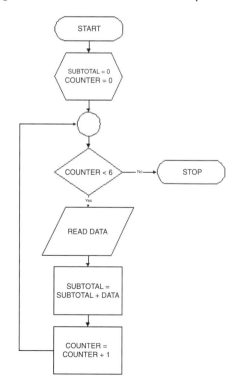

Figure 6-1: A counter controlled loop

calculator. The real-life description of that activity is much simpler:

1. Clear calculator memory.

2. Enter a number.

3. Hit the + key (repeat 2 and 3 five times).

Using this example, let's take a closer look at each of these elements.

The Body of the Loop

It's within the body of the loop that all of the action occurs. The part of the algorithm that is to be repeated is found here; these are the instructions that are going to run over and over under the control of the loop structure. For example, in the algorithm described above for summing a series of numbers the statement that actually adds the current number to the subtotal would be in the body of the loop. The instructions

```
Read DATA
SUBTOTAL = SUBTOTAL + DATA
COUNTER = COUNTER + 1
```

make up the body. Figure 6-2 highlights this section of the flowchart. There are no limitations on what actions can occur within the body of the loop. In fact, quite commonly other loops are included in the body that enclose bodies of their own, a process called *nesting*.

Figure 6-2: The loop body

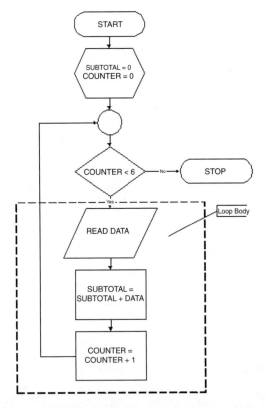

The Initialization Statements

All loop control structures have one thing in common, a control variable. The control variable is the value that is used in a logical test expression to determine if the loop continues for another iteration or if it terminates. In our calculator emulation example we are going to add six numbers. The control variable in the example is called COUNTER and this variable is used to check the number of iterations the loop has executed. Of all of the variables in your programs, initialization of the control variables is critical to the proper operation of your program. Figure 6-3 highlights the initialization statements of the loop. It contains the two program statements:

```
SUBTOTAL = 0
COUNTER = 0
```

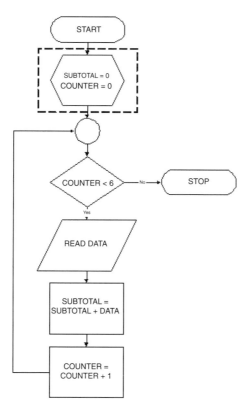

Figure 6-3: The initialization statements

The loop logic that you decide to implement will determine the data type of the control variable and how the variable is to be initialized prior to use. If a loop is to run ten times, for instance, the control variable that is tested in a counter controlled loop is likely to be initialized to zero. Starting at zero will cause the control variable in this type of loop to increment 0, 1, 2 .. 9 to 10. Comparing this control variable against the end value of 10 using an expression that tests to see if the control variable is less than 10 will result in the correct number of iterations. Any other value in the variable will cause a lesser or greater number of iterations than expected. The SUBTOTAL value is also initialized prior to entering the body of the loop to emulate the Clear Calculator Memory action. Initialization is performed at this point in the program because moving it anywhere else in the code results in incorrect results.

The Conditions for Exit

The condition that causes the termination of the loop is one of the most important decisions made in the design of the algorithm. The primary design decision for a loop control structure is how it will stop; improperly designed loops that run without termination cause such problems as locked up machines or thousands of utility bills to be sent to one customer. There are four methods used for terminating a loop:

1. Controlled by user input
2. Ask before the next iteration
3. Loop termination by a sentinel value
4. Running out of input

Figure 6-4:
Testing for
termination

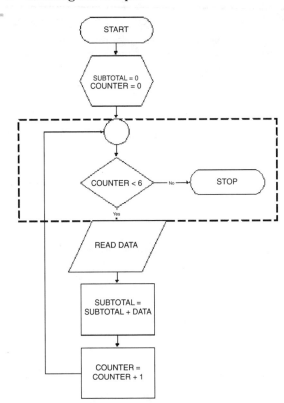

In the case of our example, the condition for exit has been programmed into the code already. The value of the control variable will never exceed 6 since this value causes termination of the loop. In Figure 6-4 the decision diamond is highlighted as this is where the loop control expression is tested for termination. If the value is less than 6, another iteration of the loop is processed. If it is equal to or greater than 6, the loop is terminated.

Let's take a closer look at the four methods of stopping the loop process.

Controlled by User Input

A counter or logically controlled loop structure, such as the one in our example, can have the number of iterations predetermined by the user. Prior to entering the body of the loop, the controlling variable can be filled with the eventual terminating value by user input. For example, in a program to average the test scores for a class, the user would be asked prior to entering the loop how many students there are. This number is tested against a running subtotal that is incremented by one each time a student score is entered. When the numbers match, the program knows that there is no more input.

This method of determining the termination value has both good and bad points. It's easy to code and implement since you have put all of the responsibility onto the user for providing you with the correct termination value. On the downside, once the user has entered the terminating value he's stuck with it. If the instructor tells the program that there are ten tests to score and then finds a couple of others lying around, the program is incapable of adapting to this new information. Once the loop has passed through ten iterations, it will terminate and ignore the professor's pleas to accept the new test scores. Only running the program a second time with the number of exams increased to 12 will solve this problem.

Ask Before the Next Iteration

The "ask before iterating" termination method takes a more flexible tack; upon completion of the body of the loop the user is asked whether or not to loop again. Using the example of the test grading program, after each score is entered the instructor would be asked if there are any more tests. If she responds to the affirmative then the loop passes through one more iteration. If the teacher says that there are no further exams to score the loop will be terminated. This method is not used in a counter controlled loop structure, only with a logically controlled loop. As you can see in Figure 6-5 this method significantly changes the logical flow of the program.

Exiting the loop in this fashion works well in programs where the loop body is very long and complex or where there will be few iterations. These prerequisites are mainly attributed to the intrusion of the query into the user's work flow. If you are grading five exams and after each one you are required to answer the question "Are there more exams to enter? Y/N" you won't mind terribly. On the other hand, if you are a teaching assistant for Astronomy 101 and have 100 or more exams to enter, that simple query becomes cumbersome. Each question and answer considerably slows down the process of your heads-down data entry. The user must also be asked a variation of this question prior to entering the loop. There may be no tests to input and it would be inappropriate for the user to enter the body of the loop for processing.

Figure 6-5: A logically controlled loop

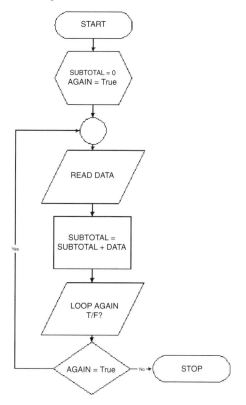

Loop Termination By a Sentinel Value

A *sentinel value* is a flag that is tested against the control variable to determine if the loop should continue for another iteration or terminate. The sentinel value itself is a constant that is designed to be significantly different from the range of values expected as a part of the input to your program. For example, we may want to modify the test scoring program so that it does not ask how many scores there are or query the user to see if there is another score for our class of 150 students. By using a sentinel value of 9999, since it's unlikely that a student will score this many points on a test, the instructor can put his head down and simply key in the test scores. When he has completed the scoring of the variable number of tests that he has, he simply keys in 9999 to terminate the loop. The program execution moves out of the loop and displays the average test score on the screen. Logically, the structure of this type of loop is similar to that shown in Figure 6-5. Rather than collecting a yes or no response to a user query, the program simply compares the last data value entered against the flag to determine whether or not to continue.

This method works well for data entry programs. In these situations we don't want the user involved in responding to screen queries during the process of entering data. The main consideration when selecting this method is to ensure that the value selected for the sentinel will never occur as a part of the data set. This is usually decided by selecting a value that is the opposite of all of the data that will be keyed. An exam score, for instance, will never be a negative number. A sentinel of −1 could be used to trigger the termination of the loop. At the other end of the spectrum, an extra credit question could easily give the student a score of greater than 100 percent, so 101 would be an inappropriate choice.

Running Out of Input

I'm not sure that this even needs to be mentioned as it is a wholly unacceptable method of terminating a loop. Running out of input simply means that when there are no more data entries, the loop terminates by a user-caused or program-generated exception. Even though the program can be designed to handle the exception and return to processing, giving up control of the execution for that moment is playing with fire. If the user is keying the data and is forced to press Ctrl+Escape or some equally obscure key combination to terminate, he is forced to perform an uncomfortable action to exit the loop. Even more common is a situation where data is read in the body of the loop from an external file and the program suddenly encounters the end-of-file marker. The loop must be prepared for this eventuality or an unrecoverable error could occur.

Fundamentals in Focus

Infinite Loops and the Variables that Create Them

When designing your loop structures it is easy to get so involved in the structure and actions of the loop that you neglect to consider the requirements of the control variable. When used with a loop control structure, the initialization of a variable becomes more important than ever as uninitialized variables are the major cause of infinite loops. The attention that they require is nothing special; simply ensure that a value is initialized in such a way that the desired actions will occur.

The for .. do control structure lets you off the hook since it will initialize its control variable by itself. On the other hand, the while .. do and repeat .. until loops may produce undesirable results if the variable used in the control expression is not properly initialized. The while .. do loop, for instance, may not execute at all or, if the control expression continues to be satisfied, it may execute endlessly.

Design the Loop Before Implementation

Be sure to consider all of these design aspects of the loop control structure prior to implementing it in your code. Loops can be notoriously difficult to debug once they are coded since the condition that is causing the problem may not occur for thousands of iterations. If you are forced to watch each one manually in order to locate the problem, programming is going to become quite a chore to you instead of the secret pleasure that it really is. Remember that there are a number of different methods for entering and exiting the loop and each has a different place in your repertoire.

The While Statement

The first of the loop control structures that we'll examine is the while statement. This statement consists of the keyword while followed by a Boolean expression and the keyword do. This complete statement is followed by the statement or compound statement that makes up the body of the loop. This loop is executed x number of times based on the evaluation of the Boolean expression. The logical representation of the Object Pascal while statement is shown in Figure 6-6.

This flowchart translates into

```
WHILE the value of X is less than or equal to 10 DO ( the following )
The Loop Body Process
        Add one to number of times the loop has run
Return to the top of the loop and test the Boolean expression again
```

Figure 6-6:
The WHILE
DO control
structure

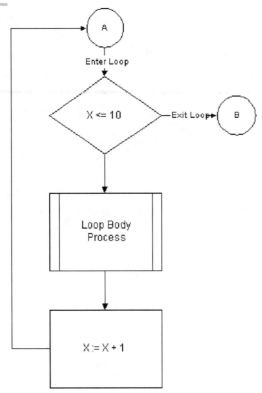

The while statement is logically controlled by the Boolean expression. As long as the expression evaluates to true, an iteration of the loop will occur. When it evaluates to false, the body of the loop is skipped and execution continues with the next line after the end of the structure.

Converting the flowchart into code is easy. The following program encompasses the entire while statement along with the other two requirements that were discussed in the design section of this chapter: initialization of the control variable and termination of the loop.

```
program lernloop;
var
   x       : integer;

begin
  x := 1;
  while x <= 10 do
  begin

    writeln(x);
    x := x + 1;

  end;
```

```
    writeln('Loop terminated');
  end.
```

The initialization of the control variable is the first action taken in the program. If the control variable is not initialized, we have an unpredictable value in the variable x when it enters the loop. When this is the case the actions of the loop cannot be logically predicted. In the program the value has been set to 1.

This control variable is the first thing that is evaluated in the while statement loop. In the sample program, the first time the program is executed the value in variable x, which equals 1, is compared with the literal 10. Since it is less than 10 and the Boolean expression evaluates to true, the body of the loop will be executed. Every statement in the body of the loop will be executed before the logic is transferred back to the while statement. In our program block, the value of x is incremented by one and then written to the screen. This variable is then returned to the Boolean expression for evaluation. After this first iteration the value is 2 and, when compared to the literal 10, causes the Boolean expression to evaluate to true again. Because of this, the loop will perform another iteration.

Skipping forward to the tenth iteration of the loop the value of x is now going to be incremented to 11. As before, the flow of the program will return to the while statement for evaluation of the Boolean expression. This time, however, the expression x <= 10 will evaluate to false. This causes the loop to skip the body and go directly to the first statement after the structure. In the case of our sample, the statement writes the line "Loop Terminated" to the screen.

Using the Debugger

Repeating structures are an excellent topic for use in introducing the integrated debugger in Delphi. A *debugger* is a tool that helps you locate and fix errors in your applications. It will let you control the execution of the program while monitoring variable values and items in data structures, and allow you to modify data values while debugging. The great thing about the Delphi environment is that these abilities are integrated into the development tools themselves and they are very easy to learn and use. To gain an introduction into the use of some of the features of the debugger we will use the *lernloop.dpr* project as the focus.

1. Reopen the project if you have closed it.

2. Instead of pressing F9 or selecting Run->Run from the menu to compile and run your program, press **F8** or select **Run->Step Over** from the menu. The program will start and pause at the first begin statement. Notice that the line is highlighted and an arrow indicates the currently processing line as shown in Figure 6-7.

Figure 6-7

3. Press **F8** two more times. The debugger will stop on the line that reads

```
writeln( x );
```

Move your cursor with the mouse over any of the x variables in the code. After a second or so a pop-up flag will appear with the current value of the variable showing. This is a great tool for examining the contents of variables throughout your program during execution.

4. Another way of watching the values of your variables is to use a Watch List window. Select **View->Debug Windows->Watches** from the menu and an empty Watch List window will appear as shown in Figure 6-8. To add a variable value to this window, press **Ins** or right-click on the window and select **Add Watch** from the context menu.

Figure 6-8

5. The Watch Properties dialog shown in Figure 6-9 appears. Enter the value **x** in the field labeled Expression. Select **OK** when finished. You can add multiple variable or object names in this list at the same time.

Figure 6-9

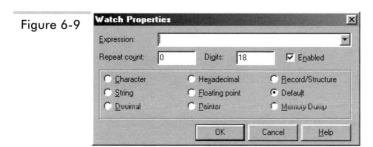

6. Now, continue pressing the **F8** key to step through your code. You can see the value of x being incremented by each iteration of the loop shown in Figure 6-10.

Figure 6-10

```
program lernloop;
var
   x      : integer;
begin
   x := 1;
   while x <= 10 do
   begin
      writeln( x );
      x := x + 1;
   end;

end.
```

Watch List
x: 5

7. It is not necessary to perform this manual control of the program until it terminates. Press **F9** and it will complete all of its processing at normal speed.

The debugger is especially useful for learning how loops process but this is certainly not its only use. As the programs in this book become more complex, your skills at debugging will come more and more into play. Taking your theoretical knowledge of how your loop structure is to process, you can use the debugger to test your idea and ensure that all of your assumptions come true. The method that we just outlined starts processing the program from the first statement. Many times you will want to skip over much of the code and focus in on a certain area. This can be done by setting a *breakpoint*, a point in the code where execution will pause and turn over control to the debugger. We'll do this now with the same program.

1. Move the cursor to the line that reads

   ```
   writeln( x );
   ```

   To create a breakpoint, click in the trough to the left of the programming statement as shown in Figure 6-11. This will place a larger, red dot there as well as a red highlight across the line.

Figure 6-11

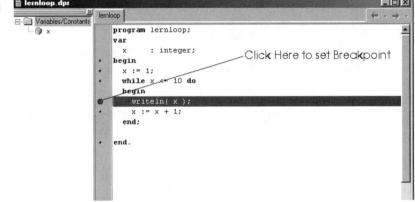

2. Press **F9** to run the program. All of the statements up to the breakpoint will be processed as normal. When execution reaches the breakpoint, it will pause and wait for your command. You can return to using the F8 key to single step through the program.

3. When you have completed your debugging you should clear the breakpoint. You can simply reverse the selection by clicking on the breakpoint indicator.

Breakpoints are flexible. Suppose you want to examine a certain part of your loop but do not want to witness the first 95 iterations of a loop. A type of breakpoint called a *conditional breakpoint* might be the answer. The execution of the program will pause at the selected line when an expression's condition is met. For example, in the *lernloop.dpr* project we would like to examine the program when the loop has completed eight iterations. To build this type of breakpoint select Run->Add Breakpoint->Source Breakpoint. In the dialog presented, type x = 8 for the condition. Now, rather than pausing on the first iteration, most of the looping will be completed before the program pauses. The debugger will watch the value of x for you and pause only when the condition is met.

Fundamentals in Focus

My Loop Didn't Run

One of the most common bugs encountered with the `while` statement is that it doesn't execute and all of the code in the body gets skipped. This often has to do with a logical part of the control structure that doesn't get committed to memory. The WHILE control structure is unique in that the body of the loop may never be executed. Why does this happen? The `while` statement tests its Boolean expression before entering the loop. If it evaluates to false, the loop will not be run and the execution will skip to the bottom of the structure. For example, modify the sample to be:

```
x := 11;
while x <= 10 do
begin

  writeln(x);
  x := x + 1;

end;
writeln('Loop terminated');
```

The first time this program is run, the expression in the loop will evaluate to false and the loop will not run. If the value of `x` was set by another process or much earlier in the program, this can be tough to debug.

The `while` statement is a logically controlled loop that determines whether or not another iteration will occur by evaluating the Boolean expression between the `while` and the `do`. Though the example shown demonstrated a loop controlled by a numeric variable, this control structure works with any Boolean expression that you can design. This can include comparing strings or characters or even a simple Boolean variable in the evaluation expression that controls the loops.

QUICK CHECK

1. Determine the output from the following code if it were embedded in a complete program.

```
x := 0;
while x <= 10 do
begin
  x := x + 1;
  writeln(x);
end;
```

2. What if the value of `x` was initialized to 1? How many iterations of the loop will occur? Is this the expected behavior?

3. Determine the output from the following code if it were embedded in a complete program.

```
choice := 'T';
while choice in ['Y','y','N','n'] do
begin
   writeln('Your choice is ',choice);
end;
writeln('Launching new application');
```

Project 1

Having the ability to repeat sections of code adds enormously to the flexibility and scope of the programs that we will be able to write. The project that we will work on now is much greater in its abilities than what we have explored in the previous pages. The program utilizes previously explored control structures and adds the capabilities of the `while` statement loop to the mix. The program will compute a loan payout based on the following requirements.

The program is a simple amortization chart for the purchase of a television costing $1,000.00. At Bertrand-Russell stores, credit is easy at fixed payments of $50.00 per month at a low, low rate of 18% annually. Under this easy payment schedule, our customers want to see how long it will take to pay off their TV before they can buy another one. The key to this program is found in the WHILE .. DO loop that is used to compute the balance and interest due each month.

```
program loanpmt;

{ ------------------------------------ }
{ program to computer installment pmts }
{ on a fixed balance. Rate and Pmt amt }
{ provided against debt of $1000        }
{                                       }
{ Compute interest and balance for each }
{ period and print these. Use a loop to }
{ repeat the payment instructions       }
{ ------------------------------------ }

const
   RATE = 0.18;
   PMT = 50.00;

var
   princ      : real;
   balance    : real;
   interest   : real;
   pmt_count  : integer;
```

```
      last_pmt    : real;

begin

  { - This data could be received from the user - }
  princ := 1000;
  balance := princ;
  pmt_count := 1;


  { - write payment report header - }
  writeln('Pmt#':5,'Payment':10,'Interest':10,'Balance':10);
  writeln('--------------------------------------------');


  { - Loop while the balance remains greater than the PMT
    amount -}
  while balance > PMT do
  begin
    interest := balance * (RATE / 12);

    balance := (balance - pmt) + interest;

    writeln(pmt_count:5, PMT:10:2, interest:10:2,
      balance:10:2);
    pmt_count := pmt_count + 1;

  end;

  { - Compute the final pmt -}
  if balance > 0 then
  begin
    interest := balance * (RATE / 12);
    balance := balance + interest;
    last_pmt := balance;
    balance := balance - last_pmt;

    writeln(pmt_count:5, last_pmt:10:2, interest:10:2,
      balance:10:2);
  end;
  readln;

end.
```

The loop is controlled by the expression

```
balance > PMT
```

and will continue until the balance falls below this amount. Why didn't we simply run this loop until the balance is zero? If the expression tested for a balance greater than zero, the final payment would not be figured correctly, generating a credit balance on the account. This is a situation that we wish to avoid. Be sure that you take details such as this into account when designing your programs.

Fundamentals in Focus

Robust Input

With the addition of looping to our tool chest, we have a new ability to improve the quality of the input statements in our programs. Program statements that gather data from the user should always screen the user's input in such a way as to prevent the entry of illegal values into the processing flow. For example, if the user is asked to confirm some action, the program should accept "Y", "y", "N", or "n" and nothing else. If the user enters a value other than those, he needs to be gently reminded of the valid values and not allowed to continue until he has entered one of the acceptable characters.

To this point, the data entry statements that would handle this query would look something like

```
write('Do you want to continue (Y/N)? ');
readln(ans)
if ans in ['Y','y'] then
  . . .
```

The only problem with a statement such as this is that the user must always select from the correct character set in order for it to work. If the character that is entered is outside of the acceptable choices, the program can fail with a run-time error.

An improved method for creating robust input statements is to trap the user in a loop that has two requirements for exit: either the user enters a value that is acceptable to the program or the user explicitly opts out of the program and any further input. The loop used for error checking uses negative logic. It is only entered if the user provides an unacceptable value. If the data provided is correct, the error-correction loop is bypassed. To modify the sample statement, a loop verifying the appropriate characters is added to the program.

```
write('Do you want to continue (Y/N)? ');
readln(ans);

while not ( ans in ['Y','y','N','n'] ) do
begin
  writeln(chr(7));
```

```
      writeln('Please enter Y or N only : ');
      readln(ans);
   end;
   if UpCase(ans) = 'Y' then
   ...
```

These additional loops might add a few lines to your programs but the benefits are well worth it in improved exception handling and more robust programs.

The For Statement

With enough creative energy applied to the design, a program can perform nearly any looping requirement with the `while` statement. One of the great advantages of the Object Pascal language is that it doesn't require you to jump through hoops to solve problems. It strives to provide the native control structures needed to implement all of the basic logical structures rather than forcing the programmer to emulate them. One of the basic loop constructs that is implemented as a control structure in Object Pascal is the FOR .. NEXT loop, defined as the `for` statement.

It performs the same task as the `while` loop with one important difference: it is a counter controlled loop.

A *counter controlled loop* will execute a specific number of times regardless of the actions that occur inside of the body. Unlike the logically controlled structure that reevaluates the Boolean value of its controlling expression after each iteration, the counter controlled loop simply steps through the series of ordinals defined for it. Figure 6-12 shows the logical representation of the `for` loop structure.

Figure 6-12:
The FOR .. NEXT control structure

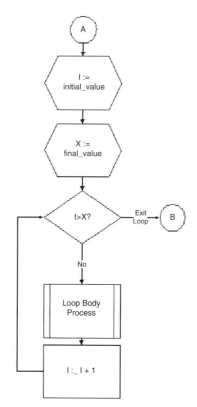

The structure makes use of two variable values, `initial_value` and `final_value`. In Object Pascal these may be either variables or constants. In the program:

```
program lrnloop2;
var
  n       : integer;
begin

  for n := 1 to 10 do
    writeln( n );
end.
```

the initial value of 1 and the final value of 10 are literals. On the first iteration of the loop the control variable n will take the initial value and will equal 1. The `for` statement in Object Pascal is self-incrementing so on the second iteration two things will occur. First, the value of n will be equal to 2 having been incremented by 1. Second, this value will be compared against the final value of 10. Since it is not greater than 10, the loop will execute again. The loop will execute the body statement, which can be a simple or a compound statement, until the final value has been incremented to 11. At that point the loop will be terminated and execution transferred to the next line after the body statement.

The `for` statement has an alternative form that controls its iterations in a different manner. In place of the keyword `to` this form uses `downto` and rather than incrementing the control variable by 1 after each iteration, the value in the control variable is decremented by 1. This gives the effect of counting down rather than up. If the control variable starts at 10, after the first iteration it will be equal to 9 and so on until completion.

Modifying the Control Variable

Unlike the logically controlled loop in which your program or your user can influence the evaluation statement to terminate the loop, the counter controlled loop must run to completion. The logical expression in a `while` statement can be manipulated by program modification of the variables used in the expression. For example, in the program:

```
program lrnloop3;
var
  ans : char;
begin
  ans := 'N';

  while UpCase(ans) <> 'N' do
  begin
    write('Continue with operation ? (Y/N) ');
    readln(ans);
```

```
    end;
  end.
```

the value of the variable `ans` can be modified at any point during the execution of the program to discontinue the loop. A counter controlled loop is not as pliable and subject to modification.

When a value has been given to the `final_value` of a counter controlled loop, the variable can be modified while the `for` control structure is running. The results, though, might not be what you expect. In the following program:

```
program lrnloop3;
var
  n  : integer;
  x  : integer;

begin
  x := 10;
  for n := 1 to x do
    writeln( n );
    x := x + 1;
    writeln( x );
  end;
end.
```

the value of x can be modified. In Figure 6-13 you can see the output from this experiment. Although the value of x was incremented it did not affect the number of iterations of the loop.

Figure 6-13

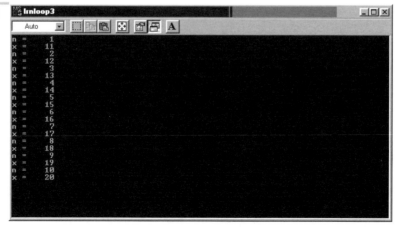

That said, <u>this is not a suggested course of action</u>! The resulting loop's output is unpredictable and this practice should be avoided. Changing the value of x has no effect on the number of iterations that the loop will make, as the values of both the control variable and the end value are stored prior to execution of the loop. <u>Under no circumstances should you attempt to modify the counter variable (n, in the</u>

<u>example above) in any way</u>. Most of the time, careful loop design will ameliorate any need to implement an early exit strategy for your loop structures. A good design rule is that you can use the variable but do not change it.

QUICK CHECK

1. Determine the output from the following code if it were embedded in a complete program.

```
for a := 'z' downto 'A' do
    writeln(a);
```

2. Determine the output from the following code if it were embedded in a complete program:

```
for x := 1 to 10 do
    for y := 10 downto 1 do
writeln( x * y );
```

Project 2

This second project for the chapter uses the `for` statement in a nested situation to create a criss-cross multiplication table. This task is simplified through the use of the counter controlled loops working one within the other. Take a look at the code and build your version of the project.

```
program multtabl;
{ ----------------------------------- }
{ Program to create a multiplication  }
{ table from two variables            }
{                                     }
{ Uses two nested FOR loops           }
{ ----------------------------------- }

var
    x           : integer;
    y           : integer;

begin
    x := 1;
    y := 2;

    writeln('---------------- Times Table --------------------');

    {- write out a header for the columns -}
    write(' ':5);
    for x := 1 to 10 do
```

```
        write(x:5);
    writeln;

  writeln('-----------------------------------------------');

    {   nest the two loops and go!  }
    for x:= 1 to 10 do
    begin
      write(x:3,' |');

      for y:= 1 to 10 do
      begin
        write(y * x:5);
      end;
      writeln;
    end;

    readln;
  end.
```

There's nothing terribly complicated about this program as is the case with a lot of software. Most programs are made up of relatively simple sets of statements that perform complex actions one step at a time. Don't forget this when your program's design seems to be spiraling out of control. The nesting of two loops allows me to generate the multiplication table one set of variables at a time. I use the formatting capabilities of the `write` and `writeln` statements to neatly form my output into rows and columns. The output of the program is shown in Figure 6-14.

 Figure 6-14

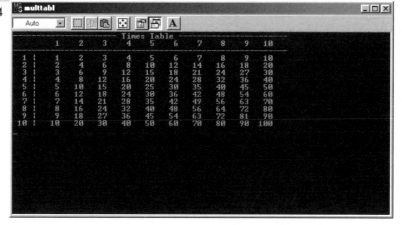

The Repeat Statement

The last Object Pascal structure that we will look at is the `repeat` statement loop structure. This is another logically controlled loop that will continue in its iterations until the Boolean expression evaluates to false. An illustration of the logic of the loop is shown in Figure 6-15.

Figure 6-15: The REPEAT UNTIL control structure

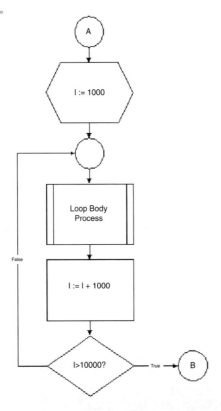

Notice that the test expression has been moved to the bottom of the structure. Both of these factors significantly change the way in which this loop is executed. First consider the `while` statement loop and the expression that controls that structure. As long as the expression evaluates to true, the loop continues to iterate. The `repeat` statement uses just the opposite logic; as long as the Boolean expression evaluates to false, the loop continues in its iterations. When the expression evaluates to true, the loop is terminated and execution skips to the line after the `until`.

Another important difference between these two logically controlled structures is in the placement of the evaluation. With the Boolean expression at the top of the `while` statement, it must be evaluated before the statement in the body of the loop can be executed. If it evaluates to false, the statement will never be processed. The `repeat` statement places its evaluation expression at the bottom of the construct, after the body statements. This means that the statements are processed at least one time before the Boolean expression is evaluated. The following program illustrates the difference:

```
program lrnloop4;
var
  keyvalue   : integer;

begin
  keyvalue := 999;
  while keyvalue <> 999 do
  begin
    writeln('Remember, key value to stop is 999');
    readln( keyvalue );
  end;
end.
```

In this code block, the loop will not be processed because in evaluating whether or not the variable `keyvalue` equals 999 the answer comes up false. This will cause the loop to skip the query for the key value. Run this using the debugging commands to follow the execution as the output will simply flash on your screen. On the other hand, the `repeat` statement will give the user at least one opportunity to get the correct value input.

```
program lrnloop5;
var
  keyvalue   : integer;

begin
  keyvalue := 999;
  repeat
    writeln('Key value to stop is 999');
    readln( keyvalue );
  until keyvalue = 999;
end.
```

No BEGIN/END pair is necessary between the `repeat` and `until`; these keywords serve this purpose in the structure.

QUICK CHECK

1. Compare the output of the following two snippets as though they were embedded in a complete program. Will the output be the same if the user inputs 10 as the response?

```
(snippet 1)
write('Enter your code : ');
readln(code)
while code <= 10 do
```

```
begin
  writeln('Iteration ', code);
  code := code + 1;
end;

(snippet 2)
write('Enter your code : ');
readln(code);
repeat
  writeln('Iteration ', code);
  code := code + 1;
until code = 10;
```

2. What if the user enters 1 as the code?

Summary

The Object Pascal structures that enable your program to repeat statements, whether simple or compound, make the programs that you develop a great deal easier to write and less limited in their functionality. Rather than artificially limiting the number of times an action such as a data entry question can occur by hard coding a series of redundant statements in a program, we know now that we can place these statements inside of a loop control structure. The loop will repeat this group of statements indefinitely until a control action, either logical or based on a counter, tells the program to stop repeating the statements and move on.

Three Object Pascal control structures were discussed for implementing looping in your programs. The first structure was the while statement. This is a logically controlled loop that controls its iterations through the evaluation of a Boolean expression placed between the while and the do. Remember that the statement that makes up the body of this loop may or may not get processed based upon the results of the evaluation. If it evaluates to false upon entrance to the loop, the body will never be executed. The opposite form of this statement is the repeat statement. Another logically controlled structure, this loop places its evaluation expression at the bottom of the structure, ensuring that the body will be executed at least one time. If the expression continues to evaluate to false, the looping action will occur. If it evaluates to true, the loop will be terminated.

A for statement is a counter controlled structure. A range of values, usually integers, is the controlling force behind this loop. The control variable is incremented by 1 each time the loop is completed and this value is then compared to the final value assigned to the statement. If the count evaluates to a false response, the loop continues to process. For those situations where a reverse count is more appropriate, we also examined the substitution of the keyword downto, which causes the control variable to be decremented on each iteration.

We also looked at the design decisions that need to be considered before any of the looping control structures can be selected and implemented within your program.

Three design considerations were highlighted for use in deciding which of the structures is appropriate for your program and determining the best way to implement it. They were the requirements of the body of the loop, the initialization statements that led into the structure, and the controls in place terminating the loop. Of the three, the termination of the loop is probably the most important decision. Infinite loops can cause many headaches and should be avoided at all costs.

TEST YOUR KNOWLEDGE

The best way to reinforce your hard gained programming skills is to put them to work. Take some time and write one or more of the following programs. Remember that the skills tested at the end of each chapter are meant to reinforce what was discussed in the chapter. For that reason, the projects are going to seem somewhat pointed and might be missing a lot of features or requirements that a production program would have. This doesn't mean, however, that you should not consider any of the other Object Pascal structures available to you.

1. Modify the Loan Payment project from this chapter so that it can accommodate user input for all of the variable values such as the total loan, the interest rate, the number of payments, etc. In addition, make the program repeat and allow the user to try out different rates and lengths as many times as they desire.

2. Create a program that allows homeowners to determine their monthly cost of ownership. The program should accept four input values: the purchase price, the annual cost of heating the home, the amount of the down payment, and the taxes per $1,000 of home value. The monthly cost will be 1/12th of the annual cost, which equals the sum of taxes, heat, and mortgage.

   The annual taxation is computed by multiplying the rate input by the user in dollars by the purchase price of the house. The mortgage cost is 10% of the balance left after deducting the down payment. If the purchase price was $100,000 and a down payment of $20,000 was made, the annual mortgage responsibility would be 10% of $80,000, or $8,000.

   Create this program in such a way that the user will be able to repeat this computation as many times as they like.

3. Create the test scoring program mentioned using two different looping methods. The first program should be a counter controlled algorithm that accepts a specific number of test scores. The output from the program should be the average, the highest score, and the lowest score.

   The second program should accept the same test score inputs and produce similar output but it should be a logically controlled loop that uses a sentinel value to control termination.

Chapter 6

Procedures and Functions

Key Concepts

- 🔑 Structuring a project's routines
- 🔑 Introduction to procedures
- 🔑 The scope of variables
- 🔑 Parameter passing with procedures
- 🔑 Introduction to functions

Introduction

All of the programs that we have developed up to this point have had one thing in common—they are all written in a linear fashion with lots of opportunities for the use of redundant code blocks. They start at the top and then process all of the instructions down to the bottom of the program and then exit. If any process needed to be repeated at different junctures of the program, the code to execute that task was simply repeated. While this works well for short, simple programs, as soon as the code begins to exceed about 60 or 70 lines it quickly becomes too complicated to follow. Starting with this chapter we're going to take a different view of a program. We're going to take a new view of the program as the sum of its obvious tasks. For example, the programs that have been written so far have commonly gathered input, processed the data, and then output the results. These tasks are tailor-made to be broken down into discrete routines.

In this chapter we're going to explore this process by discussing and putting into practice the following items:

- We'll decide what portions of your program are appropriate for breakout into separate routines.

- We examine the design considerations that are useful when you are building routines.
- The concept of the procedure, a self-contained routine, will be introduced.
- Because the variables that are going to be used will be both global and local, the concept of scope will be covered.
- We introduce scope in this chapter because your programs will use fewer global variables and begin passing data through parameters. We'll look at what a parameter is and learn how the types differ from one another.
- Finally, the code unit called a function will be discussed. There are important differences between procedures and functions and you will learn where to use which.

Hopefully you have taken the time to develop a few of the suggested programs in the previous chapters so your design skills are honed to a fine edge. By this point you are concentrating more on what it is you want to accomplish rather than being focused only on how to implement the task.

Dividing a Program into Routines

Read the following paragraph.

> The precursor to OOD Object Oriented Design was known as *top-down design* following centuries old problem solving techniques where large programming problems can be broken down into the logical subtasks and these algorithms then can be further decomposed into smaller subalgorithms and this divide and conquer strategy offers the developer a number of advantages beyond the simplification of the code produced by identifying the tasks and separating the job of coding them and each subtask can be designed coded and tested individually and once each separate piece has been verified the entire program can be assembled from these parts but this advantage can sometimes be overlooked in the hectic environment of software creation because once a subtask has been coded and tested and it is verified to be working it can be set aside with no further work required and because it stands on its own as a discrete unit no other changes in the program should ultimately affect it.

Whew! That wasn't easy. Now we're going to prepare to see the paragraph again. The new version is going to be easier to read and comprehend even though the ideas and words are nearly the same. The addition of punctuation and capitalization lend structure to the thoughts and nuances by forming sentences. From those sentences, the paragraph becomes one that leads the reader from one thought to the next before ending. Computer programs can be the same way; the code can be written in one long series of instructions from start to end or they can be broken down into discrete segments, each one focused on resolving one idea.

> The precursor to OOD (object-oriented design) was known as *top-down design*. Following centuries-old problem-solving techniques, large pro-

gramming problems can be broken down into the logical subtasks. These algorithms can then be further decomposed into smaller subalgorithms. This divide and conquer strategy offers the developer a number of advantages. Beyond the simplification of the code produced by identifying the tasks and separating the job of coding them, each subtask can be designed, coded, and tested individually. Once each separate piece has been verified, the entire program can be assembled from these parts. This advantage can sometimes be overlooked in the hectic environment of software creation. <u>Once a subtask has been coded and tested and it is verified to be working, it can be set aside with no further work required</u>. Because it stands on its own as a discrete unit, no other changes in the program should ultimately affect it.

Another advantage of the routines that we are going to create is that they can be reused. Once a common process has been designed, coded, and debugged there is no reason that it could not be used in another program or even several times within the same program. If your program simply needs the functionality offered by the routine you can view it as a *black box*. In the black box paradigm, an object performs a function while keeping the details of how the process is completed hidden within the opaque confines of the box. The user of the box is instructed on what data is required as input and what output will be generated at the back end of the box. Once these parameters are established, the user of the process does not need to be concerned with <u>how</u> the process is completed, only that it is.

On the other hand, if you have access to the source code, the structuring of code into separate routines makes the process of understanding their inner workings much easier. Rather than having to trace the execution path logically through several hundred or thousand lines of code, the routine presents a single task in high focus. You can then build your understanding of a complete program task by task. Object Pascal, like nearly all programming languages, has the ability to include these subalgorithms within the larger algorithm of a complete program. These are called procedures.

Introducing Procedures

In Object Pascal, one method of declaring a subtask is to create a *procedure*. The procedure will provide us with all of the benefits just mentioned. It will encapsulate a subroutine by structuring our code better and then provide the program with our first glimpse of code reuse. A procedure that is visible to a program's code can be called from many locations within the program, allowing it to use the routine repeatedly. An excellent example of this capability is the `writeln` procedure that has been used throughout the preceding chapters. We have no idea how it actually puts the characters onto the screen or into a file but we are able to call it from any point in our program. As long as the data passed to the procedure is correctly formatted, the internal code of the procedure will handle it without any further intervention by us.

To introduce the mechanics of the procedure into a program, we'll use the simple example shown here. This procedure will draw a boxed header when called throughout the program. The task is perfect for encapsulation as a procedure as it can be used on a repeated basis throughout a program. The output from this program is shown in Figure 7-1. After you have typed the code or loaded it from the CD-ROM, we will examine it step by step.

```
program draw_hdr;

procedure proc_header;
{ --------------------------- }
{ proc proc_header            }
{ prints a report heading     }
{ params: none                }
{ --------------------------- }

var
   i        : integer;

begin
  writeln;
  write( CHR(201) );
  for i := 1 to 25 do
    write( CHR(205) );
  writeln( CHR(187) );

  writeln( CHR( 186 ), '          RESULTS          ', CHR(186));
  write( CHR(200) );
  for i := 1 to 25 do
    write( CHR(205) );
  writeln( CHR(188) );

  writeln;
end;
```

Figure 7-1

```
begin
  proc_header;
end.
```

Before the procedure can be used, it must be declared. This definition is written in the last section of the declaration part of a program, following the type, constant, and variable declarations. The procedure definition follows a similar structure as that already used to define the program file. Before examining the sample line by line, let's establish the logical declaration of a procedure:

```
procedure procedureName( parameterList ); directives;
local declarations;
begin
  statements
end;
```

The sample starts with the header line

```
procedure proc_header;
```

which is composed of the reserved word `procedure` and the name of the procedure `proc_header`. For this first procedure there is no parameter list. The next section of the procedure contains any constant or variable declarations. Notice that these are labeled in the logical diagram as local variables, meaning that they will be visible within this procedure but not outside. There is only one in this sample and that is the variable `i`. (A discussion of parameters and scoping follows in this chapter.) When this preamble is complete, the statements that make up the actions of the procedure are written. In this example, the ASCII graphic characters are used to enclose the word RESULTS in a double lined box to be used at the beginning of an onscreen report. Finally, just like the program file, the procedure declaration is terminated with an `end` statement. Unlike the program file, the procedure is ended with a semicolon rather than a period.

Once declared as shown in the declaration section of a program file, the `proc_header` procedure is visible and can be called throughout the program. In our example, the procedure is called one time by the use of its name. This could just as easily have been ten calls to the procedure to produce the header ten times. The advantages of the creation of a procedure are easily seen here. First, we will not have to type that set of lines over and over each time a header is needed in the program; if we did, the possibility for introducing errors into the program would grow. Also, once this is written and tested, the header routine will not need to be touched again in the development process of the program; it becomes a discrete entity and we can call it repeatedly without worrying about <u>how</u> it performs its duties. Finally, if the user decides that a single line box is more appropriate, we only need to make these changes in a single place rather than in multiple locations scattered throughout thousands of lines of programming code.

It is appropriate here within this topic to introduce the topic of scope into the discussion since we have used its synonym "visibility" repeatedly through the preceding chapters without offering much support or explanation. To simplify the learning process up to this point all of the programs have made use of variables that are global in scope. This method of data passing is appropriate for some items and holds inherent risks for others. Without careful consideration of its use and an understanding of the risks involved the casual use of global variables leads to the possibility of programming problems. Globally scoped variables require micro management throughout the development and modification processes and Object Pascal offers much better methods for the transfer of values within a program. Before we talk about those, however, we need to establish an understanding of variables and their scope.

Scope

Scope is a term that defines the visibility of a data object such as a variable or procedure to the rest of the program. The measure of visibility determines in which context the identifier can be used or which version of an identifier is active. Object Pascal normally declares that the visibility of an object extends only through the block in which it is defined. There are two measures of scope: *global* and *local*. Global objects are declared in the context of the program or unit block and are visible throughout the program or unit. Local variables are defined within a class, procedure, or function and their visibility is limited to the processing that occurs within that block.

The program below shows the workings of a variable, global_x, with a global scope. When a variable is declared as global in scope, it can be accessed and modified from any point within the program.

```
program globvar;
var
  global_x    : integer;
procedure one;
begin
  global_x := 5;
end;

procedure two;
begin
  global_x := 10;
end;

procedure three;
begin
  global_x := 15;
end;

begin
  global_x := 0;
  writeln('Program starts');
  writeln('Global_X value = ', global_x);
```

```
      one;
      writeln('Global_X value = ', global_x);

      two;
      writeln('Global_X value = ', global_x);

      three;
      writeln(' Global_X value = ', global_x);
    end.
```

In this example, the value is modified four times as seen in Figure 7-2.

Figure 7-2

The first is within the main block of the program where it is assigned the value of zero. Following that, each of the declared procedures is processed and within each of these the value is modified as well. This points out an inherent strength and danger in the use of global variables; not only are they an easy way to pass values throughout your program but they are also an easy way to introduce hard to locate bugs into your design. The downside of global usage is not easy to spot in the 37 lines of the example program. The change that occurs in procedure three could just as easily have been buried in the 37,000th line of the program. Since that variable is global in scope, an inadvertent change to the value of the variable can easily occur anywhere within the program, possibly introducing unexpected results. This lack of control over the modification of the variable's value is what makes the use of too many global variables undesirable.

Some minor changes have been made to the same program as shown in the code below:

```
    program globvar2;
    var
     global_x    : integer;

    procedure one;
    var
      global_x   : integer;
```

```
begin
 global_x := 5;
end;

procedure two;
var
  global_x   : integer;

begin
 global_x := 10;
end;

procedure three;
var
  global_x   : integer;

begin
 global_x := 15;
end;

begin
  global_x := 0;
  writeln('Program starts');
  writeln('Global_X value = ', global_x);

  one;
  writeln('Global_X value = ', global_x);

  two;
  writeln('Global_X value = ', global_x);


  three;
  writeln(' Global_X value = ', global_x);
end.
```

Now, what would you expect the output to be? When this version of the program is executed, the output will be what you see in Figure 7-3.

Figure 7-3

This change in output is driven by the declaration of local variables in each of the procedures. The scope of a local variable is the unit, function, or procedure in which it is defined. When a variable is defined within the block of a procedure, memory is reserved for this identifier. As soon as the procedure is terminated, this memory location is released and the value no longer exists. We now see that the changes made within the procedures have no effect on the global variable because all of their changes are visited upon the local versions of the variable. At the completion of each of the procedure calls, the local versions of global_x are released and the global version is used in the writeln statements.

Locally scoped objects are dominant within the block that defines them. This means that their value overrides that of any similarly named global variable. In the program example both the global and local variables share the same identifier name. When the processing of the program enters the procedures, the local version of the variable global_x becomes the active object. The global variable holds its value in its originally assigned memory space while a new memory location is used for storage of the local variable's value. When the procedure is complete, the local variable's space is released and the global version is again activated.

Local variables will be visible only within the bounds of the declaring procedure. The following program contains lines that will generate compiler errors:

```
program globvar3;
var
  global_x   : integer;

procedure one;
begin
  writeln('In Proc One');
  {- this will cause an error -}
  z := 123;
end;

procedure three;
var
```

```
    z : integer;

begin
  writeln('In Proc Three');
  z := 99;
  writeln('Z = ', z );

  { - calling procedure one - }
  one;
end;

begin
  writeln('program starts');
  three;
end.
```

Though the global visibility appears to be a function of the fact that it is defined in the "wrapper" for all of the other procedures, this is not the case. Notice that procedure one is called from within procedure three and attempts to utilize the variable z. This will cause a compiler error due to the fact that variable z is visible to statements within procedure three, but it does not extend to the statements in procedure one.

Change Machine

Let's work through an example that will lead into the next facet of our discussion on procedures. The program shown in Listing 7-1 is a non-procedural program that computes the breakdown of the coins necessary to make change under one dollar.

Listing 7-1

```
program change;

var
  quarters      : integer;
  dimes         : integer;
  nickels       : integer;
  pennies       : integer;
  tot_amount    : integer;
  sub_total     : integer;

begin
  writeln('This program makes change in the most');
  writeln('efficient manner possible from your   ');
  writeln('change drawer.');
  writeln;
  write('Enter an amount less than one dollar: ');
  readln(tot_amount);
```

```
while (tot_amount  99) or (tot_amount 0) do
begin
  writeln('That amount is too high or too low!');
  write('Enter an amount less than one dollar: ');
  readln(tot_amount);
end;

sub_total := tot_amount;

if sub_total = 25 then
begin
  quarters := tot_amount div 25;
  sub_total := tot_amount - (25 * quarters);
end;

if sub_total = 10 then
begin
  dimes := sub_total div 10;
  sub_total := sub_total - (10 * dimes);
end;

if sub_total = 5 then
begin
  nickels := sub_total div 5;
  sub_total := sub_total - (10 * nickels);
end;

if sub_total = 1 then
  pennies := sub_total div 1;

writeln('** Correct Change **');

writeln('Quarters  :', quarters);
writeln('Dimes     :', dimes);
writeln('Nickels   :', nickels);
writeln('Pennies   :', pennies);

  readln;
end.
```

The tasks in this program break down fairly easily. First we must gather a figure that represents the amount of change. Once this number has been validated, each coin's value is compared to the amount of change yet accounted for. Finally, the number of coins in each denomination is output so that the machine can return the appropriate change.

Each coin's face value makes a logical subdivision point for a procedure but we will start with the data collection task first. This job encompasses two simple tasks: gather the data and validate it. The end result should be a numeric value that the rest of the program can act upon. This procedure will appear as follows:

```
procedure get_change;
{ ----------------------------- }
{ proc get_change                }
{ this will collect and validate }
{ the amount of change from the  }
{ user                           }
{ ----------------------------- }
begin
      write('Enter an amount less than one dollar: ');
   readln(tot_amount);

   while (tot_amount > 99) or (tot_amount < 0) do
   begin
     writeln('That amount is too high or too low!');
     write('Enter an amount less than one dollar: ');
     readln(tot_amount);
   end;
end;
```

Now that this functionality has been encapsulated within a procedure, it would be possible to use this throughout the rest of the program.

The next item that requires attention in this program are the conversion tasks where the number of coins in each denomination is computed. Each of the coin types is handled in the same fashion so we will only look at a single example procedure.

```
procedure num_quarters;
{ ----------------------------- }
{ proc num_quarters              }
{ This proc will compute the     }
{ number of quarters in the change}
{ amount                         }
{ ----------------------------- }
begin
  if sub_total >= 25 then
  begin
    quarters := sub_total div 25;
    sub_total := tot_amount - (25 * quarters);
  end
  else
    quarters := 0;
end;
```

This procedure is specific to the quarters; is it possible that one procedure could handle all coin types? The short answer is yes, but we need to learn a little more about data passing before we can implement this change. Listing 7-2 shows the completed program. You will see that the main body of the program has been vastly simplified and is much easier to understand, goals that every programmer should aspire to.

Listing 7-2

```pascal
program change;
var
    quarters      : integer;
    dimes         : integer;
    nickels       : integer;
    pennies       : integer;
    tot_amount    : integer;
    sub_total     : integer;

procedure get_change;
{ ------------------------------ }
{ proc get_change               }
{ this will collect and validate }
{ the amount of change from the  }
{ user                           }
{ ------------------------------ }
begin
  write('Enter an amount less than one dollar: ');
  readln(tot_amount);

  while (tot_amount  99) or (tot_amount 0) do
  begin
    writeln('That amount is too high or too low!');
    write('Enter an amount less than one dollar: ');
    readln(tot_amount);
  end;
end;

procedure num_quarters;
{ ------------------------------ }
{ proc num_quarters             }
{ This proc will compute the    }
{ number of quarters in the change}
{ amount                         }
{ ------------------------------ }
begin
  if sub_total = 25 then
```

```
     begin
       quarters := sub_total div 25;
       sub_total := tot_amount - (25 * quarters);
     end
     else
       quarters := 0;
end;
procedure num_dimes;
{ ------------------------------ }
{ proc num_dimes                 }
{ This proc will compute the     }
{ number of dimes in the change  }
{ amount                         }
{ ------------------------------ }
begin
   if sub_total = 10 then
   begin
     dimes := sub_total div 10;
     sub_total := sub_total - (10 * dimes);
   end
   else
     dimes := 0;
end;

procedure num_nickels;
{ ------------------------------ }
{ proc num_nickles               }
{ This proc will compute the     }
{ number of nickles in the change }
{ amount                         }
{ ------------------------------ }
begin
   if sub_total = 5 then
   begin
     nickels := sub_total div 5;
     sub_total := sub_total - (5 * nickels);
   end
   else
     nickels := 0;
end;

procedure num_pennies;
{ ------------------------------ }
{ proc num_pennies               }
{ This proc will compute the     }
{ number of pennies  in the change}
```

```
{ amount                               }
{ ----------------------------- }
begin

  if sub_total = 1 then
    pennies := sub_total div 1
  else
    pennies := 0;

end;

begin
  writeln('This program makes change in the most');
  writeln('efficient manner possible from your   ');
  writeln('change drawer.');
  writeln;

  { -- call get_change procedure -- }
  get_change;
  sub_total := tot_amount;

  num_quarters;
  num_dimes;
  num_nickels;
  num_pennies;

  writeln('** Correct Change **');

  writeln('Quarters  :', quarters);
  writeln('Dimes     :', dimes);
  writeln('Nickels   :', nickels);
  writeln('Pennies   :', pennies);

  readln;
end.
```

Though some benefits have been achieved there are still problems remaining with the program. All of the variables remain global in scope, a necessity since the procedures use this conduit to compute and pass the modified data back to the program. The difficulty in this approach is just what we mentioned earlier; it would be very simple to make an error in one of the procedures and inadvertently change the value of a variable to an incorrect number. There must be a better way of handling this.

Parameters

Procedures and functions have the ability to accept data values through a locally scoped object called a *parameter*. Parameters give the procedure the ability to directly receive data values through a conduit that doesn't rely on the use of global variables. The result is a program that exercises much greater control over the data objects within it. Before we get into the specifics and types of parameters that are available for our use, we will modify the *change* program with a new procedure:

```
procedure Output( qtrs: integer; dms: integer; nkls: integer;
pns: integer);
begin
  writeln('** Correct Change **');

  writeln('Quarters  :', qtrs);
  writeln('Dimes     :', dms);
  writeln('Nickels   :', nkls);
  writeln('Pennies   :', pns);
end;
```

This procedure encapsulates all of the processing for the output statements in the program so that it can be called repeatedly if necessary. Notice how the procedure declaration has been modified. Following the procedure name is now a list of parameters bracketed by parentheses. The parameters, local to the procedure, have a name and a data type declared, the same as all of the other variables we have used. Data will be passed into these new variables for use within the procedure.

The order of the parameter list is very important when the procedure is called within the program. The line that calls the change procedure is

```
output( quarters, dimes, nickels, pennies );
```

If the values that are passed from the calling statement to the parameters of the function are not matched up with the order of the receiving parameters, one of two things will occur. The program will either issue incorrect output, for instance if the pennies and quarters values are swapped, or a compiler error will occur if the data types of the parameter and value do not match. In the case of the example, everything is right where it should be. When the procedure is called, the value contained in the variable quarters is copied to the parameter qtrs. This local object is then used within the change procedure to display the number of quarters in the change pile.

So what happens to the variable quarters? Is it now empty, having deposited its contents into qtrs? No, the contents of the variable were simply copied into the parameter, leaving them intact in the original variable. This is known as *passing by value*. Once the parameters have been passed a copy of the value from the original variable, the procedure is free to modify and manipulate it in any way it pleases without having any effect on the original variable. This is a marked difference from the handling of variables in the programs we have developed up to now in which any modification made to the value of the global variable was reflected throughout the program. By using parameters to get the value into the procedure instead of utilizing the global variable we can exercise much more control over the values.

Fundamentals in Focus

Order in the List!

I cannot emphasize enough the importance of the ordering of both the formal parameter list and the actual parameter list. Many beginning programmers get tripped up when using parameters for the first time and Object Pascal does nothing to help you. The compiler will follow your instructions to the letter and replace the first parameter in the formal parameter list with the first actual parameter and so on through the list. The only time you will hear a peep out of it will be when the two parameters are not of compatible data types.

Consider what will happen if a program uses a procedure to process your next monumental pay raise. It would look something like this

```
procedure ModifyPay( OldRate:real, NewRate:real )
```

Since both of the parameters are of the same data type (real) the parameter OldRate will easily accept your new pay rate and vice versa. Without careful attention to the programming, you will be mighty unhappy come pay day.

The *change* program has been modified further as shown in Listing 7-3 to encapsulate all of the functionality into a set of procedures.

Listing 7-3

```
program change;
var
   quarters     : integer;
   dimes        : integer;
   nickels      : integer;
   pennies      : integer;
   tot_amount   : integer;
   sub_total    : integer;

procedure get_change( var change_amt:integer );
{ ----------------------------- }
{ proc get_change               }
{ this will collect and validate }
{ the amount of change from the  }
{ user                          }
{ ----------------------------- }
begin
   write('Enter an amount less than one dollar: ');
```

```
   readln(change_amt);

   while (change_amt  99) or (change_amt 0) do
begin
    writeln('That amount is too high or too low!');
    write('Enter an amount less than one dollar: ');
    readln(change_amt);
   end;
end;

procedure num_quarters(var in_sub:integer; var qtrs:integer );
{ ------------------------------ }
{ proc num_quarters             }
{ This proc will compute the    }
{ number of quarters in the change}
{ amount                        }
{ ------------------------------ }
begin
  if in_sub = 25 then
  begin
    quarters := in_sub div 25;
    in_sub := tot_amount - (25 * quarters);
  end
  else
    quarters := 0;
end;

procedure num_dimes( var in_sub: integer; var dms: integer );
{ ------------------------------ }
{ proc num_dimes                }
{ This proc will compute the    }
{ number of dimes in the change }
{ amount                        }
{ ------------------------------ }
begin
  if in_sub = 10 then
  begin
    dimes := in_sub div 10;
    in_sub := in_sub - (10 * dimes);
  end
  else
    dimes := 0;
end;

procedure num_nickels(var in_sub:integer; var nkls: integer );
{ ------------------------------ }
```

```
{ proc num_nickles              }
{ This proc will compute the    }
{ number of nickles in the change }
{ amount                        }
{ ----------------------------- }
begin
  if in_sub = 5 then
  begin
    nickels := in_sub div 5;
    in_sub := in_sub - (5 * nickels);
  end
  else
    nickels := 0;
end;


procedure num_pennies(var in_sub:integer; var pns:integer );
{ ----------------------------- }
{ proc num_pennies              }
{ This proc will compute the    }
{ number of pennies  in the change}
{ amount                        }
{ ----------------------------- }
begin

  if in_sub = 1 then
    pennies := in_sub div 1
  else
    pennies := 0;

end;

procedure Output( qtrs: integer; dms: integer; nkls:
integer; pns: integer);
{ ----------------------------- }
{ proc output                   }
{ This proc will output the result}
{ of the change computation     }
{ ----------------------------- }
begin
  writeln('** Correct Change **');
  writeln('Quarters  :', qtrs);
  writeln('Dimes     :', dms);
  writeln('Nickels   :', nkls);
  writeln('Pennies   :', pns);
end;
```

```
procedure Header;
{ ----------------------------- }
{ proc header                   }
{ Output the header information  }
{ ----------------------------- }
begin
  writeln('This program makes change in the most');
  writeln('efficient manner possible from your   ');
  writeln('change drawer.');
  writeln;
end;

begin
  header;

  { -- call get_change procedure -- }
  get_change(tot_amount);
  sub_total := tot_amount;

  num_quarters(sub_total, quarters);
  num_dimes(sub_total, dimes);
  num_nickels(sub_total, nickels);
  num_pennies(sub_total, pennies);

  output(quarters, dimes, nickels, pennies);

  readln;
end.
```

These look a little different though. The *formal parameters*—the parameter list in the procedure heading—now contain an additional word, `var`. The parameters shown here in the `num_quarters` procedure are called *variable parameters*.

```
procedure num_quarters( var in_sub: integer; var qtrs: integer
);
{ ----------------------------- }
{ proc num_quarters             }
{ This proc will compute the    }
{ number of quarters in the change}
{ amount                        }
{ ----------------------------- }
begin
  if in_sub >= 25 then
  begin
    quarters := in_sub div 25;
    in_sub := tot_amount - (25 * quarters);
```

```
          end
        else
           quarters := 0;
     end;
```

Variable parameters have a unique property; they are two-way conduits into and out of the procedure. This allows the procedure to manipulate the data received through the receiver parameter and then return a value back through the same parameter. This type of parameter passing is known as *passing by reference*. By doing this we can finally begin to overcome much of the need for the global variables, the eventual goal of program development.

Listing 7-4 is an example of what we are trying to achieve within our programs.

Listing 7-4

```
program change;
var
    tot_amount    : integer;

procedure get_change( var change_amt:integer );
{ ------------------------------ }
{ proc get_change               }
{ this will collect and validate }
{ the amount of change from the  }
{ user                          }
{ ------------------------------ }
begin
  write('Enter an amount less than one dollar: ');
  readln(change_amt);

  while (change_amt  99) or (change_amt 0) do
  begin
    writeln('That amount is too high or too low!');
    write('Enter an amount less than one dollar: ');
    readln(change_amt);
  end;
end;

procedure Output( qtrs: integer; dms: integer; nkls:
integer; pns: integer);
{ ------------------------------ }
{ proc output                   }
{ This proc will output the result}
{ of the change computation      }
{ ------------------------------ }
begin
```

```
    writeln('** Correct Change **');
    writeln('Quarters  :', qtrs);
    writeln('Dimes     :', dms);
    writeln('Nickels   :', nkls);
    writeln('Pennies   :', pns);
end;

procedure Header;
{ ----------------------------- }
{ proc header                   }
{ Output the header information  }
{ ----------------------------- }
begin
  writeln('This program makes change in the most');
  writeln('efficient manner possible from your   ');
  writeln('change drawer.');  writeln; end;

procedure make_change(in_amt : integer);
{ ----------------------------- }
{ proc make_change( in amount ) }
{ Computes the amount of change }
{ from the var in_amt           }
{ ----------------------------- }

var
  quarters     : integer;
  dimes        : integer;
  nickels      : integer;
  pennies      : integer;

begin

  header;

  if in_amt = 25 then
  begin
    quarters := in_amt div 25;
    in_amt := in_amt - (25 * quarters);
  end
  else
    quarters := 0;

  if in_amt = 10 then
  begin
    dimes := in_amt div 10;
    in_amt := in_amt - (10 * dimes);
```

```
    end
  else
    dimes := 0;

  if in_amt = 5 then
  begin
    nickels := in_amt div 5;
    in_amt := in_amt - (5 * nickels);
  end
  else
    nickels := 0;

  if in_amt = 1 then
    pennies := in_amt div 1
  else
    pennies := 0;

  output(quarters, dimes, nickels, pennies);

end;

begin

  get_change(tot_amount);
  make_change(tot_amount);

  readln;
end.
```

The program now has a single global variable and the main block of the program has been reduced to two lines:

```
begin
  get_change( tot_amount );
  make_change( tot_amount );
end.
```

The get_change procedure will gather the data from the user and place it into the tot_amount variable. This variable is then passed into the make_change procedure where the values are computed and output. Each of the coin variables is now protected and controlled a local variable within the procedure.

QUICK CHECK

1. Determine the output from the following program.

```
program Follow;
```

```
var
  x, i : integer;
procedure Crank( in_x, in_i : integer);
var
  n : integer;
begin
  for n := in_i to in_x do
    writeln( n );
  in_x := n;
end;
begin
  x := 5;
  i := 1;
  crank( x, i );
  writeln('X = ', x);
end.
```

2. If the formal parameters in procedure `Crank` are modified to be var parameters, what would the output be?

Functions

Procedures have done an excellent job of encapsulating and structuring the tasks within our program. By adding parameters to the mix, we were able to do away with many of the problems associated with the global variables by directly passing the values through the parameters. The variable parameters, however, make us perform sometimes uncomfortable manipulations of code in order to accommodate this method of returning the results of the computations. A program construct called a *function* does a much better job of handling this. A procedure call in Object Pascal is a statement, and like any other statement it performs an action when called. Functions, on the other hand, are expressions and again, just as any other expression, they will always return a value.

Functions are declared in much the same manner as procedures, usually in the same place in a program and interspersed with their brethren. The function name is nearly always followed by an ordered list of parameters. These are exactly the same as the parameters used with procedures. There are two major differences in the design of a function. The first is that since functions must always return a value from their processing, the data type of the return value must be declared following the function name and parameter list. The second requirement of the function's design is that at some point within the body of the function, the name of the function or the predefined variable `result` must appear on the left-hand side of an assignment statement. It is through this mechanism that the result of the function computation is returned.

A simple example will set the stage for further development. The following snippet builds a function called `squared` that returns a valued "squared," or multiplied once by itself:

```
function squared( i : integer ): integer;
begin
  squared := i * i;
end;
```

You'll notice right off the bat that the reserved word `function` is used to begin this declaration. The identifier that follows must abide by all of the naming rules that have previously been discussed. The parameter list follows the examples seen in the procedure segments. The parameter names are followed by a colon and the data type and, if there is more than one, they must be separated by semicolons. The entire function declaration then becomes similar to a simple variable declaration because immediately after the closing parenthesis is another colon and a data type. This data type definition tells the compiler what to expect in return when the function is called. `Squared` will return an integer every time it is run so it can only be used in places where an integer is appropriate. The return type can be any of the types `integer`, `real`, or `char`, or any of the string types.

The functionality of this routine is easy to understand. It will take whatever integer value is passed through the `i` argument and square it. A function returns its results through the use of the function's name, in this case `squared`. For that reason the processing results in the factor of i * i being assigned to `squared`. This odd process makes more sense when the statement that calls the function is seen.

```
x := squared(9);
```

In essence, the value of `squared` is being assigned to variable `x`. This simple function doesn't make this clear but you are not limited to a single assignment statement within the body of the function. You may have a decision structure, for instance, that returns one of two alternative values. What must be remembered is that the assignment statement to the function name should terminate the function's processing.

The addition of the function to our repertoire will make the processing in the *change* program vastly simpler. The first thing that we can do away with is the need for those variable parameters. The var parameters were used to return values from the processing within the procedures. The functions themselves will provide this return value so the declarations will be easier to implement. To begin exploring the possibilities, we're going to go back to the now familiar *change* program and see what can be modified. A good place to start would be with the handling of the coins. Each coin's value is tested and the module is required to return the number of coins that would best fit into the remaining amount of change so the task is ideal for encapsulation as a function. The task for handling nickels would look like this:

```
function make_nickels( in_change: integer ): integer;
{ ****************************** }
{ FUNCTION: make_nickels          }
{ ARGS: in_change - amount of chg }
{ RETURNS: number of nickels      }
{ ****************************** }
```

```
begin
  if in_change >= 5 then

    make_nickels := in_change div 5

  else
    make_nickels := 0;

end;
```

The way that the task is processed has not changed much from the procedure version. The argument accepts the amount of change and converts it into a return value representing the number of coins that go into making up that amount. The value of the number of coins is assigned to the `make_nickels` identifier through which it returns to the calling statement.

Fundamentals in Focus

Result

The vast majority of the function examples in this book utilize the traditional Pascal method of returning a value from a function and that is to assign the return value to the function name. This method has been improved upon in Delphi. In the Delphi environment, a predefined variable exists called `Result`. It can be used in place of the function name when returning a value.

```
function foo():integer;
begin
  Result := 5;
end;
```

The advantage of using this variable is that you can change the name of the function without having to modify other parts of your code. In essence, this provides the same advantage that using a constant declaration has over using several literals spread throughout your code.

Where we see the most change is in the output process. Listing 7-5 shows the modified *change* program.

Listing 7-5

```
program change;


{ ------------------------------ }
{ FUNCTION Version               }
{ ------------------------------ }
```

```pascal
function get_change : integer;
{ ------------------------------ }
{ FUNCTION: get_changes         }
{ ARGS: none                    }
{ RETURNS: amt of change entered }
{ by the user                   }
{ ------------------------------ }
var
  change_amt  : integer;
begin
  write('Enter an amount less than one dollar: ');
  readln(change_amt);

  while (change_amt  99) or (change_amt 0) do
  begin
    writeln('That amount is too high or too low!');
    write('Enter an amount less than one dollar: ');
    readln(change_amt);
  end;
  get_change := change_amt;
end;


procedure Header;
{ ------------------------------ }
{ proc header                   }
{ Output the header information  }
{ ------------------------------ }
begin
  writeln('This program makes change in the most');
  writeln('efficient manner possible from your   ');
  writeln('change drawer.');
  writeln;
end;

function make_quarters( in_change: integer ): integer;
{ ***************************** }
{ FUNCTION: make_quarters      }
{ ARGS: in_change - amount of chg }
{ RETURNS: number of quarters  }
{ ***************************** }
begin
  if in_change = 25 then

    make_quarters := in_change div 25
```

```pascal
    else
      make_quarters := 0;

end;

function make_dimes( in_change: integer ): integer;
{ ****************************** }
{ FUNCTION: make_dimes            }
{ ARGS: in_change - amount of chg }
{ RETURNS: number of dimes        }
{ ****************************** }
begin
  if in_change = 10 then

    make_dimes := in_change div 10

  else
    make_dimes := 0;

end;

function make_nickels( in_change: integer ): integer;
{ ****************************** }
{ FUNCTION: make_nickels          }
{ ARGS: in_change - amount of chg }
{ RETURNS: number of nickels      }
{ ****************************** }
begin
  if in_change = 5 then

    make_nickels := in_change div 5

  else
    make_nickels := 0;
end;

function make_pennies( in_change: integer ): integer;
{ ****************************** }
{ FUNCTION: make_pennies          }
{ ARGS: in_change - amount of chg }
{ RETURNS: number of pennies      }
{ ****************************** }
begin
  if in_change = 1 then

    make_pennies := in_change div 1
```

```
        else
          make_pennies := 0;
end;

procedure make_change;
{ ------------------------------ }
{ proc make_change( in amount )   }
{ Computes the amount of change   }
{ from the var in_amt             }
{ ------------------------------ }

var
  sub_amt      : integer;

begin

  header;

  sub_amt := get_change;

  writeln('** Correct Change **');

  writeln('Quarters  :', make_quarters( sub_amt ) );
  sub_amt := sub_amt - (make_quarters( sub_amt ) * 25);

  writeln('Dimes     :', make_dimes( sub_amt ) );
  sub_amt := sub_amt - (make_dimes( sub_amt ) * 10);

  writeln('Nickels   :', make_nickels( sub_amt ) );
  sub_amt := sub_amt - (make_nickels( sub_amt ) * 5);

  writeln('Pennies   :', make_pennies( sub_amt ) );
end;

begin

  make_change;

  readln;
end.
```

Wait a minute! Look carefully at that listing; there appears to be something missing. There are no longer any global variables used in the program and the main body of the program has been reduced to a single line. Nearly all of the processing occurs in the new make_change procedure:

```
procedure make_change();
var
  sub_amt        : integer;

begin

  header;

  sub_amt := get_change();

  writeln('** Correct Change **');

  writeln('Quarters  :', make_quarters( sub_amt ) );
  sub_amt := sub_amt - make_quarters( sub_amt );

  writeln('Dimes     :', make_dimes( sub_amt ) );
  sub_amt := sub_amt - make_dimes( sub_amt );

  writeln('Nickels   :', make_nickels( sub_amt ) );
  sub_amt := sub_amt - make_nickels( sub_ amt );

  writeln('Pennies   :', make_pennies( sub_amt ) );


end;
```

The amount of change entered by the user is now assigned to a local variable within this procedure so we no longer have to worry about it being inadvertently modified. Notice that the function calls to the coin processing tasks are used directly within another statement. A function can be used anywhere that is appropriate for its return value. In these cases we can place the coin functions anywhere an integer is an appropriate value. This extends to the subtotal lines below each output line and you can even place a function call into the parameter list of a procedure or function call. See the example in the next Quick Check section.

Fundamentals in Focus

Stay Focused

You will realize by this point that a function can do anything that a procedure can, but that doesn't mean that it should. A function's task is to return a single value and you should remain true to this concept. You might be tempted to utilize the abilities of variable parameters to return more than one value but in doing so you can create a program that is difficult to debug and maintain. Before you approach a problem with this kind of solution, consider your design very carefully. If you find that this is the only way to solve a programming task, it may be that you have not decomposed the problem sufficiently.

Functions can change global variables, get input from the user, and write data to the screen. These extra features are called **side effects** and each one detracts from the clarity of your program. Look at your design a second time and determine if it can be simplified further so that the function performs a single task and returns a single value. If the complexity of the problem is such that the problem requires a procedure and multiple variable parameters to solve correctly, simply declare the correct number of parameters. This will be much cleaner than using the single return value of the function plus additional variable parameters to return the other values.

QUICK CHECK

1. What is the output of the following program if the user inputs a value of 5?

```
program Clarity;

function Cubed( in_val : integer ): integer;
begin
  cubed := in_val * in_val * in_val;
end;

procedure Handler;
var
  i   : integer;
begin
  write(' Enter an integer value : ');
  readln( i );

  writeln( cubed( cubed( i ) ) );

end;

begin
  handler;
end.
```

2. Was the output value what you expected? Why not? What effect does the size of the user value have to do with the output?

Summary

Object Pascal programs take a giant step forward when the code is structured into procedures and functions. The resulting programs morph from long linear lists of statements riddled with redundant code and the danger of inadvertent modification of variable values lurking around every corner to objects of beauty in the eyes of coding professionals. Each of the discrete tasks being performed within the program is efficiently encapsulated within a function or procedure, ready to be called into action and then quietly fade into the background. The ability to pass data between these objects using parameters does away with the need for long lists of global variables and their inherent problems.

The procedure is an Object Pascal statement that encapsulates a specific task within a program. That task can be performed throughout a program as long as the procedure is in scope. Procedures are the workhorse objects in an Object Pascal program. A function also encapsulates a specific task within a program. The difference between it and the procedure is that it will always return a value. Several steps are followed in creating this compartmentalized efficiency, the first being simply deciding what portions of your program are appropriate for structuring into routines. There is no right or wrong answer to this issue; rather it is a matter of discovering what provides the most control and the highest performance. The decision as to what variables are appropriate for global scope usage and which should be localized within a procedure or function takes careful consideration. The performance and readability of your code is effected by clean data passing so selecting and implementing the appropriate parameters will make the difference between a dog of a program and a model that will engender the admiration of your fellow programmers.

TEST YOUR KNOWLEDGE

Your programs are going to take on a whole new look now and it will be very important to reinforce the skills of developing procedures and functions and then assembling them into a working program. A good way to start this process is working on something familiar, similar to the path that we followed in developing the procedures and functions within this chapter. Consider taking the programs that were developed in the previous chapter and reworking them so that no global variables are necessary. Two ideal candidates for modification are the Loan Payment and Cost of Ownership programs, each of which contain a number of formulas that would be better handled as functions. Once you have worked on something with predictable results, try one or all of these problems.

1. Modify the Change Machine program that was developed in this chapter to accommodate both dollars and cents. This will require that the input variable be modified to be a `real` data type rather than `integer`. This change alone will cascade throughout the entire program. Be sure to expand the functions to include the necessary bill denominations up to the maximum amount that you set for the program. Allow the user to repeat the program as many times as they want to.

2. Develop a badly needed program to aid people when they are haggling over the price of a new car. The user will input the base price of the automobile and the list price of the options that the consumer wants. The program will output the lowest price that the dealer will be willing to accept based on the following facts: The competitive dealer environment in the area will accept a price of 2% over invoice plus options for their inventory. You know that the cost of the options is one-half of the suggested retail price shown on the sticker. There is a $300 non-negotiable delivery surcharge on all cars and trucks that cost over $30,000 that must be computed into the final price. The user should be able to repeat the process as many times as necessary.

3. Write a useful conversion utility that will convert between the common weights and measures used in the United States and the metric system measurements used elsewhere. The user should first be given a choice between converting from U.S. to metric or metric to U.S. Then they should be asked if they want to convert lengths or weights. The program should perform the following conversions:

   ■ Convert a length in feet and inches into the equivalent length in meters and centimeters. There are 0.3048 meters per foot and 100 centimeters in a meter.

   ■ Convert a weight in pounds and ounces into the equivalent weight in kilograms and grams. There are 2.2046 pounds in a kilogram and 1000 grams in a kilogram.

   ■ The user should be able to repeat the entire process or subprocess as many times as they want to.

Units and Abstract Data Types

Key Concepts

- What is a unit?
- Putting units to use
- Defining abstract data types
- Ordinal data types
- Enumerated data types

Introduction

As your development skills continue to grow, the programs that you write will soon expand to be of an unwieldy length. Writing all of your code in a single file leads to two dilemmas. First, it becomes harder and harder to keep track of all of the code within that file, and second, it is exceptionally difficult to share your work with anyone else. This is where Object Pascal units come in. Creating a unit will enable you to separate your program into files that contain procedures and functions that are logically associated. The main body of the program can then be compiled together with these units, calling those procedures and functions as it needs them. This organizational tool solves both problems. It makes the program easier to work with since it is in much smaller discrete segments, and you can share the compiled segments with other programmers.

This chapter is also going to delve into the topic of *abstract data types*. These are user-defined data types designed by the programmer to improve the clarity of your programming solution. Once designed, the new data types are then built from the fundamental data types covered in the preceding chapters. In addition to data abstraction we are going to look at two data types in greater detail that were mentioned in an earlier chapter. Object Pascal implements ordinal and enumerated data types natively. To this end we'll cover a variety of topics, including the following:

- Since this is a new structure that we are going to introduce into our programs, we'll first need to determine what a unit is.

- Once the unit is defined, the appropriate usage of the structure is going to be explored. The advantages and disadvantages of using units in your programming will become more apparent through the construction of the sample programs.

- After defining what an abstract data type is they'll be put to use in some example programs to cement the concept.

- Ordinal data types play an integral role in the way that a lot of Object Pascal control structures function, making a knowledge of this type critical to your success in programming. A more in-depth definition and examples will explain how and why they're used.

- Enumerated data types also lend additional clarity and function to your Object Pascal programs. We will explore their special place and usage in your programs.

Your Object Pascal programming skills should be coming along quite nicely at this point. This chapter marks the transition to more advanced topics so be sure that you understand the fundamentals presented on the earlier pages before moving on. Everything that we cover from here on out will require a sound understanding of the basics in order to successfully assimilate the new information, so don't cheat yourself. How are those programming exercises coming?

Units

Borrowing an allusion from the last chapter, picture this paragraph being written without the benefit of capitalization, spacing, or punctuation. This organization was necessary to convey the ideas of the sentences within the chapter. Now picture the entire book as one long chapter. Rather than grouping like-focused paragraphs together to create topical breaks, the text would simply run on and on until it ended. This is not the ideal organizational tool when trying to provide information to people. The ability to create subsections of the entire work also benefits me as the writer and the publisher as we have the option of pulling out chapters that don't work and rearranging them to make the book flow better. Programs can easily grow this way as well, as the developer includes every required function or procedure within a single program file. Scrolling back and forth from the top to the bottom of this lengthy file significantly slows the development process while building your program. Indirectly, this method of development also leads to problems as the programmer has to continually verify that new modifications didn't break any of the old ones.

The unit in Object Pascal serves a similar organizational task to the programmer as the chapter does for the writer. Pascal facilitates the separation of sections of code into discrete files and then uses the compiler to reassemble the pieces that are needed into a single executable file. A *unit* is a logically associated grouping of declarations and definitions that is compiled separately from the main program file. With the use of the appropriate inclusion statement, the public code contained within the unit is accessible by the program file and other units. Code reuse is a second advantage of the separately compiled unit. Units can act as libraries for reusable components that can be made available to other programs and programmers. Again, the correct inclusion statement in a program file links a unit into your program, giving you the benefit of someone else's expertise and labor.

One further advantage of the unit file is information hiding. This factor is occasionally overshadowed by the modularity and reuse discussions even though it is equally important. Recall the black box discussion that we pursued with regard to functions and procedures. A user of the function or procedure was insulated from the internal workings of the object, only needing to provide the correct parameters and prepare to receive the results. Units offer the same capabilities on a much larger scale. A compiled unit can contain constants, variables, data types, procedures, functions, and even a main body, all of which can be hidden from the calling unit or program. The caller needs only to know the interface syntax to utilize the public functionality contained within the unit. She doesn't need to know or understand the inner workings of the file.

Coding the Unit

Let's begin our examination of the unit by looking at the logical structure of the file itself. After viewing it as a whole, we will delve into the details of the new sections that appear within it.

```
unit < identifier >;
interface
uses < list of units >;

{ PUBLIC DECLARATIONS }

implementation
uses < list of units >;

{PRIVATE DECLARATIONS }
{Procedure and Function code }

initialization
{ initialization code }

finalization

{ finalization code }
end.
```

This looks a lot like the program file that we are very familiar with but with a lot of new syntax thrown in. That observation is essentially correct. Each unit is still contained in its own .PAS file and compiled separately. The unit keyword at the top of the file tells the compiler that this will not be an executable file but rather a shared library. In traditional Pascal programming all of the code files in a project were built as .PAS files. Delphi veers from this traditional course. The units are built as .PAS files and then compiled into .DCU (Delphi Compiled Unit) files while the main program file, as we have seen, is built in a .DPR file. The best way to break the skeleton of the unit file down is by examining each section in turn.

The Interface Section

The aptly named interface section defines the public parts of the unit. The elements defined in this section of the file are visible to the programs or other units that use this unit. This section starts with the reserved word `interface` and ends when the keyword `implementation` appears. Constants, data types, variables, and routines can be defined within the unit's interface section. Something unique that we haven't seen prior to this is the way that the procedures and functions are defined in this section. Only the procedure's header is defined here. The body of the procedure or function is written in full in the implementation section.

Uses

Another new term enters the Object Pascal vocabulary in the context of our discussion of units, and that is `uses`. The `uses` statement is the linking device that programs and other units utilize to indicate that they use a procedure, function, class, or other data element contained within a specific unit. In the snippet

```
program SampProg;
uses SampUnit;
...
```

the program *SampProg* is going to use code contained in the unit `SampUnit`. When the compiler sees this `uses` statement it will search for the unit indicated and compile the necessary contents of the unit file into the executable.

`Uses` is not limited to a single unit file per call. If you use multiple units they can be itemized in a comma-separated list. The number of units that can be included is limited only by the maximum statement length. When a `uses` statement is used within another unit, the compiler action remains the same. Calling units from other units further insulates the objects from the main program file.

The Implementation Section

The implementation section has two jobs within the unit. First, it contains the full definitions of all of the functions and procedures declared in the interface segment. The routine definitions in this part may be written in one of two ways depending on the approach you took with them in the interface section. If you declared a procedure with a full parameter list:

```
interface
function Squared( in_num: integer ): integer;
...
```

then the definition in the implementation part can be defined using the minimalist form:

```
implementation
function Squared;
```

Though this sparse definition is legal, it is not the recommended approach. The compiler, however, will not complain. See the currency converter example that follows for the preferred approach.

The second task of the implementation part is to facilitate the data hiding capabilities of the unit. Remember that variables that were declared within procedures and functions were local in scope and not visible to the rest of the program; they were only accessible within the body of the procedure or function in which they were defined. The same holds true for any objects including variables, constants, procedures, or functions that are defined within the implementation section of the unit and not exposed through the interface section. These program elements are local in scope to the unit and are not exposed to a program or unit that uses the unit. Within a unit, rather than being called local they are referred to as private. The advantage of this design is that the developer of the unit may modify these objects to her heart's content as long as the public interface remains the same. This concept is known as *procedural abstraction*; the internals of procedures and functions are hidden from the eyes of the user who need only be concerned with what the procedure does, not how it does it.

The Initialization Section

The initialization section of a unit does just what you would expect it to do from its name. This section is used to initialize any data structures or open data files that the unit uses. Additionally, it can initialize any data structures that are exposed through the interface section. Depending on the dialect of Object Pascal you use, this section can be implemented in a couple of different ways. In older implementations, any `begin` and `end` pair that is placed between the reserved word `implementation` and the `end-period` automatically acts as a de facto initialization section. Delphi, on the other hand, explicitly defines a specific section in the unit headed by the keyword `implementation` which is followed by no punctuation.

When does the initialization fire? All of the statements in the initialization section are processed when the unit is called by the `uses` statement. When a series of units is listed after the `uses` statement, the initialization sections are processed in the order in which they are listed. For example, the statement

```
uses MyStuff, MyMath, MyStrings;
```

would process the initialization section MyStuff, then MyMath, and then finally MyStrings. This sequencing is important to remember if there are any dependencies between the units and their data objects.

The Finalization Section

This unit section performs just the opposite actions of the initialization section; it releases the resources that were initialized when the unit was called. Because of this, it is only allowed in units that have an initialization section. The processing of the finalization section is performed in the reverse order in which the units were initialized. The familiar statement

```
uses MyStuff, MyMath, MyStrings;
```

would process the finalization statements in the order of MyStrings, MyMath, and then finally MyStuff.

The Currency Converter

To demonstrate the construction and usage of the unit we're going to build a program that converts currency from United States dollars to the currency of various nations and vice versa. This processing shouldn't be too terribly difficult to devise. The logical requirements of the program are straightforward:

A. Determine which direction the conversion will take. U.S. dollars to foreign currency or the currency of another country into U.S. dollars are the two options.

B. Get the amount of money from the user.

C. Ask the user to specify the country involved.

D. Perform the conversion and display the results.

In looking at the tasks required of this program I am looking with an eye towards those routines and objects that could be easily reused again in other programs. Those that I identify as being suitable for a library are going to be segregated into a unit. In this case, the most obvious choices are those procedures, functions, and objects that directly perform the currency conversions.

Below is a complete listing of the convert unit. After you have typed this in we'll examine the details. There is going to be some minor adjustment to the steps that we have followed necessary to build a unit as opposed to a program file. Create a new project following the same process used in the previous chapters: Select File->New and select the Projects tab. We can continue to use the Console Application template. Start a new directory for this chapter called Chapter8 and allow the template to be written there. Instead of saving the project by changing the name, we also need to modify the extension of the file. Name the file *convert* and then from the Save As Type drop-down box, select Delphi Unit(*.pas) as the file type.

```
unit convert;

interface

  procedure USConvert;
  procedure FOREIGNConvert;
```

```
implementation
  CONST
    AUSTRALIA = 1.5642;
    CANADA = 1.4672;
    FRANCE = 6.2961;
    KOREA = 1186.40;

  Procedure USMenu(var country: char);
  { ------------------------------------------------------ }
  { PROC USMenu                                            }
  { ------------------------------------------------------ }
  Begin
    writeln('Convert to ...');
    writeln('(A)ustralian Dollars');
    writeln('(C)anadian Dollars');
    writeln('(F)rench Francs');
    writeln('(K)orean Won');
    writeln;
    write('Selection : ');
    readln(country);

    while ( not (upcase(country) in ['A','C','F','K']) ) do
    Begin
      writeln('Please select a choice from the menu.');
      readln(country);
    End;
  End;

  Function US_Australian( in_dollar : real ): real;
  { ------------------------------------------------------ }
  { FUNCTION US_Australian                                 }
  { ------------------------------------------------------ }
  Begin
    US_Australian := in_dollar * AUSTRALIA;
  End;

  Procedure USConvert;
  { ------------------------------------------------------ }
  { PROC USConvert                                         }
  { PUBLIC Proc                                            }
  { ------------------------------------------------------ }
  var
    amount_US      : real;
    country_code   : char;
    out_amount     : real;
```

```
        Begin

          amount_US := 0;
          out_amount := 0;

          write('Amount US $: ');
          readln(amount_US);

          USMenu(country_code);

          If ( upcase(country_code) = 'A' ) Then
          begin
            out_amount := US_Australian( amount_us );
            writeln('Australian Dollars ', out_amount:6:2);
          end;

        End;

        Procedure FOREIGNConvert;
        { ------------------------------------------------------ }
        { PROC FOREIGNConvert                                    }
        { PUBLIC Proc                                            }
        { ------------------------------------------------------ }
        begin
          writeln('FOREIGN conversion stub');
        end;

    end.
```

Save your work and then compile the unit by selecting Project->Compile *convert*. This will not create an executable file but rather will produce a file with the .DCU extension that can be called by other files within a Delphi project.

The interface section lists two public procedures:

```
    interface
      procedure USConvert;
      procedure FOREIGNConvert;
```

These are the only routines or data objects that will be available for use by our calling program. By encapsulating all of the task functions within the privacy wrapper of the implementation section we will be able to modify them at will without requiring that the calling program also be modified to accommodate the changes.

Now we will write a program that utilizes the unit that we just wrote. For this part of the exercise you are going to build a project as we have previously, creating a project file. This is going to be an executable program when it is completed.

```
    program exchange;
```

```
uses convert;
var
  choice : char;
  again  : char;

begin
  choice := ' ';
  again := 'Y';

  repeat
    writeln('   CURRENCY CONVERTER   ');
    writeln;

    writeln('(U).S. -> Foreign or (F)oreign -> U.S. ?');
    readln( choice );
    while( not(choice in['U','u','F','f'] )) do
    begin
      writeln('Incorrect choice: please F/U');
      readln(choice);
    end;

    if( upcase(choice) = 'U' ) then
      USConvert
    else
      FOREIGNConvert;

    write('Run conversion again Y/N? ');
    readln(again);
  until upcase( again ) = 'N';
end.
```

Save your work and run the project. Remember, referring back to the unit file if you have to, that only the Australian conversion has been coded in this example. Figure 8-1 shows a sample session converting one U.S. dollar into Australian currency.

Figure 8-1

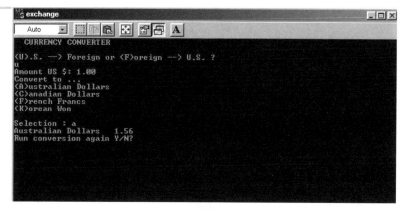

You'll immediately notice that aside from the housekeeping of presenting the program to the user, the program file does little meaningful work. All of the action is through one of the two procedure calls in the IF .. THEN .. ELSE control structure:

```
if ( upcase( choice ) = 'U' then
   USConvert
else
   FOREIGNConvert;
```

Referring back to the listing of the unit file, remember only those items that are exposed through the interface section are visible to the calling program. If the program was to try to call the function US_Australian for instance, an error would be generated by the compiler. Why is this designed in this fashion? For one thing, we want to present a very simple call to the user of the unit. This improves their ability to utilize the functionality of the unit without having to worry about how it is done. The routines and data objects that are hidden in the implementation section are ours to manipulate at will without affecting the end user of the unit. The constant definitions that contain the exchange values are a good example. These hidden objects are defined as constants in this version of the unit. A more likely scenario is that these rates would be read from a data file each time the program is used so that the most recent changes can be used. If these were public data elements there is a chance that they could be used by the programmer throughout the main program, limiting our ability to modify their usage in the future.

Fundamentals in Focus

Procedure or Function Stubs

You will notice in the convert unit that the implementation of the procedure FOREIGNConvert is not complete. The way that the procedure is written as shown in called a stub. There is no functionality in the procedure; it is merely a placeholder so that the rest of the program can be written and tested. This is a good practice to use during the development phase of your program.

When the program file is compiled, it will evaluate the uses statement and locate the convert unit. The unit is then parsed to determine the routines and data objects that are exposed through the interface. If necessary, the unit will be compiled on its own before being assimilated into the program. One of the more important aspects of the unit object is that you can distribute it to your users as a compiled file without providing the source code along with it. This not only prevents snooping eyes from copying your masterful code but it keeps the not-so-talented coders from making a mess of your program and then requesting that you clean it up.

On Second Thought

As we look at the design of our conversion routines, the thought strikes us that not all of the users of the tools are going to want to perform both types of conversions. If the user only needs one type of conversion, say foreign currency into U.S. dollars, the unit that we are developing will saddle them with a lot of unnecessary overhead. For this reason we are going to divide the routines into two separate units, one for U.S. to foreign conversions and the other for foreign to U.S. Won't that be a problem for our current users who currently have their working programs compiled with a single `uses` call to the `convert` unit? Not if we design it carefully with this factor in mind.

The second unit for this project is called `FO2USCon` and is listed below. Remember that you are creating a unit file and not an executable when you set up the template.

```pascal
unit FO2USCon;

interface
  function Australian_US( in_dollar: real ) : real;
  procedure FOREIGNMenu( var country: char );

implementation
  CONST
    AUSTRALIA = 0.6393;
    CANADA = 0.6816;
    FRANCE = 0.1588;
    KOREA = 0.000843;

  procedure FOREIGNMenu;
  { --------------------------------------------- }
  { PROC FOREIGNMenu                              }
  { --------------------------------------------- }
  begin
    writeln('Convert from ...');
    writeln('(A)ustralian Dollars');
    writeln('(C)anadian Dollars');
    writeln('(F)rench Francs');
    writeln('(K)orean Won');
    writeln;
    write('Selection : ');
    readln(country);

    while(not (upcase(country) in ['A','C','F','K']) ) do
    begin
      writeln('Please select a choice from the menu.');
      readln( country );
    end;
  end;

  Function Australian_US;
```

```
{ ------------------------------------------- }
{ FUNCTION Australian_US                       }
{ ------------------------------------------- }
begin
  australian_US := in_dollar * AUSTRALIA;
end;
end.
```

This new unit is called in the implementation section of the `convert` unit which serves to keep the routines in `FO2USCon` hidden from the main program. The modifications are simple:

```
unit convert;
interface
 procedure USConvert;
 procedure FOREIGNConvert;

implementation
 uses fo2uscon;
 ...
```

They are hidden despite the fact that both the procedure and function declared in the `FO2USCon` unit are listed in the interface section of the unit. This declaration is necessary so that the routines are visible to the unit that calls it. Notice in the listing that the forward declaration of the function and procedure have the full definition listed in the interface section and a shorter declaration in the implementation section, the opposite of what we used in the `convert` unit. Remember, this is legal but not recommended. The stub that was used for the procedure `FOREIGNConvert` can now be fleshed out as shown below:

```
procedure FOREIGNConvert;
{ ------------------------------------------- }
{ PROC FOREIGNConvert                          }
{ PUBLIC Proc                                  }
{ ------------------------------------------- }

var
  amount_foreign : real;
  country_code   : char;
  out_us_amount  : real;

begin
  amount_foreign := 0;
  out_us_amount  := 0;

  write('Foreign Amount : ');
  readln( amount_foreign );
```

```
      FOREIGNMenu( country_code );
      if ( upcase( country_code ) = 'A' ) then
      begin
        out_us_amount := Australian_US( amount_foreign );
        writeln( 'U.S. Dollars ', out_us_amount:6:2);
      end;
    end;
```

A bonus of the unit used in the construction of the program and our design which stubbed in the function previously is that we don't need to modify the program file to use the new functionality. Simply recompile the executable section of the program and test the new function. Figure 8-2 shows the new functions of the program in action.

Figure 8-2

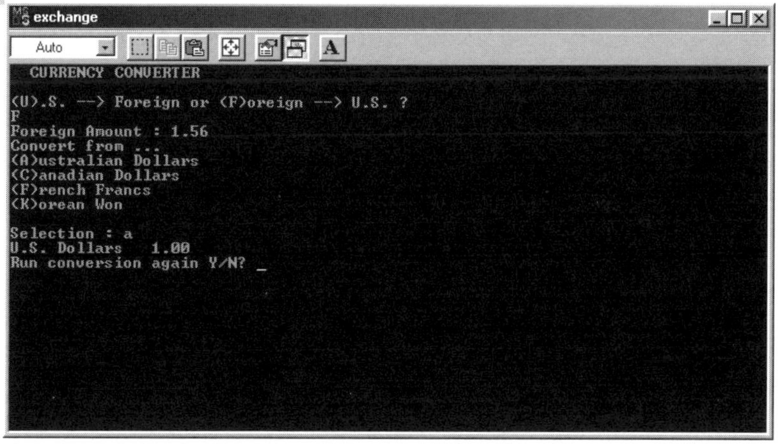

QUICK CHECK

1. In what order are the declarations required within a unit?
2. How are the data hiding facilities of a unit implemented?

Units Summary

The unit gives the developer another method of encapsulating her code and, better yet, a way of distributing that code in precompiled libraries that are safe from the user's ability to modify the source code. By carefully planning the unit structure the eventual user of the code can simplify his program and only compile into the executable file those functions that are needed for the program. The unit provides excellent data hiding characteristics, that is, the user need never see the complex internals of our code. She can concentrate on what she wants to accomplish rather than how it is done. In the next chapter, where we are going to talk about object-oriented programming, you will notice the evolutionary changes from this data structure that lead directly to the class. Before we move forward too far, however, we want to look at some data types in more detail, starting with a look at abstract data types.

Abstract Data Types

Our discussion of data types thus far could easily lead you to view a data type as being the values that make it up. For example, an `integer` type will have a set of values associated with it: 1, 2, 10, 20, and so on. What is not so easy to remember is that data types are much more than the values alone. The complete definition of a data type includes the range of operations that are permitted upon those values as well because without a defined set of operations there would be nothing that we could do with variables, functions, etc., of the data type. The `integer` type, for example, supports a range of operations that include the +, −, *, MOD, and DIV operators as well as a few others. An *abstract data type* (ADT) is another term used to describe a data type where the programmer who is using it does not have access to the underlying details of how the operations work. Well, this is certainly true of the data types that we have examined so far. We do not know how Object Pascal handles the + or − operation on an integer, for example. All of the data types that we have mentioned in this book then are considered to be abstract. One of the great strengths of the language is that it gives the programmer the ability to define custom data types so that the code's readability and clarity can be improved. Ideally, these custom data types will be defined as abstract data types.

If you package a new data type and the definitions for its operations into a unit, the data type becomes usable throughout your programs just as you would use one of the predefined types now. Compiling the unit as a part of a program gives you the ability to define procedures and functions that manipulate the new data element. The unit can play an important part in controlling how the users of your data type approach it. If you utilize the ability of the unit to hide the details of how the data type's operations work, your user will be limited to utilizing it only in the fashion in which you intended rather than trying new and interesting ways of using it. This process of hiding is known as *data abstraction* and a data type defined in this way, with the details of the operations hidden from view, is the abstract data type we are discussing.

Defining a New Data Type

Defining a new data type starts with a type declaration. This statement takes the form:

```
type
   type_identifier = type_definition;
```

where `type_identifier` is any valid identifier other than a reserved word and `type_definition` is any defined data type. Let's start simply by defining a simple substitution

```
type
```

```
money = real;
```

The new data type `money` can be used throughout the program in which it is visible, just as you would an `integer`, `char`, or especially a `real`. A simple data type definition like this would be made for purposes of clarity in the program. A programmer reviewing the code would develop a better understanding of the purpose of the design when it is correlated with money rather than the difficult concept of a `real` data element.

Fundamentals in Focus

Complete Unit Notation

We have finally completed discussion of all of the declarations that you will use within a program or unit. The order in which these declarations are arranged within the program is important and it should be:

1.   Constant declarations

2.   Type declarations

3.   Variable declarations

4.   Procedure and function declarations

With the addition of the `type` statement to your vocabulary, this ordering really makes sense. You would have to define the type of a new variable, for example, before you could declare a variable of that type.

`Money` will inherit all of the operations of the `real` data type. A programmer will be able to use the +, −, *, or / operators to compute amounts of money, and all of the format specifiers that have been used in conjunction with the `writeln` procedure will continue to affect the output when the `money` type is used. Once you have defined a new type such as this you should be careful to be consistent in its use. Your program must be careful in differentiating it from its base type `real`. For instance, if you are creating a function that results in this new type, the parameters and local variables should be of this type as well. Don't mix and match the abstract data type and the base data type even though you know the result will be the same. Remember, we are trying to add clarity to the program.

Ordinal Data Types

In Object Pascal, a data type whose values are specified in a list is known as an ordinal data type. A list connotes a specific set of members that has a specific ordering to it. The simplest ordinal data type that we will encounter is the `Boolean`. The membership of that list is confined to false and true. The Object Pascal operator < can be used with ordinals to determine the ordering of the list. Testing the Boolean members

```
false < true
```

with the < operator will result in a Boolean result of true; false comes before true in the list. (This is not meant to indicate that no other operators can be used; they all can.) The type char has another easily defined membership and order, the list being composed of elements such as 'A', 'B', and 'C'. Again, testing the order of these elements is a matter of testing the relationship with the expression

```
'B' < 'C'
```

which results in a Boolean true result. Though the list of integer data types would be quite long, extending as far as any number line will go, the list has a very obvious ordering to it.

While we easily recognize the ordering of the integer ordinal type based upon the numeric value of the members, the list of char becomes a little less obvious when all of the possible values are considered. Remember that the char data set is composed of all of the characters recognized as members of the character set in use. Where do characters such as 'Z', '$', and 'b' fall in the continuum of the list? The answer is driven by the character set that is selected as the representation of the characters. In an example that fits well with our experience base, the ordering is based upon the ASCII character set. In the ASCII set, the uppercase characters are all defined first, followed by the lowercase letters. This results in evaluations such as

```
'A' < 'a'          'Z' < 'a'
```

resulting in a Boolean true.

Beyond their positioning in a list and the ability to determine the predecessor and successor of every item, what use is the ordinal data type to the programmer? Well, alphabetization comes immediately to mind as a use for the characteristics of this data type. We have also seen numerous examples of comparing one integer value to another to generate a Boolean result throughout the book. There are a couple of less obvious uses that Object Pascal has for the ordinal as well. The for statement uses the ability to traverse a list from one end to the other using the ordering of the elements to perform the looping operations. The following program contains a loop controlled by a character control variable rather than the numeric variables we have used previously. Try this and see if the results are what you expect:

```
program charloop;
var
  c : char;
begin
  for c := 'A' to 'Z' do
    writeln ( c );
end.
```

This usage may seem unusual until you realize that the characters between 'A' and 'Z' are easily used to move up the list going from one to the next in sequence. Using the characters rather than the usual integer counters may allow you to create more intuitive code rather than forcing the reader into an uncomfortable process of correlation between the numbers and the character that they are to represent.

Enumerated Data Types

An enumerated type really comes down to nothing more than a list of identifiers. The values of an enumerated type have none—values that is. The only things they have are their position and their name, much like deposed royalty. Despite this seeming lack of value, enumerated types can add extraordinary clarity to your program. To see how this is possible let's look at an example of a user-defined type. The following declaration declares a new data type called `ball`:

```
type
   ball = (Basketball, Football, Baseball, Volleyball);
```

Your program now has the use of a new data type called `ball`. This data type has four possible values attributed to it: Basketball, Football, Baseball, and Volleyball. The type declaration for an enumerated type will always follow this template: the name of the data type followed by a list of comma-separated identifiers enclosed in parentheses.

Of course, once you have defined this new data type you can create variables of that type and then put those variables to use. Using the previously declared `ball` data type, the statement

```
var
   equipment : ball;
```

declares a variable `equipment` of the new data type. Once the variable has been declared you are free to assign acceptable values to it. A simple assignment statement would be

```
equipment := baseball;
```

The utility of this data type may be even less apparent when you are reminded that the values of type `ball` are not strings and they cannot be output or read in as input.

The CASE structure is a good place to demonstrate the use of a user-defined enumerated type. In the following example, the program uses non-intuitive integers to represent the choices within the structure:

```
sport_type := 3;
case equipment of

  1 :{User choice basketball}
     writeln('Basketball');

  2 :{User choice football}
     writeln('Football');

  3 :{User choice baseball}
     writeln('Baseball');
```

```
    4 :{User choice volleyball}
        writeln('Volleyball');
  else

    writeln('Unknown sport');
  end;
```

Taking a different approach, we can create an enumerated type that will make the program far easier to understand (especially if the choices extend beyond the four shown). Try this sample program:

```
program sports
type
  ball = (Basketball, Football, Baseball, Volleyball);

var
  equipment      : ball;

procedure out_ball( in_sport : ball );
begin
  case in_sport of
    Basketball :
        writeln('Hoops');

    Football :
        writeln('Pigskin');

    Baseball :
        writeln('The Pill');

    Volleyball :
        writeln('Beach Games');
  else

    writeln('Unknown sport');
  end;
end;

begin
  for equipment := Volleyball downto Basketball do
    out_ball( equipment );
end.
```

The CASE structure is certainly not the only use for an enumerated type. Remember that the FOR .. DO loop structure can use an enumerated type for the control of the loop. By themselves, enumerated types have few inherent operations and no input or output abilities. To make better use of the newly defined type, you might want to consider wrapping the type definition, some input and output processes, and any necessary operations into a unit. This creates a true abstract data type that your users or programs can simply put to use without worrying about how the magic is performed.

QUICK CHECK

1. Which of the following are legal type declarations?

```
type
  Range = 1..20;
  Numbers = 1 .. MAXINT;
  Lowercase = 'a'..'z';
  RealNums = 1.2 .. 4.5
  Day = (Mon, Tue, Wed, Thu, Fri, Sat, Sun);
  Weekday = Mon .. Fri;
```

2. Identify which of the following are ordinal data types.

```
integer      char      real      Boolean      string
0..20        'a'..'c'            (Tue, Wed, Thu)
```

Summary

Your Object Pascal skill set has grown now to the point at which you are ready to begin writing much longer programs. Before you read this chapter, however, you were only prepared to write programs that would grow to lengths that made them difficult to maintain. The dual dilemmas of writing all of your code in a single file, namely keeping track of all of the code within that file and maintaining it, and secondly the inability to share your work with anyone else were addressed by our discussion of units. A unit enables you to break your program into discrete pieces containing data types, procedures, and functions that the main body of the program or even other units can call.

The topic of abstract data types was also discussed. These are data types that are user defined with the express purpose of adding readability and clarity to your programming efforts. They are generally built from the fundamental data types that we talked about in an earlier chapter and have used exclusively to this point in the book. In addition to general data abstraction we also worked with two specific types that are a part of every Object Pascal implementation, ordinal and enumerated data types. All of this encapsulation will lead directly into a programming tool we will study in a later chapter—object-oriented programming. Having assimilated the information in this chapter will give you an enormous head start on understanding the concept and practices of this programming approach. Before we get to it, however, we need to develop a couple of additional data structures.

TEST YOUR KNOWLEDGE

At the end of Chapter 6 we mentioned that your programs would take on a whole new look but this statement is even more true with your newfound knowledge. By this point in your studies you will have come to recognize the importance of putting your new skills to the test by developing one or both of the following problems. If you get stuck, go back into the text and use those examples as the basis for your own code.

1. Develop a program that tests your fellow programmers' knowledge of the Boolean expression. Each test question will generate a simple expression that consists of two integers with a Boolean operator between them, such as:

    ```
    33 > 44
    ```

    The user will respond with a keystroke that indicates true or false. Your program should track the number of true or false responses and ask the user if they want to continue. When the user responds that they have finished the test, you should display the number of correct and incorrect answers and the percentage of correct answers.

    The operators used in the program will come from the following list

    ```
    <,  >,  <=,  >= ,  = ,  <>
    ```

    and the operands on either side will come from another pair of lists. List 1 is composed of:

    ```
    2,  4,  6,  3
    ```

    and list 2 is composed of the integers:

    ```
    1,  4,  5,  2,  7
    ```

    Your program should cycle through all of these lists of operators and operands in something that resembles random fashion.

2. Create a unit that encapsulates a new data type called `animal`. The unit should allow the calling program to encounter different actions based upon whether the animal is a mammal or non-mammal. Limit the number of animals represented so that the scope doesn't get out of hand. Use this new unit as a test program similar to the one you developed above.

Chapter 9

Arrays

Key Concepts

- ⊶ Using single-dimensional arrays
- ⊶ The Pascal string
- ⊶ Using multidimensional arrays

Introduction

In the previous chapter you learned that the simple data types that Object Pascal supports can be modified into new, user-defined data types that will add function and clarity to your programs. We are going to expand upon that foundation and create a structured data type, a complex data type built from Object Pascal's simple data types. An array is going to add to our programs the ability to address a collection of values with a single reference. The first structure that we are going to look at is known as a single-dimensional array, a close cousin of the simple list data structure.

This chapter is tightly focused on the array structure in both of its varieties, single- and multidimensional. This single focus is necessary because arrays are often misunderstood and therefore misused. The truth is, arrays are one of the more flexible and useful data structures available to the programmer as long as they are utilized correctly. In addition to the single-dimensional array, we will examine the declaration and usage of arrays with multiple dimensions. This type of structure requires careful algorithm design, within that section we will see numerous code examples to aid your understanding. The chapter will approach these topics as follows:

- The array as a concept will be defined first and we will determine where it is appropriately used in a program.
- Declaring and putting to use a single-dimensional array will follow the theory.
- The traditional Pascal string data type fits nicely into this chapter since it has much in common with the single-dimensional array.

■ Finally, we are going to look at a structure called a multidimensional array and how it is useful to the developer.

The programming that we explore in this chapter will make use of all of the fundamental skills you have worked on up to this point, especially your skills with the loop. The algorithms presented in the second half of the chapter will also be necessarily complex as we examine multidimensional arrays, so take your time and work your way through the examples. Practicing your coding on projects guaranteed to be successful is a good way to build your confidence as well as your skills.

The Array

You are assigned the rather mundane task of writing a program to find the average cost of the things that you purchase each day. Your extensive analysis of the problem indicates that you purchase no more than five items per day, making the resolution a simple exercise. The solution is a program that will have five variables, all of which will be summed and then averaged:

```
program avgprice;
var
   p1          : real;
   p2          : real;
   p3          : real;
   p4          : real;
   p5          : real;
   sum         : real;
   avg         : real;
   x           : integer;

begin
   write('Enter price 1 : ');
   readln(p1);

   write('Enter price 2 : ');
   readln(p2);

   write('Enter price 3 : ');
   readln(p3);

   write('Enter price 4 : ');
   readln(p4);

   write('Enter price 5 : ');
   readln(p5);

   sum := p1 + p2 + p3 + p4 + p5;
   avg := sum / 5;
```

```
writeln('The total of your purchases is $',sum:0:2);
writeln;
writeln('The average cost of your purchases is $',avg:0:2);

readln;

end.
```

This is certainly not the most efficient piece of code ever devised but it meets all of the requirements stated for the program. In order to accommodate the five different values that must be collected, we declared five variables, p1 through p5, to hold the incoming dollar amounts.

While the solution will solve the current problem, consider what is necessary when modifications are requested. In its current incarnation the user is forced to enter five responses regardless of the number of purchases made each day. This is easily solved by nesting a series of IF .. THEN control structures through the program that will skip the questions if there are no numbers to be entered for a purchase. With five different variable identifiers there is no easy way to loop in this program, so the redundant lines are necessary. Now look at that program and envision what is needed to expand the five values to 50 or more. We can expand the number of variables to the new number needed, though it would be tedious. The same action could be applied to the query/response blocks that gather the figures. The point is that the code would become more and more inefficient as the number of data elements grew.

Object Pascal offers a very efficient alternative for situations such as this called the array. An *array* is a collection of elements of like data type that is referred to by a single name. Using that identifier, each individual element within the collection is referred to by an *index* value that correlates to the position of a specific item within the list. Declaring an array is a two-step process. First, a new data type must be declared within the type segment of the program or unit, and then a variable of the new data type is declared. To modify the *AvgPrice* program, we will start by adding the declarations:

```
program avgpric2;
type
  PriceArray = array[ 1..5 ] of real;
var
  prices : PriceArray;
begin
  ....
```

The type definition for the array breaks down as follows. The identifier PriceArray is the name of the new type, which is followed by the array type definition. The reserved word array is followed by a range or subrange enclosed in square brackets that determines the size and the subscripts of the array. In this case there are going to be five slots reserved in the array. To complete the declaration, the subscript definition is followed by the keyword of and the data type that will be stored in each of those slots, in this case `real`. This is referred to as the *component type*.

This declaration results in five elements, or *subscripted variables*, that are referred to as

```
prices[1], prices[2], prices[3], prices[4], prices[5]
```

in order to differentiate them from the normal variables that we have used up to this point. The numeral enclosed in the square brackets following the identifier is the *subscript*. (This number is actually an expression and does not need to be a single integer as shown in the example.) These variables can be used just like any other variable type:

```
prices[3] := 29.99;
x := prices[5];
readln(prices[1]);
writeln(prices[2]);
```

The only limiting factor involved with the subscripted variables is that the subscript expression must be an ordinal data type.

We will make a simple modification to our *AvgPrice* program to see how the values are stored in memory with the array structure:

```
program avgpric2;
type
   PriceArray = array[ 1..5 ] of real;

var
   prices : PriceArray;
   sum         : real;
   avg         : real;

begin
   write('Enter price 1 : ');
   readln(prices[1]);

   write('Enter price 2 : ');
   readln(prices[2]);

   write('Enter price 3 : ');
   readln(prices[3]);

   write('Enter price 4 : ');
   readln(prices[4]);

   write('Enter price 5 : ');
   readln(p[5]);
```

```
sum := prices[1] + prices[2] +
prices[3] + prices[4] + prices[5];
avg := sum / 5;

writeln('The total of your purchases is $',sum:0:2);
writeln;
writeln('The average cost of your purchases is $',avg:0:2);

readln;

end.
```

In this version, we have replaced the individual variables with their subscripted counterparts. What does change when the array is used is how the data is stored in memory. Figure 9-1 is a graphical representation of the new array variables as they are stored in adjacent locations in RAM. The array alone represents this collection of values, with each subscript pointing to a specific box within the list.

Prices[1]	Prices[2]	Prices[3]	Prices[4]	Prices[5]
29.99	33.52	124.99	1.09	.66

Figure 9-1: An array in memory

Fundamentals In Focus

Initialization is a Must

If you will recall several chapters back we discussed the necessity for initializing all of your variables prior to use. This prevented undesired side effects from creeping into your program. The same is even more important for an array since it is very possible that you will not always utilize all of the possible memory locations in the list. If your program does not initialize all of the subscripted variables, they can easily take their value from the underlying memory location, possibly leading to incorrect results or program failure.

Taking Advantage of the Subscript

A program can capitalize on the sequential nature of the ordinals that make up the subscript range. This range is not limited strictly to integers as the example uses; it can be a range or subrange of any ordinal data type. The types Boolean, char, and any other ordinal types defined can make up the range of subscripts as in:

```
names = array['A' .. 'F'] of char;
numbers = array[ 10 .. 20 ] of integer;
possibility = array[ Boolean ] of char;
```

When declared as variables, each of these arrays will have a slightly different subscript range than we have seen in the examples up to now. If declared as:

```
var
   name      : names;
   number    : numbers;
   possible  : possibility;
```

the name variable will have six subscripts, name['A'], name['B'], through name['F']. The number array will have ten subscripts, number[10], number[11], through number[20], and the possible array will have two subscripted variables possible[false] and possible[true]. Each of the subscripted variables is capable of holding one element of its assigned data type.

As I mentioned, we can utilize the sequential nature of the ordinal variable when working with arrays. We'll make another round of modifications to the *AvgPrice* program to demonstrate this:

```
program avgpric3;
type
   PriceArray = array[ 1..5 ] of real;

var
   prices : PriceArray;
   sum    : real;
   avg    : real;
   x      : integer;
   go     : char;

begin
   x   := 1;
   avg := 0;
   sum := 0;

   {- initialize the array - }
         for x := 1 to 5 do
     prices[ x ]  := 0;

   { - process user response - }
   write('Enter any prices today ? (Y/n) : ');
   readln(go);

   x := 1;
   if go in ['Y','y'] then
   begin
```

```
      while ( x <= 5) and (go in ['Y','y']) do
      begin
        write('Enter price : ');
        readln(prices[x]);

        x := x + 1;

        if x <= 5 then
        begin
          write('Enter another? (Y/n): ');
        readln( go );
        end;
      end;

      {- sum the values entered -}

      for x := 1 to 5 do
        sum := sum + prices[x];

      avg := sum / 5;

      writeln('The total of your purchases is $',sum:0:2);
      writeln;
      writeln('The average cost of your purchases is $',avg:0:2);
    end
    else
      writeln('No purchases today.');
      readln;

  end.
```

The first modification that you will notice is the initialization of the array's elements and how this task is performed. Because the subscripted variables are adjacent to one another in the list, a loop can be used to traverse the list. Remember that the value enclosed in the square brackets is an expression and therefore can accept a variable.

```
        {- initialize the array - }
            for x := 1 to 5 do
        prices[ x ] := 0;
```

In this example we use the properties of the `for` statement to step through the subscripts one by one and then assign the value of 0 to each variable. The control variable x starts with a value of 1 and is incremented sequentially to the value of 5 automatically by the loop structure. This action is the same as the group of assignment statements:

```
prices[1] := 0;
prices[2] := 0;
....
prices[5] := 0;
```

but a lot more efficient, especially when the size of the array grows to be a hundred or so elements.

Fundamentals in Focus

Index Out of Range

One of the most common errors that Object Pascal programmers make is to reference a subscript value that is out of the range defined for the array. If you have defined an array with a range of subscripts that go from 1 to 5:

```
scores = array[1 .. 5] of integer;
```

and you attempt to reference a subscript that is less than 1 or greater than 5, Object Pascal will generate an error message that reminds you that your subscript 'value is out of range.'

This common error usually occurs when reading the first or last elements due to the ordinal requirement of the range or subrange. It will also occur frequently during operations that are filling the array; it is very easy to get to the end of the array and attempt to add just one more element. Be sure that your code implements the necessary safeguards to prevent these types of errors from occurring at run time. An excellent addition to your programs is a constant that indicates the top of the list.

The data collection of the purchase prices has also been enclosed within a loop. This control structure allows the user to determine how many elements of the array are filled on those days when fewer than five items are bought. This possibility points up the importance of the initialization. Figure 9-2 shows the array before and after three values have been entered. If subscripts 4 and 5 are not initialized, there is a very real possibility that garbage values could enter the program. This problem would not exist if all five spots are filled on each execution of the program but you should design your programs to compensate for every possible situation.

After initialization

Prices[1]	Prices[2]	Prices[3]	Prices[4]	Prices[5]
0	0	0	0	0

After data entry

Prices[1]	Prices[2]	Prices[3]	Prices[4]	Prices[5]
33.33	44.44	55.55	0	0

Figure 9-2: The Prices array after initialization and data entry

This situation also points up a logical design flaw that needs to be addressed in the *AvgPrice* program to prevent incorrect output. The avg value is being computed by dividing the sum by the maximum size of the array, currently set to five. This leads to an incorrect result if the array is only partially filled. To fix this error, the function average is added to the program:

```
function Average( in_array : pricearray ): real;
{ ----------------------------- }
{ func Average                  }
{ Param: in_array               }
{ Accepts array and finds average }
{ from the filled elements       }
{ ----------------------------- }
var
  count        : integer;
  x_sum        : real;

begin

  count := 1;
  x_sum := 0;

  while (in_array[count] > 0) and (count <= 5) do
  begin

    x_sum := x_sum + in_array[count];
    count := count + 1;

  end;

  average := x_sum / (count - 1);

end;
```

The function takes as a parameter the complete array prices. The completed program *AvgPric4* is shown below:

```
program avgpric4;
type
  PriceArray = array[ 1..5 ] of real;

var
  prices       :PriceArray;
  sum          : real;
  avg          : real;
  x            : integer;
  go           : char;
```

```pascal
function Average( in_array : pricearray ): real;
{ ----------------------------- }
{ func Average                  }
{ Param: in_array               }
{ Accepts array and finds average }
{ from the filled elements      }
{ ----------------------------- }
var
  count      : integer;
  x_sum      : real;

begin

  count := 1;
  x_sum := 0;

  while (in_array[count] > 0) and (count <= 5) do
  begin

    x_sum := x_sum + in_array[count];
    count := count + 1;

  end;

  average := x_sum / (count - 1);

end;


begin
  x    := 1;
  avg  := 0;
  sum  := 0;

  {- initialize the array - }
  for x := 1 to 5 do
    prices[ x ] := 0;

  { - process user response - }
  write('Enter any prices today ? (Y/n) : ');
  readln(go);

  x := 1;
  if go in ['Y','y'] then
  begin
    while ( x <= 5) and (go in ['Y','y']) do
```

```
      begin
        write('Enter price : ');
        readln(prices[x]);

        x := x + 1;

        if x <= 5 then
        begin
          write('Enter another? (Y/n): ');
          readln( go );
        end;
      end;

      {- sum the values entered -}

      for x := 1 to 5 do
        sum := sum + prices[x];

      writeln('The total of your purchases is $',sum:0:2);
      writeln;
     writeln('The average cost of your purchases is $',average( prices ):0:2);

    end
    else

      writeln('No purchases today.');

    readln;
  end.
```

Once the data type `pricearray` has been defined it can be used in any situation that requires a data type, and the parameter declaration is no exception. When the function is called, the entire array is passed to the function. When the entire array is referred to like this it is known as an *array variable*. If you needed to pass only a single subscripted variable such as `prices[2]` the parameter is declared as a single instance of the component type; in this case a `real`. For example, the function `compare` shown here:

```
  function Compare ( in_1 : real; in_2 : real ): real;
  ....
```

would accept a subscripted variable passed as:

```
  larger := compare( prices[x], prices[x+1]);
```

As long as we are discussing functions, it should be noted that Object Pascal does not support returning an array data type from a function.

Fundamentals in Focus

Array Passing and Memory Management

When passing an array as a parameter to a function or procedure, remember to take into consideration the differences between passing by reference and passing by value. When you pass an array via a value parameter, in other words a normal parameter as shown in the previous example, remember that you are making a copy of that data for local usage. This means that a second copy of the entire array is placed into memory during the duration of the function or procedure processing. The variable parameter, on the other hand, passes a pointer to the actual array, precluding the need for a second copy.

Though memory management is not as crucial as it once was it is still your job as the programmer to ensure that your program does not terminate abnormally due to a memory overrun. Aside from the need to manage the amount of memory used, consider the efficiency of passing large data objects back and forth during the execution of the program. A large array would certainly slow the execution of your program. Consider the two alternatives available to you; a variable parameter that does not copy the array might be slightly more risky but add a lot in terms of the speed of your program.

QUICK CHECK

1. Identify the correct type definitions.

   ```
   Type
      counter = [99 .. 225] of integer;
      answers = [1 .. 10] of Boolean;
      codes   = ['z' .. 'A'] of integer;
      cash    = [1 .. 25] of reals;
   ```

2. Write the appropriate type and variable declarations for arrays that fit the following scenarios.

   a. Collect 50 test scores with a possible range of 0 to 100.

   b. Set up a test key for an exam that has 75 true or false questions.

   c. Create an array for a program that records the gender makeup of a company's workforce.

3. The following snippet is supposed to print out to the screen all of the elements of the array `grades`. It is failing. What is wrong with it and what changes need to be made in order to make it work?

   ```
   for x := 1 to 100 do
      writeln('Grade' ,x, grades);
   ```

Pascal Strings

Strings—how did this section get into a chapter about arrays? Well, the answer goes back to the original implementations of Pascal that supported only one string data type. The current Delphi implementation supports multiple string types. This section discussing string manipulation specifically references the traditional fixed-length string. If you can put this functionality to use in your program you must be certain to include the proper compiler directive to ensure that these types of strings are used. The reason that this material is included in this chapter is that traditional Pascal strings are very similar in structure and action to an array of characters. The properties of the two data elements are similar; each has a set of subscripted elements and each element, in the case of the string, can be used in place of a single `char` variable.

The string variable declaration

```
var
   BookTitle   : string[15];
```

allocates a block of memory sufficient to store 15 contiguous characters. When an assignment is made to this variable

```
booktitle := 'Object Pascal';
```

it is stored as shown in Figure 9-3.

| 13 | O | b | j | e | c | t | | P | a | s | c | a | l | | |

Figure 9-3: The Object Pascal short string

The most important difference between the short string and an array is the first byte in the string. The first byte denotes the length of the string, in this case 13. The length byte exists in the zero subscript of the string variable and can be read through an assignment statement such as

```
x := ord( title[0] );
```

The length of the string is much easier to obtain using the `length` function. `Length` returns the number of characters actually stored in the string without the need for your program to reference the zero subscript.

```
x := length( title );
```

Because each of the elements of the string is also accessible through its subscript value, the replacement or extraction of specific characters is simplified. For example, the snippet:

```
title[1] := 'A'
writeln( title );
```

will result in the output "Abject Pascal." Another use for this characteristic is to modify a property of the characters contained at each subscript. The following code will convert the entire string to its uppercase representation:

```
program capper;
var
   x              : integer;
   title          : string[15];

begin

   title := 'Object Pascal';
   writeln( title );

   for x := 1 to length( title )   do
      title[x] := upcase( title[x] );

   writeln( title );

end.
```

After looking at this program it appears that the functionality could be useful in other situations and for that reason it would be better implemented as a function. The design of the function would be simple.

```
function AllUpCase( in_str : string[15] ): string[15];
var
   x      : integer;

begin

   for x := 1 to length( in_str ) do
     in_str[x] := upcase(in_str[x]);
   allupcase := in_str;

end;
```

The only problem is, you cannot pass a string definition as shown as a parameter to a function or procedure. This limitation is compiler based. To pass these string references you must define a new type and then use that type in your parameter and return value declarations. The following code will fix this problem:

```
type
   string15 = string[15];
   ....

function AllUpCase( in_str : string15 ) : string15;
   ....
```

Delphi offers an even simpler solution through the use of the default string type. This string is dynamically allocated and does away with the sizing requirements.

```
program capper2;

var
 title     : string;

function AllUpCase( in_str : string ) : string;
var
   x          : integer;
begin
   for x := 1 to length( in_str ) do
     in_str[x] := upcase( in_str[x] );

   allupcase := in_str;
end;

begin
   writeln('Capper 2');
   title := 'Object Pascal';
   writeln( title );

   writeln( allupcase(title) );

end.
```

An added advantage of the 32-bit version that is shown in this version of the program is that strings of any size can be accommodated, unlike the fixed-length strings shown earlier. When using zero byte strings, any characters that exceed the defined length of the string are truncated.

Complex Array Structures

As your programming advances you are going to find that arrays are one of the more useful data structures implemented through Object Pascal. As we will see in the sections to come that cover more advanced algorithms, using arrays for searching and sorting makes the handling of these tasks much simpler. Often though, the single-dimensional array does not adequately allow us to model the data that we are trying to store. An example would be the text on this page. Laying the characters end-to-end in a list would destroy the spatial relationships that make it readable: the spacing, the paragraphs, etc. The page would be better modeled on a grid so that things such as the indentation and other formatting could be retained. To facilitate this modeling, Object Pascal supports multidimensional arrays.

Multidimensional Arrays

A multidimensional array models a matrix rather than a list. A matrix has two dimensions, rows and columns, and Object Pascal supports an array definition that includes two or more indices. Suppose that your program needed to store a full screen of text. The standard text screen measurements are 25 rows down and 80 columns wide across. This means that there can be 2000 characters on the screen at any one time and that a matrix to store it would require this many subscript values. The multidimensional array declaration for this would be:

```
type
   screen = array[ 1..25, 1..80 ] of char;

var
   textscreen : screen
....
```

It is not required that the declaration order be row/column but this is the traditional Object Pascal ordering.

Referencing each element in this matrix requires two subscripts. Figure 9-4 shows a part of the array with the proper addresses in each cell. To reference the value stored in the element 1,1 the array variable must provide both offsets.

```
textscreen[1,1] := 'a';
```

1,1	1,2	1,3	....
2,1	2,2	....	....
3,1	....	....	....
....	....	....	....

Figure 9-4: The multidimensional array TextScreen

As with the single-dimensional arrays, the subscript range can be defined as any valid ordinal range or subrange and the component type can be any valid data type.

The algorithms for processing multidimensional arrays are not much more complicated than their single-dimensional relatives. The initialization process, for example, makes use of nested loops to accomplish its task:

```
program matrix;

const
   MAXROWS = 25;
   MAXCOLS = 80;

type
   TextMatrix = array[1..MAXROWS, 1..MAXCOLS] of char;
```

```
var
   screen      : TextMatrix;
   r           : integer;
   c           : integer;

begin
   r := 1;
   c := 1;

   for r := 1 to MAXROWS do
      for c := 1 to MAXCOLS  do
         screen[ r, c ] := ' ';

end.
```

Follow along on this next programming example that will put the matrix to work and utilize its unique characteristics to simplify the program's design.

The Airline Reservation Project

This project makes use of the matrix to model a set of airline seats, albeit a very small airline. The seating area is composed of six rows of seats numbered row one through row six. Each row has six seats across labeled seat A, B, C, D, E, and F. This problem could probably be solved using six individual single-dimensional arrays but the matrix models it much more naturally. Figure 9-5 gives a good visual picture of the real-life layout of the objects.

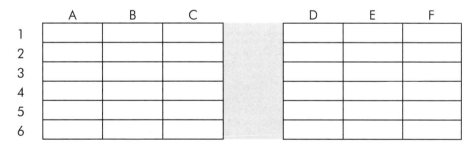

Figure 9-5: The airline seat layout

The first step then is to create the data object that will match this in the most natural way. The definition for the array is straightforward:

```
const
   MAXROWS = 6;
   MAXCOLS = 'F';
```

```
type
    RowsCols = array[1..MAXROWS, 'A'..MAXCOLS] of char;

var
    seats       : RowsCols;
    ....
```

Notice that the type definition for the array uses two types of subranges to define the matrix. The rows are defined numerically as you would expect but we use the actual seat letters to identify the columns. This will make operations more natural and easy to follow.

With all data structures that are put into use in a program, the first step is to initialize them to a fixed value. In the case of the airline seats the program places an "o" in each empty seat. The code for this step is a simple nested structure that uses ranges that match those of the matrix:

```
{ - Initialize array - }
for r := 1 to MAXROWS do
  for s := 'A' to MAXCOLS  do
      seats[ r, s ] := 'o';
```

The use of constants makes modification of the program a much easier chore. One other fundamental tool is needed before looking at the operational tasks that need to be handled and that is the drawing of the seat matrix on the screen. A procedure called DrawSeats will handle this repetitive chore. (Note that this program was originally written for Turbo Pascal 7.0 and makes use of a procedure from the CRT unit, clrscr. This clears the screen and repositions the cursor at 0,0 for the redraw. If you are writing strictly in Delphi, you should comment these lines out.)

```
procedure DrawSeats;
{ ---------------------------------------------- }
{ Draw the seat matrix with any updates          }
{ ---------------------------------------------- }
var
  row          : integer;
  seat         : char;

begin
  clrscr;
  writeln('A':10,'B':5,'C':5,'D':5,'E':5,'F':5);

  for row := 1 to MAXROWS do
  begin
    write(row:5);
    for seat := 'A' to MAXCOLS  do
      write(seats[ row, seat ]:5);
      writeln;
```

```
          end;

   end;
```

The use of a procedure makes sense in the program because every time an update is made to the reservations matrix it should be reflected right away. The simplest way to do that is to redraw the entire array onscreen so that the modifications can be seen.

Making a Reservation

The first real task that needs to be accomplished is adding a reservation. This action has two steps to it: locate the seat and determine whether or not it is already reserved and then reserve it or return the bad news to the reservations clerk. When the matrix was initialized, an "o" was written into each location; this is what should be displayed for each seat prior to any reservations being made. The user will enter a row and seat combination that will be parsed and broken down into two variables that can be used as the subscript values for the element desired.

```
procedure AddSeats;
{ --------------------------------------------- }
{ Writes a reservation to seat                  }
{ --------------------------------------------- }

var
   rs           : string[2];
   row          : integer;
   seat         : char;
   error        : integer;
begin
   write('Enter row/seat desired (RS) : ');
   readln(rs);

   val(rs[1], row, error);

   if (row > 0) and (row <= MAXROWS) then
   begin
     if (upcase(rs[2]) >= 'A') and (upcase(rs[2]) <= MAXCOLS)
then
       begin
         seat := upcase(rs[2]);
         if seats[row, seat] = 'o' then
         begin
            seats[ row, seat ] := 'X';
            writeln('Seat Assigned');
         end
         else
```

```
          begin
            writeln('Seat already assigned');

          end;
        end
        else
          writeln('Invalid seat letter');
      end
      else
        writeln('Invalid row number');

      writeln('Press a key ...');
      readln;
    end;
```

The user inputs a string at the prompt with a length of two characters. Anything past that length will be discarded because our design has utilized this property of the fixed-length string. The row and seat identifiers must be separated because the row identifier must be converted into an integer value to match the row subrange. This action is performed by the `val` procedure. The seat letter is already in the proper format, needing only capitalization. The string is parsed using the ability to identify specific positions within the string by supplying a subscript value after the string identifier. If the string supplied by the user does not contain a correctly formatted row-seat combination, an error message is issued and the screen is redrawn for the next action.

If the row-seat combination is validated, the seat status can be directly queried by supplying the array identifier and subscript values. If it contains an "o," it is not reserved and the contents of the element will be modified to contain an "X." On the other hand, if it contains an "X," the seat is reserved and the appropriate notification is passed back to the user. The matrix is redrawn to the screen to reflect the changes and the program waits for the next instruction.

Removing a reservation is exactly the opposite process of making one. The user must provide a valid row-seat combination and, using this, the contents of the specified element will be examined. If the seat is reserved, the "X" will be replaced by an "o." If the seat requested has never been reserved, the user will receive the appropriate notification but no changes will be made to the contents of the element. The complete program is shown in the following listing.

Listing 9-1

```
program reserve;
{ ------------------------------------ }
{ TURBO PASCAL ONLY!!!!               }
{ Uses CRT and CLRSCR = DOS Only      }
{ ------------------------------------ }
{uses crt;                            }
```

```
const
   MAXROWS = 6;
   MAXCOLS = 'F';

type
   RowsCols = array[1..MAXROWS, 'A'..MAXCOLS] of char;

var
   seats      : RowsCols;
   r          : integer;
   s          : char;
   action     : char;

procedure DrawSeats;
{ ----------------------------------------------- }
{ Draw the seat matrix with any updates           }
{ ----------------------------------------------- }
var
   row        : integer;
   seat       : char;

begin
  {clrscr;}
  writeln('A':10,'B':5,'C':5,'D':5,'E':5,'F':5);

  for row := 1 to MAXROWS do
  begin
    write(row:5);
    for seat := 'A' to MAXCOLS  do
      write(seats[ row, seat ]:5);
      writeln;
  end;

end;

procedure AddSeats;
{ ----------------------------------------------- }
{ Writes a reservation to seat                    }
{ ----------------------------------------------- }

var
  rs         : string[2];
  row        : integer;
  seat       : char;
  error      : integer;
```

```pascal
begin
  write('Enter row/seat desired (RS) : ');
  readln(rs);

  val(rs[1], row,error);

  if (row  0) and (row MAXROWS) then
  begin
    if (upcase(rs[2]) = 'A') and (upcase(rs[2]) MAXCOLS) then

    begin

      seat := upcase(rs[2]);
      if seats[row, seat] = 'o' then
      begin
        seats[ row, seat ] := 'X';
        writeln('Seat Assigned');
      end
      else
      begin
        writeln('Seat already assigned');

      end;
    end
    else
      writeln('Invalid seat letter');
  end
  else
    writeln('Invalid row number');

  writeln('Press a key ...');
  readln;

end;

procedure RemoveSeats;
{ --------------------------------------------- }
{ Removes a reservation from a seat             }
{ --------------------------------------------- }

var
  rs         : string[2];
  row        : integer;
  seat       : char;
  error      : integer;
```

```
begin
  write('Enter row/seat to change (RS) : ');
  readln(rs);

  val(rs[1], row,error);

  if (row  0) and (row MAXROWS) then
  begin
    if (upcase(rs[2]) = 'A') and (upcase(rs[2]) MAXCOLS) then

      begin

        seat := upcase(rs[2]);
        if seats[row, seat] = 'X' then
        begin
          seats[ row, seat ] := 'o';
          writeln('Reservation Removed');
        end
        else
        begin
          writeln('Seat not assigned');

        end;
      end
      else
        writeln('Invalid seat letter');
  end
  else
    writeln('Invalid row number');

  writeln('Press a key ...');
  readln;

end;

begin

  { - Initialize array - }
  for r := 1 to MAXROWS do
    for s := 'A' to MAXCOLS  do
      seats[ r, s ] := 'o';

  action := 'D';
```

Chapter 9

```
      while not (action in ['X','x']) do
      begin

        DrawSeats;

        write('(A)dd, (R)emove, (D)isplay, E(X)it : ');
        readln( action );

        case UpCase(action) of

          'A'  : AddSeats;

          'R'  : RemoveSeats;

          'D'  : DrawSeats;
        else
          writeln('Incorrect choice, press a key');
        end;

      end;

    end.
```

I Wanna Window Seat!!!

Ever accommodating, the program needs one more function to provide some additional customer service to the flying consumer. If they request either seat A or seat F in any row, they are looking for a window seat. A similar preference is applied to seats C and D in each row, the aisle seats. If the customer requests one of these seats in a particular row and it is filled, the program will automatically search out the next available suitable seat. For example, if the passenger requests seat 1A and it is filled, the program should search from 2A through 6A before attempting a match in seat F on the other side of the plane. The matrix structure makes this search process quite simple since your search will involve movement within a single data structure.

Before coding a solution to this problem, you should establish the business rules that pertain to the task. Will the search attempt the same row on the other side of the plane first or will it run sequentially down one side of the plane prior to moving to the first row on the other side? If the search starts in the middle of the rows will it continue when it reaches the last row by starting over at the top of the same row? There are numerous questions like these that affect every program you will write so it is important to establish them prior to coding. By performing the necessary analysis BC (Before Coding), no matter how tedious and difficult it may be, you will have a much better chance of satisfying your users with your initial productions and will not be put in a position of having to extensively recode your program. For this problem, the search will simply start at the top of the selected side of the plane and continue until the bottom is reached and then it will proceed to the opposite side of the plane.

Two changes are needed to implement this modification. The first is the addition of the necessary procedure to handle this task. The procedure FindWindow is shown below:

```
procedure FindWindow( var f_row : integer; var f_seat :
char);
{ --------------------------------------------- }
{ Finds an alternative window seat              }
{ --------------------------------------------- }
var
  row         : integer;
  seat        : char;
  found       : Boolean;
  totalck     : integer;

begin

  totalck := 0;
  found := false;

  row := 1;
  seat := f_seat;

  while not found do
  begin

    if seats[ row, seat ] = 'o' then
    begin
      f_row := row;
      f_seat := seat;
      found := true;
    end
    else
      row := row + 1;

    if (row = MAXROWS+1) and (seat = 'A') then
    begin
      row := 1;
      seat := 'F'
    end;

    if (row = MAXROWS+1) and (seat = 'F') then
    begin
      row := 1;
```

```
          seat := 'A';
      end;

   totalck := totalck + 1;
   if totalck = 12 then
      found := true;

   end;
end;
```

Once again, this procedure takes advantage of the sequential structure of the matrix to simplify the actions needed. The only other change needed is to add a call to the procedure:

```
      ....
writeln('Seat already assigned');

      { - Find another window seat - }
      if (seat = 'A') or (seat = 'F') then
      begin
         writeln('Searching for window seat ....');
         t_row := row;
         t_seat := seat;

         FindWindow( row, seat );

         if (t_row = row) and (t_seat = seat) then
            writeln('No more window seats available.')
         else
         begin
            seats[ row, seat ] := 'X';
            writeln('Seat ',seat,' in row ',row,' assigned.');
         end;
      end;
      ....
```

The same design is utilized to implement the search for an aisle seat. The completed *reserve2* program is shown in Listing 9-2.

Listing 9-2

```
program reserve2;
{ ----------------------------------- }
{ TURBO PASCAL ONLY!!!!               }
{ Uses CRT and CLRSCR = DOS Only      }
{ ----------------------------------- }
uses crt;
```

```
const
   MAXROWS = 6;
   MAXCOLS = 'F';

type
   RowsCols = array[1..MAXROWS, 'A'..MAXCOLS] of char;

var
   seats       : RowsCols;
   r           : integer;
   s           : char;
   action      : char;

procedure DrawSeats;
{ --------------------------------------------- }
{ Draw the seat matrix with any updates         }
{ --------------------------------------------- }
var
  row         : integer;
  seat        : char;

begin
  clrscr;
  writeln('A':10,'B':5,'C':5,'D':5,'E':5,'F':5);

  for row := 1 to MAXROWS do
  begin
    write(row:5);
    for seat := 'A' to MAXCOLS  do
      write(seats[ row, seat ]:5);
      writeln;
  end;

end;

procedure FindWindow( var f_row : integer; var f_seat : char);
{ --------------------------------------------- }
{ Finds an alternative window seat              }
{ --------------------------------------------- }
var
   row         : integer;
   seat        : char;
   found       : boolean;
   totalck     : integer;
```

```
begin

  totalck := 0;
  found := false;

  row := 1;
  seat := f_seat;

  while not found do
  begin

    if seats[ row, seat ] = 'o' then
    begin
      f_row := row;
      f_seat := seat;
      found := true;
    end
    else
      row := row + 1;

    if (row = MAXROWS+1) and (seat = 'A') then
    begin
      row := 1;
      seat := 'F'
    end;

    if (row = MAXROWS+1) and (seat = 'F') then
    begin
      row := 1;
      seat := 'A';
    end;

    totalck := totalck + 1;
    if totalck = 12 then
      found := true;

  end;
end;
procedure FindAisle( var f_row : integer; var f_seat : char);
{ --------------------------------------------- }
{ Finds an alternative aisleseat               }
{ --------------------------------------------- }
var
  row        : integer;
  seat       : char;
  found      : boolean;
```

```
    totalck    : integer;

begin

  totalck := 0;
  found := false;

  row := 1;
  seat := f_seat;

  while not found do
  begin

    if seats[ row, seat ] = 'o' then
    begin
      f_row := row;
      f_seat := seat;
      found := true;
    end
    else
      row := row + 1;

    if (row = MAXROWS+1) and (seat = 'C') then
    begin
      row := 1;
      seat := 'D'
    end;

    if (row = MAXROWS+1) and (seat = 'D') then
    begin
      row := 1;
      seat := 'C';
    end;

    totalck := totalck + 1;
    if totalck = 12 then
      found := true;

  end;
end;

procedure AddSeats;
{ --------------------------------------------- }
{ Writes a reservation to seat                  }
{ --------------------------------------------- }
var
```

```pascal
        rs          : string[2];
        row         : integer;
        seat        : char;
        error       : integer;
        t_row       : integer;
        t_seat      : char;

begin
    write('Enter row/seat desired (RS) : ');
    readln(rs);

    val(rs[1], row,error);

    if (row  0) and (row MAXROWS) then
    begin
      if (upcase(rs[2]) = 'A') and (upcase(rs[2]) MAXCOLS) then

      begin

        seat := upcase(rs[2]);
        if seats[row, seat] = 'o' then
        begin
          seats[ row, seat ] := 'X';
          writeln('Seat Assigned');
        end
        else
        begin
          writeln('Seat already assigned');

          { - Find another window seat - }
          if (seat = 'A') or (seat = 'F') then
          begin
            writeln('Searching for window seat ....');
            t_row := row;
            t_seat := seat;
            FindWindow( row, seat );
            if (t_row = row) and (t_seat = seat) then
              writeln('No more window seats available.')
            else
            begin
              seats[ row, seat ] := 'X';
              writeln('Seat ',seat,' in row ',row,' assigned.');
            end;
        end;
```

```
                      { - Find another aisle seat - }
                  if (seat = 'C') or (seat = 'D') then
                  begin
                    writeln('Searching for aisle seat ....');
                    t_row := row;
                    t_seat := seat;
                    FindAisle( row, seat );
                    if (t_row = row) and (t_seat = seat) then
                      writeln('No more aisle seats available.')
                    else
                    begin
                      seats[ row, seat ] := 'X';
                      writeln('Seat ',seat,' in row ',row,' assigned.');
                    end;
                  end;
              end;
          end
          else
            writeln('Invalid seat letter');
      end
      else
        writeln('Invalid row number');

      writeln('Press a key ...');
      readln;

end;

procedure RemoveSeats;
{ ------------------------------------------- }
{ Removes a reservation from a seat           }
{ ------------------------------------------- }

var
  rs          : string[2];
  row         : integer;
  seat        : char;
  error       : integer;

begin
  write('Enter row/seat to change (RS) : ');
  readln(rs);

  val(rs[1], row,error);
```

```pascal
        if (row  0) and (row MAXROWS) then
        begin
          if (upcase(rs[2]) = 'A') and (upcase(rs[2]) MAXCOLS) then

          begin

            seat := upcase(rs[2]);
            if seats[row, seat] = 'X' then
            begin
              seats[ row, seat ] := 'o';
              writeln('Reservation Removed');
            end
            else
            begin
              writeln('Seat not assigned');

            end;
          end
          else
            writeln('Invalid seat letter');
        end
        else
          writeln('Invalid row number');

        writeln('Press a key ...');
        readln;

      end;

      begin

        { - Initialize array - }
        for r := 1 to MAXROWS do
          for s := 'A' to MAXCOLS  do
            seats[ r, s ] := 'o';

        action := 'D';

        while not (action in ['X','x']) do
        begin

          DrawSeats;

          write('(A)dd, (R)emove, (D)isplay, E(X)it : ');
          readln( action );
```

```
     case UpCase(action) of

       'A'  : AddSeats;

       'R'  : RemoveSeats;

       'D'  : DrawSeats;
     else
       writeln('Incorrect choice, press a key');
     end;

   end;

 end.
```

Fundamentals in Focus

Running Out of Memory

Depending on the complexity of your design, it is possible for a multidimensional array to take up an extraordinary amount of memory. Be sure that you consider the size of the elements and the number of instances to be used during the design phase. A two-dimensional matrix of 100 rows by 100 columns creates 10,000 elements, while an array of 1,000 by 1,000 sets aside 1 million elements. Multiply that number by the size of the data type, currency for example, which is stored in an 8-byte block, and you will see how quickly memory can get eaten up.

QUICK CHECK

1. Given the following array declaration, write the code to perform the tasks indicated.

```
type
  table = array[ 'A'..'Z', 'a'..'z' ] of real;

var
  DataStore    : table;
```

   a. Initialize the array to zeroes.
   b. Fill the array with random values.
   c. Total each row and display the sum.
   d. Total diagonally from subscript A, a to Z, z and display the product.

Chapter 9

2. Write the type declaration for an array that stores 52 weeks of Sunday through Saturday dates in a way that can be intuitively referenced, i.e., Week5, Wednesday. Initialize the array with the correct dates for the year 2000.

Summary

Expanding on the experiences from the previous chapter in which you learned that the simple data types could be used to build new, user-defined data types, this chapter took that knowledge one step further to create a structured data type, a complex data type built from Object Pascal's simple data types. The array gives programs the newfound ability to address a collection of values with a single reference. By utilizing the subscripted properties of the structure, the programs that we write are able to either drill down directly to the specific data element needed in the collection or work sequentially through the entire set.

The single-dimensional array emulates a list of data elements. Each ordinal subscript points to a single element in the list, making it easy for a program to deal with an element and those adjacent to it. The multidimensional array is an expansion of the single-dimensional array with row, column, and even Z axis subscripts. The multiple dimensions allow a program to model a matrix of values, again with a single reference, that puts your programs much closer to reality than some of the contorted logic that might otherwise be necessary. Arrays are extremely flexible and useful structures that should be an innate part of every programmer's toolbox. Taking the time to experiment and understand the structure and how it works will add immeasurably to your programming skills.

TEST YOUR KNOWLEDGE

1. Expand the reservations program shown earlier to accommodate an airplane with the full complement of 32 rows of seats. Once you have accomplished this task, expand the program again to handle a week's flights.

2. Write a program to play bingo. The bingo card will have five rows and five columns to create a matrix of 25 elements. This card will be filled with random integers numbered from 1 to 50 with no repeating elements. Once the card is filled with numbers, the random process will start over and emulate the process of selecting the numbers called for the game. When a number is called your program should examine the contents of the "card" and determine if any of the numbers match. If they do your program must make note of this fact and then check to see if a "Bingo" has occurred. For the purposes of this game, any complete line, horizontally, vertically, or diagonally, will be considered a winner. A winner should be announced by displaying the word "BINGO" on the screen. The player should also be able to quit at any time.

Records and Other Data Structures

Key Concepts

- Using the Object Pascal record
- Using variant records
- Object Pascal data structures: the stack and the queue

Introduction

The arrays that were encountered in the last chapter are very useful to the programmer in modeling real-life data collections. We looked at two varieties of the array, the single- and multidimensional structured data types that brought specific advantages to our designs and programs. In taking a second look, however, the structure has one big limitation: the array is a collection of *like* data elements. It must be composed of a single data type, whether that be all reals or all chars or all something. Sometimes reality dictates that disparate elements be grouped together under a single name. For this purpose Object Pascal defines a data structure called the record. A *record* is a data structure made up of different data types but, like the array, it is referred to by a single identifier. There are two types of records recognized by Object Pascal: the standard record and the variant record. In this chapter we will define them and put both of the structures to use.

This chapter will also look at a couple of basic data structures. A data structure is a way of organizing data that is specific to accomplishing a task. We examined lists (through the array) in the last chapter and within these pages we are going to add definitions for both the queue and the stack. These two structures are often thought of as simple lists but they have a number of variants that make them very flexible. We'll examine them in the context of this chapter, as the record often makes an ideal vehicle for modeling them. The approach for this chapter will be:

■ The record will be defined in concept to ensure that it is the appropriate design choice for the problem that needs to be solved. Full decomposition of a problem is necessary since a record should not be used where a simpler data structure would suffice.

■ The Object Pascal statements necessary for declaring and utilizing the record will be explained and written as we work through an example program to cement your understanding.

■ The stack will be explained as a LIFO structure, giving you an idea about its appropriate usage. A stack ADT unit is developed to demonstrate how the structure can be implemented in Object Pascal.

■ The queue, a FIFO structure, is compared and contrasted and another useful ADT unit is designed and written to support this structure.

The programming examples and problems are becoming longer and more complex in step with your developing programming proficiency. The material from this chapter on in the book can be a bit abstract without a good foundation in the fundamentals of Object Pascal, so be sure that you are up to speed before trying out this new material. As a reminder, please feel free to substitute other projects for those listed at the end of the chapters. If you practice on something you are more familiar with, the process of correlating the abstraction of the programming languages with your design thoughts goes much quicker. Many programming students have gotten hung up on simply understanding the written definitions of the problems and neglect to focus on the language elements that they are trying to learn.

The Record Structure

Real-life objects often have many characteristics that describe them. Each of us has a different name, weight, hair and eye color, taste in music, etc., but all of these things together are all a part of the magic that is you. This variety sometimes makes real-life objects difficult to model in a programming environment since we must apply a unique data type to each element. While our experience tells us that we can simply assign different element types to different variables, we also realize from our use of the array that it is very convenient to refer to a collection of elements by a single name. In Object Pascal it is possible to define a structured type that contains a diverse set of element data types; these structures are called records.

Our programming assignment for this chapter is to create a piece of software that will help me manage my student rosters. For each student in my classes I must track four pieces of information: their name, their student identification number, their attendance in class, and the scores that they receive on their tests and assignments. This data collection looks like this:

```
Name: Gallardo, Brianna
ID #: 090590
Attendance: P, P, P, P, P, P, P ,P ,P
Scores: 10, 10, 9, 10, 10, 10
```

At first glance, we might try to solve this with individual variables but we would quickly be overwhelmed by the number needed for a class of 35 people. Discarding that approach, we might consider the array. Because the array is designed to be a collection of like data elements, we would need to define a different type and a separate array for each piece of data. This would be equally tedious for a large collection of student information.

The Object Pascal *record* is a structured data type that is designed to contain a collection composed of different typed data elements. Each of the elements, which are referred to as *fields*, has two parts to it: the identifier for the field and a data type. The fields can be defined as being of any legal Object Pascal data type, including the array. To define a record that will contain the student information we mentioned above, it might appear as

```
type
  StudentRec = record
    LastName    : string[20];
    FirstName   : string[15];
    StdtId      : integer;
    Attendance  : array[1..20] of char;
    Scores      : array[1..8] of integer;
  end;
```

The type definition begins with the record identifier, StudentRec, followed by an equal sign and the reserved word record. Following this keyword are the field definitions. The compiler will continue to assume that the statements that follow record are field definitions until it encounters an end. Once the type has been defined, as in the other user-defined types we have seen, it can be used to declare variables of this type. In this case I am going to declare a sufficient number of variables to meet the number of students I have:

```
var
  Stud1 : StudentRec;
  Stud2 : StudentRec;
  ....
  Stud35 : StudentRec;
```

Each of these variables contains all of the simpler data types defined in the type definition; we only need a way to get to them to make it useful. An Object Pascal record's fields are accessed via a process called *dot notation*. This method of addressing the fields is very intuitive. If, for instance, you wanted to type a student's last name into a variable you would type the variable identifier, a dot (period), and the field identifier. For instance, the lines:

```
Stud1.LastName := 'Shea';
Stud1.FirstName := 'Eddie';
```

would assign the values 'Eddie' and 'Shea' to the component variables FirstName and LastName, respectively.

When referenced via dot notation, the component variables are of the simple data type set in their definition. The variable `Stud1.LastName` can be used in any place that a variable of type `string[20]` can be used. The program below will fill one `StudentRec` type variable and then print the values:

```
program students;

type
  StudentRec = record
  LastName       :string[20];
  FirstName      :string[15];
  StdtId         :integer;
  Attendance     : array[1..10] of char;
  Scores         : array[1..8] of integer;
end;

var
  Stud1        : StudentRec;

  count        : integer;
  scoresum     : real;

begin

  write('Enter student last name : ');
  readln(Stud1.LastName);

  write('Enter student first name : ');
  readln(stud1.FirstName);

  write('Enter student ID number  : ');
  readln(stud1.StdtId);

  for count := 1 to 10 do
  begin
    write('Enter day ',count,' attendance : ');
    readln(stud1.Attendance[count]);
  end;

  for count := 1 to 8 do
  begin
    write('Enter score ',count,': ');
    readln(stud1.Scores[count]);
  end;

  { Now simply print it out }
```

```
    writeln('Name : ',stud1.LastName,', ',stud1.FirstName);
    writeln('ID # : ',stud1.StdtId:0);

    for count := 1 to 8  do
    begin
      writeln('Test Score ',count,' = ',stud1.Scores[count]);
      scoresum := scoresum + stud1.Scores[count];
    end;
    writeln('Average test score = ', (scoresum / 8):0:2);

end.
```

When this program is executed and the data entered into it, it is creating the data structure shown in Figure 10-1.

Stud1 record variable

LastName										
FirstName										
StdtId										
Attendance										
Scores										

Figure 10-1: The StudentRec record structure

After this series of statements

```
    write('Enter student last name : ');
    readln(Stud1.LastName);

    write('Enter student first name : ');
    readln(stud1.FirstName);

    write('Enter student ID number  : ');
    readln(stud1.StdtId);
    ....
```

the data will appear as follows:

Record value

LastName	Gallardo									
FirstName	Brendon									
StdtId	9090									
Attendance	P	P	P	A	P	P	P	P	P	P
Scores	10	9	9	9	10	10	10	10		

Just as we did with the array, the record structure is addressed as a single unit that includes all of the individual data fields within it. The assignment statement:

```
Stud2 := Stud1;
```

assigns all of the values in the fields of variable `Stud1` to `Stud2`. The same holds true when a record is passed as a parameter to a procedure or function. The following code snippet shows a new function to average the test scores in the record:

```
function AvgScores( in_rec : StudentRec ): real;
{ ------------------------------------------------- }
{ AvgScores - returns the average score from the }
{ record.array of test scores                      }
{ ------------------------------------------------- }
var
   x          : integer;
   scoresum   : real;

begin
   scoresum := 0;
   for x := 1 to 8  do
   begin
      scoresum := scoresum + in_rec.Scores[x];
   end;
   AvgScores := scoresum / 8;
end;
```

When this function is called in the program we use the simple record variable to pass the entire structure into the function:

```
writeln('Average test score = ', AvgScores( stud1 ):0:2);
```

QUICK CHECK

1. Write the type declaration for a record called `Book` that has one field of type `real`, one of type `integer`, and one field of type `string[15]`.

2. Write a type declaration for a baseball player record that includes the player's name, number, position, batting average, RBIs, and hits.

3. What would the output be from the following code if it were embedded in a properly constructed program?

```
type
   rec = record
      field1 : string[10];
      field2 : integer;
   end;
```

```
var
  rec1    : rec;
  rec2    : rec;

rec1.field1 := 'McCloud';
rec1.field2 := 22;
rec2.field1 := 'Posey';
rec2.field2 := 9;
writeln(rec1.field1, rec1.field2:2);
writeln(rec2.field1, rec2.field2:2);
rec1 := rec2;
writeln(rec1.field1, rec1.field2:2);
```

Arrays of Records

If we continue to follow this design, the *students* program would have to be hundreds of lines in length simply to accommodate the data entry and display statements for 35 students. Even at that it would not be a very efficient design. The truth is, a single record variable is very rarely used for storing collections of data like this. It is a much more common practice to utilize groups of records, and one way of managing them in a program is to create an array of records. The type definition for the sample program is modified to read:

```
const
  CLASS_SIZE = 35;

type
  StudentRec = record
  LastName      :string[20];
  FirstName     :string[15];
  StdtId        :integer;
  Attendance    : array[1..10] of char;
  Scores        : array[1..8] of integer;
end;

  AllRecords = array[ 1..CLASS_SIZE ] of StudentRec;

var
  Studs     : AllRecords;
```

The array `AllRecords` is defined to have 35 elements of type `StudentRec`. The array variable is then defined in the `var` section as `studs`.

This compound structure is known as a nested structure and addressing the individual components can become rather complex. The component variables will continue to be referenced as we have seen but with a deeper hierarchy of extension. For example, to assign a value to the `LastName` component of the `StudentRec` record in the array `studs` you would write:

```
studs[ i ].LastName := 'Gallardo';
```

A statement for referencing a nested array:

```
readln(in_array[rec].Scores[x]);
```

becomes easier to understand if you work your way slowly through the statement and identify the individual component parts.

Putting the Records to Work

We're going to take a different approach to this project and actually plan ahead for the reuse of the code base and the data structures. Since I teach many different courses, I don't want to have to re-create these structures and procedures in a program to support each one. For this reason, we are going to create an abstract data type that can be used over and over by placing the data structure and its supporting code into a unit. The compiled unit can then be linked into any program that wants to use it. Do you remember what an abstract data type is? It is a data type where the programmer (and program) using it has no knowledge of the underlying details of how it works. The unit that we are going to create will expose the structures and procedure headers but will hide the implementation from the user.

A little planning always goes a long way towards a successful implementation. Before we start coding we'll take a moment to analyze what we want to accomplish so that all of the functionality that we need is incorporated correctly into the ADT. (This is the antithesis of a normal team of programmers: "You start coding and I'll go find out what they want!") For each student the program should collect the following data:

```
Name (Last name and First name)
Student Identification Number
Test scores (Up to eight of them)
```

The maximum group size for my classes will be 35 students. The program will use a record structure so that all of the related information is stored together in a single data structure and, to keep the class together, all of these individual records will be stored in an array sized to match the class size.

What common actions will be needed for the student data record? Well, we know right off the bat that we will have to be able to add the records to the array. When the records have been added, the contents of the array should be displayable. What data should the user see? The complete student record including the first and last name of the student, the student's ID number, and all of the test scores that have been recorded. In addition, it would be very useful to display the average test score for each student. Finally, if the records require modification, the user should be able to specify a record and then modify the student's data. Do all of these functions belong in the unit? There is no hard and fast rule regarding what does and does not belong in the unit. If the unit is destined for wide distribution, the programmer may want to include every conceivable function that any niche user could ever want. On the other hand, since this will be used locally our design might call for only the basic functions to be encapsulated within the unit. Any specialty tasks will be handled by extending the functions in the program files.

The Data Structures

The data structure that the program will be centered around is an array of records. The definitions for these will be very similar to the examples we have been looking at on the previous pages.

```
unit students;

INTERFACE

  const
    { - Maximum class size - }
    CLASS_SIZE = 35;

  type

    StudentRec = record
    LastName      : string[20];
    FirstName     : string[15];
    StdtId        : integer;
    Scores        : array [1..8] of integer;
  end;

    AllRecords = array[ 1..CLASS_SIZE ] of StudentRec;
```

The two basic data structures, the record and the array, are defined in the interface section of the unit so that they have a global scope. By defining a constant to represent the size of the class I accomplish two things: First, the program has a fixed ending value for many of the computations that are required. Second, if the maximum size of the classes changes drastically it will only be necessary to modify this single variable rather than searching out every incidence of 35 throughout the program.

Adding a Record

The process of adding data to a record within the array seems like a simple process on the surface, but it needs to be examined to be sure that this is a true assumption. The first thing that needs to be determined is how the records will be added to the array. The records could be added all at once, one after the other until finished or the array is full or, the more likely choice, the user will add them as a discrete activity mixed in with other actions. Each approach takes a different design to accomplish. If the records were going to be added one after the other, the data entry statements could simply be placed within a loop that terminated upon user choice or when it was full. The approach that this unit takes is more dynamic and gives the user much more freedom in their actions.

The design calls for the user to have the ability to add a single record and then go on to other activities. In order to accomplish this the program must be able to determine where the next available empty slot in the array is. This task could be handled by a variable that is global in scope but another approach is to dynamically seek the next available slot. The advantage of this approach is that in the long term, it simplifies the program. Figure 10-2 shows why.

(A) Located at the end of the list

A	B	C	D	E	

(B) Located in the middle and end of the list

A	B		D	E	

Figure 10-2: Locating the next available record

If a list allows maintenance of its members, it is possible that specific records from the middle of the list could be deleted. If the availability variable always points to the end of the list, then code must be written to constantly keep the members packed as shown in (A). If member C is removed, both D and E will have to be moved toward the front of the list. If a seek process is used to determine where the first blank spot is, then when the list looks like (B), the empty spot can be located and filled. The next seek will then find the end of the list and it will go from there.

This is the design that is going to be implemented for the AddStudent procedure. The students unit will use two code blocks for this task.

```
procedure AddStudent( var in_array : AllRecords );
var
   x              : integer;
   go_on          : boolean;
   ans            : char;
   rec            : integer;

begin

   rec := findlast( in_array );

   if rec >= class_SIZE then
      writeln('List Full. Cannot add another student.')
   else
   begin
```

```
        with in_array[rec] do
  begin
    write('Enter student last name : ');
    readln(LastName);

    write('Enter student first name : ');
    readln(FirstName);

    write('Enter student ID number  : ');
    readln(StdtId);

    x := 1;
    go_on := true;

    while (go_on) and (x <= 8) do
    begin

      write('Enter score ',x,': ');
      readln(Scores[x]);

      write('Enter another ? (Y/n) : ');
      readln(ans);
      if not (upcase(ans) in ['Y','y']) then
        go_on := false;

      x := x + 1

    end;
   end;
  end;
 end;
```

Procedure AddStudent calls the private function FindLast. Since the function is defined only within the implementation section, the user will never have direct access to this code. The benefit to the developer is that we can modify it as we please without worrying about how it will affect the users of our unit. Once an empty place for the record is located, a simple question and answer session with the user fills the array. When the test scores are input, the user is asked if he wants to continue adding scores, allowing him to terminate the data entry in the event that there are fewer than eight scores.

The With Statement

A new statement was introduced in the AddStudent procedure listing, the with statement. The with statement is shorthand that tells the compiler that all of the statements enclosed within it are referring to the same object. The syntax for the complete `with` statement is:

```
with object or record do
    ....
end;
```

Using `with` in a program provides a shorthand way of referring a group of statements to a single object. When the statements are bracketed by the `with` structure, the compiler assumes that every reference is to a complex structure identified in the object section. For example, the `AddStudent` procedure includes these lines:

```
with in_array[rec] do
     begin
             write('Enter student last name : ');
             readln(LastName);

             write('Enter student first name : ');
             readln(FirstName);
     ....
     end;
```

Following the `with` reserved word and up to the `end`, each of the component references is assumed to be a part of the `in_array` structure. This shorthand simplifies and shortens the code that you will have to write. In the sample shown, the statements are able to refer to the component variables of the record `LastName`, `FirstName` without the necessity of fully qualifying each one.

If a program refers to another object within this statement it must be fully qualified, meaning that full dot notation identifying the object and the field is necessary to avoid compiler errors. Another, more subtle benefit of the `with` statement is increased efficiency. Since any indexing or pointer dereferencing is performed only once, before the processing statements occur, the code is slightly more efficient. This action also prevents changes to the reference of the object during the execution of the statements.

Displaying a Student

The procedure `ShowStudent` is designed a little differently to infuse a level of flexibility into the task of displaying a student's record. The program has several places in which it is necessary to display the contents of a student record and each one is slightly different. The user might want to see one specific student or she might want to see all of the students in a list, for a printout perhaps. Also, prior to modifying a record it would be helpful to list its current contents. To allow this flexibility, the design calls for the procedure to operate on a single record rather than working with the entire array. The location and looping operations are left to external code blocks. When designing and building a unit for wide use, the procedures and functions should be as simple as possible in their base composition. Design them to always be flexible enough to allow the user to extend them to fit the function into a specific task.

The code for ShowStudent is simple and straightforward. The procedure accepts as an input parameter a single record of type StudentRec:

```pascal
procedure ShowStudent( in_rec : StudentRec );
var
   x              : integer;

begin

  with in_rec do
  begin
    writeln;
    writeln('Name : ',LastName,', ',FirstName);
    writeln('ID # : ',StdtId:0);

    x := 1;
    writeln(' ----- Test Scores ----- ');
    while (Scores[x] >= 0) do
    begin
      write( '#',x:0,' ', Scores[x]:3,' ' );
      x := x + 1;
    end;
    writeln;
    writeln('Average test score = ',
AvgStudentScore(in_rec):0:2);
  end;
end;
```

With future flexibility as the watch word for this project, this procedure also calls the private function AvgStudentScore to return the average of the student's test scores. This separation of tasks would allow the program to leave this number out in situations where it is not needed, such as in an editing session.

Modifying a Student Record

The final big task of the program is to provide the ability to modify a specific student record. This operation is a little more complex since it will require three distinct tasks: The program must locate the student record desired, display the current contents, and allow the user to modify the contents and save the changes back into the array. The integrity of the data is of paramount importance in this section of the program; the contents of a record must be protected against inadvertent modification. To aid in this pursuit two steps will be taken. The operations will only take place on a temporary record rather than the actual record, and the user will also have to commit the changes rather than having them instantly modified.

Listing 10-1 shows the completed Students unit.

Listing 10-1

```pascal
unit students;
{ ------------------------------------------------ }
{ Students - Abstract Data Type for record of     }
{ type StudentRec                                 }
{ Exposes an array of records to user of unit     }
{ ------------------------------------------------ }

INTERFACE

  const
    { - Maximum class size - }
    CLASS_SIZE = 35;

   type

    StudentRec = record
          LastName       : string[20];
          FirstName      : string[15];
          StdtId         : integer;
      Scores         : array [1..8] of integer;
         end;

  AllRecords = array[ 1..CLASS_SIZE ] of StudentRec;
  { -------------------------------------------- }
  { Function / Procedure Headers                 }
  { -------------------------------------------- }

  procedure AddStudent( var in_array : AllRecords );
  { -------------------------------------------- }
  { Proc AddStudent - adds a single student      }
  { Param: StudentRec Record structure           }
  { -------------------------------------------- }

  procedure ShowStudent( in_rec : StudentRec );
  { -------------------------------------------- }
  { Proc ShowStudent - display student record    }
  { Param: StudentRec Record Structure           }
  { -------------------------------------------- }

  procedure InitStudents( var in_array : AllRecords );
  { -------------------------------------------- }
  { Proc InitStudents - initialize an array of   }
  { records of type StudentRec                   }
  { Param: Array of StudentRec                    }
```

```
{ ----------------------------------------- }

procedure ModifyStudent( var in_array : AllRecords);
{ ----------------------------------------- }
{ Proc ModifyStudent - display and modify a     }
{ student record                                }
{ Param: Array of StudentRec                     }
{ ----------------------------------------- }
```

IMPLEMENTATION

```
function AvgStudentScore( in_rec : StudentRec ): real;
{ =================================================== }
{ Func AvgStudentScores - returns the avg score       }
{ for a single student record                         }
{ Param: StudentRec record structure                  }
{ Return: real = avg score                            }
{ Note: initialization sets all test scores to        }
{ -1 to handle partially filled array                 }
{ =================================================== }
var
   x          : integer;
   scoresum   : real;

begin
   scoresum := 0;
   x := 1;
   while (in_rec.Scores[x] = 0) and (x 8) do
   begin
      scoresum := scoresum + in_rec.Scores[x];
      x := x + 1;
   end;
   AvgStudentScore := scoresum / (x-1);
end;


function FindLast( var in_array : AllRecords ) : integer;
{ =================================================== }
{ Func FindLast - locates the last open record slot   }
{ Param: AllRecords array                             }
{ Return: the subscript of the last open record or EOL }
{ =================================================== }
var
   i          : integer;

begin
```

```
      i := 1;
      while (in_array[i].lastname  '') and (i CLASS_SIZE) do
        i := i + 1;

      findlast := i;
  end;

  procedure AddStudent( var in_array : AllRecords );
  { ======================================================= }
  { Proc AddStudent - adds data to an empty record          }
  { Param: AllRecords array                                 }
  { Writes student data into the first blank record slot    }
  { Uses FINDLAST function to provide record #              }
  { ======================================================= }
  var
    x            : integer;
    go_on        : boolean;
    ans          : char;
    rec          : integer;

  begin

    rec := findlast( in_array );

    if rec = class_SIZE then
       writeln('List Full. Cannot add another student.')
    else
    begin

      with in_array[rec] do
      begin
        write('Enter student last name : ');
        readln(LastName);

        write('Enter student first name : ');
        readln(FirstName);

        write('Enter student ID number  : ');
        readln(StdtId);

        x := 1;
        go_on := true;

        while (go_on) and (x 8) do
        begin
          write('Enter score ',x,': ');
```

```
            readln(Scores[x]);

            write('Enter another ? (Y/n) : ');
            readln(ans);
            if not (upcase(ans) in ['Y','y']) then
              go_on := false;

            x := x + 1

        end;
      end;
    end;
  end;

  procedure ShowStudent( in_rec : StudentRec );
  { ======================================================= }
  { Proc ShowStudent - displays student record and avg test score }
  { Param: single student record                           }
  {======================================================= }
  var
    x             : integer;

  begin
    with in_rec do
    begin
      writeln;
      writeln('Name : ',LastName,', ',FirstName);
      writeln('ID # : ',StdtId:0);

      x := 1;
      writeln(' ----- Test Scores ----- ');
      while (Scores[x] = 0) do
      begin
        write( '#',x:0,' ', Scores[x]:3,' ' );
        x := x + 1;
      end;
      writeln;
      writeln('Average test score = ', AvgStudentScore
        (in_rec):0:2);
    end;
  end;

  procedure InitStudents( var in_array : AllRecords );
  { ======================================================= }
  { Proc InitStudents - intializes the AllRecords array     }
```

```
{ Param: Allrecords array                                            }
{ NOTE: The initialization values may be modified to set up}
{ the array differently if necessary. Other functions use  }
{ the blank in LastName and the -1 in Scores so be careful }
{ ======================================================== }
var
   i          : integer;
   c          : integer;

  begin

    for i := 1 to CLASS_SIZE do     begin
      in_array[i].FirstName := '';
      in_array[i].LastName  := '';
      in_array[i].StdtId    := 0;

      for c := 1 to 8 do
        in_array[i].Scores[c] := -1;

    end;
  end;
function FindRecord(var in_array: AllRecords; in_name:
 string): integer;
{ ======================================================== }
{ Func: FindRecord - locates a record based on LastName field    }
{ Param: AllRecords array                                        }
{        In_name = LastName to locate                            }
{ Returns: record number                                         }
{======================================================== }

var
  rec_count  : integer;
  locate     : integer;
begin
  rec_count := 1;
  locate := 0;
  while (in_array[rec_count].lastname  '') and (rec_count
    CLASS_SIZE) do
  begin

    if in_array[rec_count].lastname = in_name then
      locate := rec_count;
    rec_count := rec_count + 1;
  end;
  FindRecord := locate;
end;
```

```
procedure ModifyStudent( var in_array : AllRecords);
{ ========================================================= }
{ Proc: ModifyStudent - modify the contents of a student record }
{ Param: Allrecords array                                   }
{ USES FindRecord function to return the found record number }
{ ========================================================= }
var
  lastname    : string;
  f_rec       : integer;
  temprec     : StudentRec;
  commit      : char;
  more        : char;
  x           : integer;
  what_to_mod: char;

begin
  write('Enter Student Last Name :');
  readln( lastname );

  f_rec := findrecord( in_array, lastname);
  if f_rec = 0   then
    writeln('No matching records.')
  else
  begin
    ShowStudent( in_array[f_rec]);

    { - Copy the current info to a temporary record - }
    temprec := in_array[f_rec];

    more := 'Y';
    while more in ['Y','y'] do
    begin
      with temprec do
      begin
        writeln;
        writeln('Select which (F)ield to modify');
        writeln('(L)astname    : ',LastName);
        writeln('(F)irstname   : ',FirstName);
        writeln('(S)tudent ID  : ',StdtId);
        writeln('or specify a Score number');

        for x := 1 to 8 do
            write('#',x:0,' ',Scores[x]:3,' ');
      end;
      writeln;
      write('Field/Score ==== ');
```

```
readln(what_to_mod);
  case upcase(what_to_mod) of
    'L': begin
           writeln('Last Name :',temprec.LastName);
           write('New value : ');
           readln(temprec.LastName);
         end;

    'F': begin
           writeln('First Name :',temprec.FirstName);
           write('New value : ');
           readln(temprec.FirstName);
         end;

    'S': begin
           writeln('Student ID :',temprec.StdtId);
           write('New value : ');
           readln(temprec.StdtId);
         end;

    '1': begin
           writeln('Score 1 :',temprec.Scores[1]);
           write('New value : ');
           readln(temprec.Scores[1]);
         end;

    '2': begin
           writeln('Score 2 :',temprec.Scores[2]);
           write('New value : ');
           readln(temprec.Scores[2]);
         end;

    '3': begin
           writeln('Score 3 :',temprec.Scores[3]);
           write('New value : ');
           readln(temprec.Scores[3]);
         end;

    '4': begin
           writeln('Score 4 :',temprec.Scores[4]);
           write('New value : ');
           readln(temprec.Scores[4]);
         end;

    '5': begin
           writeln('Score 5 :',temprec.Scores[5]);
```

```
                    write('New value : ');
                    readln(temprec.Scores[5]);
                end;

          '6': begin
                    writeln('Score 6 :',temprec.Scores[6]);
                    write('New value : ');
                    readln(temprec.Scores[6]);
                end;

          '7': begin
                    writeln('Score 7 :',temprec.Scores[7]);
                    write('New value : ');
                    readln(temprec.Scores[7]);
                end;

          '8': begin
                    writeln('Score 8 :',temprec.Scores[8]);
                    write('New value : ');
                    readln(temprec.Scores[8]);
                end;
        else
          writeln('Invalid field choice.');
        end;

        write('More changes (Y/n)? ');
        readln(more);
      end;

      write('Commit the changes (Y/n) ? ');
      readln(commit);

      if commit in ['Y','y'] then
        in_array[f_rec] := temprec
      else
        writeln('Abandoning changes.');

    end;
  end;

end.
```

In the ModifyStudent procedure the first step taken is to call the function FindRecord with the last name of the student whose record is to be modified. When the record is located, it is copied to a record variable called temprec. By operating only on this temporary record, the program will prevent corruption to the array data should something happen during the edit process. This is a good practice to follow anytime stored data is being modified, whether it be in an array or in a file or database. The user is then given the opportunity to modify the specific fields that they want to change and are then asked to commit the changes.

The program *nsa240* is listed below and contains the code from which the executable program is created. It's very short and simple because it draws all of its data structures, procedures, and functions from the Students unit. If we were going to distribute this unit to a wide range of users it could be compiled and distributed without the source code, effectively hiding the implementation of the functions. This would prevent the users from modifying the code and possibly causing problems that we would end up supporting.

```
program nsa240;

uses
   students;

var
  MyKids      : AllRecords;
  ans         : char;
  count       : integer;

begin

  { - Initialize array MyKids - }
  InitStudents( MyKids );

  ans := ' ';
  while not ( ans in ['X','x']) do
  begin
    write('(A)dd Student, (S)how Students, (M)odify Student,
E(x)it : ');
    readln(ans);

    case upcase(ans) of
      'A' :
          begin
            { - Add Students to the array -}
            AddStudent( MyKids );
          end;
      'S' :
          begin
            { display the students }
            count := 1;
            while (count <= CLASS_SIZE) and
(MyKids[count].LastName <> '') do
```

```
                        begin
                          ShowStudent( mykids[ count ] );
                          count := count + 1;
                        end;
                    end;
                'M' :
                    begin
                        ModifyStudent( mykids );
                    end;
                'X' :
                    begin
                        writeln('Quitting ...');
                    end;
            else
                writeln('Invalid menu choice');
            end;

        end;

    end.
```

If you have carefully coded the program and unit files you should be able to run the executable. In Figure 10-3 we take the first step in testing the program by adding a student record.

To verify that the record has been stored, the (S)how Students option has been selected as shown in Figure 10-4.

Figure 10-3

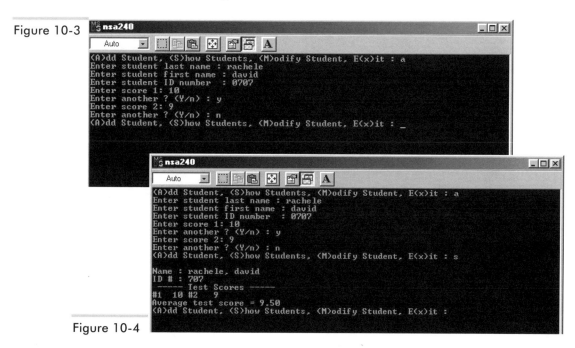

Figure 10-4

To test the other features of the program we need to add a couple more students:

```
Lee, Jong Hwon
0656
#1   10   #2   10

Bates, Britney
0885
#1   9   #2   9
```

As we see in Figure 10-5, there is a minor problem with the database entry for student David Rachele. I neglected to capitalize his first or last name and when I search for the record using the proper case I receive no matching records in response. To fix this I will use the (M)odify Student option, using the incorrect case to locate the record and fix it. This session is shown in Figure 10-6.

Figure 10-5

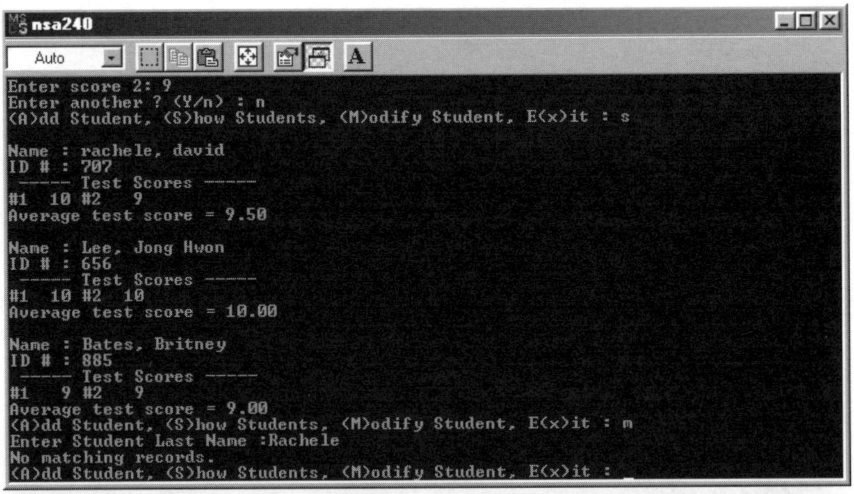

Figure 10-6

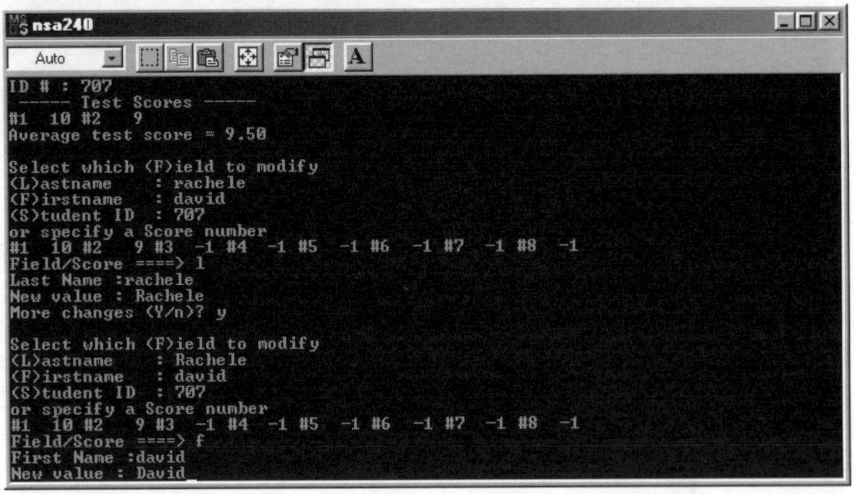

The program has some obvious interface issues that will be easily solved using the rich Delphi VCL. What is important to remember for this and nearly all of the projects in the book is that the interface alone will not provide the functionality that you are learning to program. The display and input and output issues will change, but the fundamental algorithms will remain the same.

Fundamentals in Focus

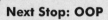

Next Stop: OOP

Study the unit and its design carefully. If you grasp the design and the reasons behind the private and public functions you will discover that object-oriented programming is not as complex as it seems. Object Pascal implements objects through similar structures and the overall structure changes very little. Take an extra minute or two and really understand how this project comes together. It will pay off big in the upcoming chapters.

Variant Records

Object Pascal supports a form of the record structure that can vary its size and contents as the situation warrants; this is called a *variant record*. A variant record can define fields that vary from instance to instance. This form of the record structure is an interesting combination of the record type we are familiar with and the enumerated data type we looked at in a previous chapter. Before the Object Pascal definition is explained, let's set up a situation in which this might be useful. If a huge sports fan came to you to create a program that would allow him to create a record for each of his favorite athletes and their statistics, this might be an excellent situation in which to use the variant record type. Since each sport maintains different sets of statistics particular to their sport, the record structure could not be the same for each player. There would be common information for each person: name, number, etc., but then you would need different fields that are dependent on the player's sport. For example, the baseball player will record his batting average and the number of hits he is credited with while the basketball player will maintain statistics on the minutes played and their field goal percentage.

Defining the variant record is a two-step process. The first step is to define an enumerated type that will be used within the record structure. This follows the same pattern as all other enumerated types we have defined.

```
type
    sport = (Baseball, Basketball);
```

The variant record uses this enumerated type in a form of the CASE structure that only works within the record structure. The `record` for the ball players will be defined as:

```
type
  sport = (Baseball, Basketball);
  player = record
     Name     : string[35];
     Uniform  : string[2];
     case game : sport of
        Baseball :
                  ( RBI : integer;
                        hits : integer);
           Basketball :
                  ( minutes : integer;
                     fg_perc : real);
  end;
```

Everything in this definition up to the reserved word `case` is the standard record definition and in this context is called the *fixed part*. References to these component variables will be exactly the same. The *variant part* starts with the reserved word `case` and continues until the `end` is reached.

The identifier `game` that follows the case is called the *tag field identifier*. It takes the data type that follows the colon; in this case it is of the enumerated type `sport`. Every record will have this component and the value in it will determine which of the variable fields is exposed. For instance, if the component variable is assigned the value `Baseball` then the fields RBI and hits will be available for use. The *playlist* program below shows the variant record defined above in use. The program doesn't really do anything except give you a platform to experiment with the record form.

```
program playlist;

type
  sport = (Baseball, Basketball);
  player = record
     Name     : string[35];
     Uniform  : string[2];
    case game:
      sport of
  Baseball :
                ( RBI  : integer;
              hits : integer);

     Basketball  :
     ( minutes : integer;
       fg_perc : real);
end;

var
  player1    : player;
  player2    : player;
```

```
begin

  with player1 do
  begin
    name := 'Curtis Leskanic';
    uniform := '16';

    {- set the variant type -}
    game := Baseball;

    rbi := 1;
    hits := 2;
  end;

  with player2 do
  begin
    name := 'Nick Van Exel';
    uniform := '22';
    game := Basketball;
    minutes := 122;
    fg_perc := 0.500;
  end;

  writeln(player1.Name,' RBI =', player1.RBI);
  writeln(player2.Name,' MINUTES =', player2.minutes);

end.
```

Variant records are not a necessity in your Object Pascal code book but they are available for situations in which they are appropriate. They can use less memory than would be required if you were to define fields to match every conceivable situation, so in tight memory situations these structures might be the ticket. They also serve to point out once again the richness of the language and its inherent flexibility for meeting different needs.

QUICK CHECK

1. Write the type declaration for a variant record called `clips` that can contain an instance of a writer's publications. There are two types of items that the writer produces, books and articles. The common information for each record will be the writer's name. If the record represents an article, it should contain the name of the publication that published it, the date it was published, and the number of words. If the piece was a book, then the publisher's name, the title of the book, and the page count must be captured.

2. Write a short program that uses the record designed above and stores ten of them in an array.

The Stack and the Queue

The data structure called the list has made numerous appearances in the book thus far. A list is nothing more than a collection of items in which you can examine and work with each item individually. An array is a list, and a very convenient one at that. Using the properties of these lists we have collected data together and manipulated it as a group and as individual elements. Two basic data structures that all programmers should be familiar with are the stack and the queue, both of which derive from the list. One thing that needs to be clear before we touch on these topics; these structures are not specific to Object Pascal nor any language in particular. These are logical structures that help to solve problems. We use the tools and syntax of the languages to implement them.

The Stack

A *stack* is a special form of a list where the elements of the list are only put on and taken off of the top of the list. This is known as a LIFO structure, an acronym that stands for Last In First Out. The archaic, but very effective, visual representation for explaining the stack is to liken it to a stack of plates in a cafeteria. When the plates are taken off of the stack they are taken only from the top. When clean plates are brought to replace those used, they are placed on the top of the stack only, pushing the plates already there down toward the bottom of the stack. Conceivably, the plate at the bottom of the stack may never get used.

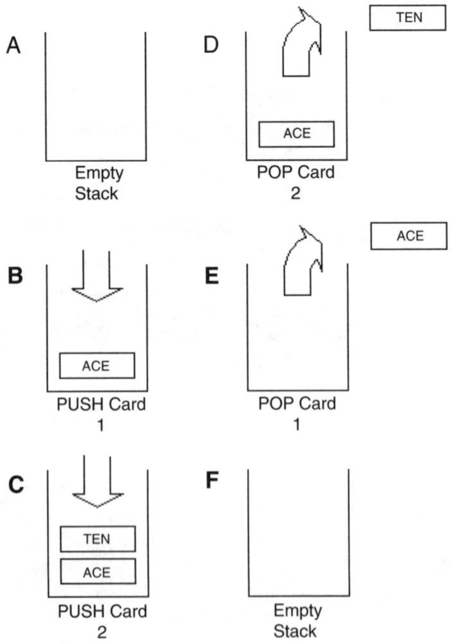

The data structure is a direct implementation of this logic. Figure 10-7 lays out the characteristics and operation of the stack with a couple of playing cards in a solitaire game.

The rules are simple: cards must be played on the top of the stack and can only be removed from the top of the stack. There are two very simple operations supported for the stack: push and pop. Step A shows the empty stack structure. Notice that there is only one way into and out of the structure, through the top. The first operation is to PUSH card 1, the Ace, onto the stack. Step C PUSHes the second card, the Ten, onto the stack. At this point the only card visible to us, and therefore our program, is the card on the top of the stack.

Figure 10-7: The stack

Step D performs the first POP operation and removes the Ten from the stack. The Ace is now visible to us and in step E, the Ace is POPped from the stack. Finally, in step F, the stack has returned to its empty state. Nothing to it, right? This simple structure is used for many computing operations; entire computer languages (FORTH) have been built around this concept. There are any number of ways that this structure can be implemented in a program: a linked list, a series of discrete variables, etc. The project that demonstrates this is at the end of a chapter about records so we might as well use that structure to emulate the stack. The record will encapsulate the two items of importance to the program when dealing with the stack, the stack structure itself and the sentinel that holds the pointer to the top of the stack.

The structure and definition of the stack record is:

```
const
  MAXSIZE = 10;

type

  stack = record
     top      : integer;
     elements : array[1..MAXSIZE] of char;
  end;
```

By encapsulating the elements and top as components of a record, a program can create as many stacks as necessary simply by declaring variables of this type. The record definition is a part of the ADT unit `stacker` shown in Listing 10-2. Also defined within this unit are the two operations procedures needed for a stack, `push` and `pop`.

Listing 10-2

```
unit stacker;
{ -------------------------------------------- }
{ UNIT Stacker - ADT for Stack structure      }
{ PUBLIC                                       }
{     push                                     }
{     pop                                      }
{     init_stack                               }
{ PRIVATE                                      }
{     full                                     }
{     empty                                    }
{ -------------------------------------------- }

INTERFACE
  const
    MAXSIZE = 10;
```

```
type

   stack = record
    top      : integer;
    elements : array[1..MAXSIZE] of char;
   end;

procedure push( var in_stack: stack; in_elem : char );
{ -------------------------------------------------------- }
{ proc push - push an element onto the stack              }
{ Param: in_stack = stack record                          }
{        in_elem = character to be pushed                 }
{ -------------------------------------------------------- }

procedure pop( var in_stack: stack; var out_elem : char );
{ -------------------------------------------------------- }
{ proc pop - pop an element from the stack                }
{ Param: in_stack = stack record                          }
{        out_elem = the element popped from the stack     }
{ -------------------------------------------------------- }

procedure init_stack( var in_stack : stack );
{ -------------------------------------------------------- }
{ proc init_stack - initialize the stack record           }
{ param: in_stack - stack record                          }
{ -------------------------------------------------------- }

IMPLEMENTATION

function full( var in_stack : stack ): boolean;
{ ======================================================== }
{ func full - determine if the stack is full              }
{ param : in_stack - stack record type                    }
{ return: true if full, false otherwise                   }
{                                                          }
{ ======================================================== }
begin
    full := (in_stack.top = MAXSIZE);
  end;

function empty( var in_stack : stack ) : boolean;
{ ======================================================== }
{ func: empty - determine if the stack is empty           }
{ param: in_stack - stack record type                     }
{ return: boolean - true if empty, false if members       }
{                                                          }
```

```
{ ======================================================== }
begin
   empty := (in_stack.top = 0);
end;


procedure push( var in_stack: stack; in_elem : char );
{ ======================================================== }
{ proc: push - push operation for stack structure         }
{ param: in_stack = stack record                          }
{        in_elem  = element to be pushed                  }
{ return: N/A                                             }
{ NOTE: calls func full to determine if filled            }
{ ======================================================== }
begin
   if not full( in_stack) then
   begin
      in_stack.top := in_stack.top + 1;
      in_stack.elements[in_stack.top] := in_elem;
   end
   else
      writeln('Stack overflow .. item not added.');
end;


procedure pop( var in_stack: stack; var out_elem : char );
{ ======================================================== }
{ proc: pop - pop operation for stack structure           }
{ param: in_stack = stack record                          }
{        out_element = returned element from stack         }
{ return: N/A                                             }
{ NOTE: uses func empty to determine no elements          }
{ ======================================================== }
begin
   if not empty( in_stack ) then
   begin
      out_elem := in_stack.elements[in_stack.top];
      in_stack.top := in_stack.top - 1;
   end
   else
      writeln('Stack Underflow .. no more items.');
end;


procedure init_stack( var in_stack : stack );
{ ======================================================== }
{ proc: init_stack - initialize stack components          }
{ param: in_stack - stack record                          }
{ return: N/A                                             }
```

Chapter 10

```
{                                                                 }
{ ======================================================= }
var
    count       : integer;
begin
    with in_stack do
    begin
      top := 0;
      for count := 1 to MAXSIZE  do
        elements[count] := ' ';
    end;
  end;
end.
```

The push operation must accomplish two things. First, before accepting any assignment to the stack, it must test the `top` component variable to determine if the stack is full. When a stack is full and an attempt is made to add an additional element, a condition known as stack overflow is created. The program must not add elements to a full stack, so the first step in the following code listing is to examine the status of the stack:

```
procedure push( var in_stack: stack; in_elem : char );
begin
  if not full( in_stack) then
  begin
    in_stack.top := in_stack.top + 1;
    in_stack.elements[in_stack.top] := in_elem;
  end
  else
    writeln('Stack overflow .. item not added.');
end;
```

It performs this action by calling the private function `full`. If the stack is not full then an element will be added. Since the variable `top` always points to the top element, not the next empty element, the program needs to increment the `top` variable immediately before adding the value through the following assignment statement.

The pop operation is equally straightforward. Its task is to remove the top element from the stack. A condition that the pop operation must be concerned with is stack underflow, removing items past the bottom of the stack. A function that tests for an empty state is also included and called from the `pop` procedure before attempting to pop a value. The pop operation is performed in the opposite order of the push. The value is popped and then the `top` variable is decremented.

Let's Play Cards

The stack is an excellent structure to use as the basis for designing a solitaire type card game. The classic Klondike solitaire game, shown in Figure 10-8, could be set up as eight stack records. Since you must work with the card on top at all times, the push and pop operations are analogous to all of the card moves that you might make.

Figure 10-8

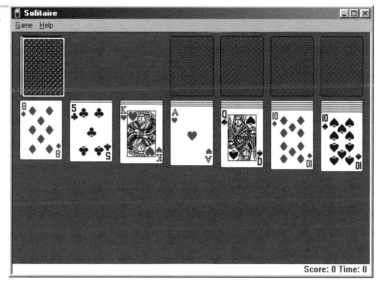

The following program, *cards*, is the rudimentary beginnings of a card game. Using a menu, the user can place individual cards onto the stack or pop them off of the stack.

```
program cards;
uses
  stacker;

var
  pile1      : stack;
  x          : integer;
  ans        : char;
  card       : char;

begin

  { - initialize card pile - }
  init_stack( pile1 );

  ans := ' ';
  while not ( ans in ['Q','q']) do
  begin
  write('(B)uild Pile, (D)raw Card, (Q)uit : ');
  readln(ans);
```

```
case upcase(ans) of
  'B' :
        {- Build the draw pile -}
        begin
        write('Add a card to the pile (A,K,Q,J,1,9,8,7,6,5,4,3,2)');
          readln( card );
          push(pile1, UpCase(card));
        end;

  'D' :
        begin
          pop( pile1, card);
          writeln('Card drawn : ', card );
        end;

  'L' :
        {- secret key for programmer test -}
        begin
          for x := pile1.top downto 1  do
            writeln( pile1.elements[x] );
        end;
  'Q' :

  else
     writeln('Invalid menu choice');
  end;

end;

end.
```

Notice the "secret" menu command (L) that allows you to display the contents of the stack from top to bottom. Don't be afraid to include debugging tools such as this in your programs.

The Queue

A very close cousin to the stack is known as the queue. This structure works on a different principle known as FIFO, First In First Out. Staying with the food-service analogy, think of the line of people waiting to be served. The first person in line gets served first, the second next, and so on until the last person in line is served. People who are arriving at the cafeteria add themselves to the back of the line. As a programming structure, the queue has a wider appeal than the stack since a number of real-life situations can be modeled very well with it. The type of queue that our example unit is going to model is called a circular queue because it loops around and reuses spots vacated when an item is removed from the front of the list. It works very well when you know the maximum number of spots you are going to need in the list.

From a programming perspective the code is a bit more complicated. However we choose to implement the queue of values, there are now two sentinels that need to be maintained, the front and the back of the list. In addition, since we are implementing a circular queue and the values for front and back may be out of order for a simple comparison operation, we must maintain a variable containing the number elements in the list. Figure 10-9 graphically depicts the queue and its actions.

Follow the diagram as we step through a series of transactions. Upon initialization the queue is empty, as shown in step A, the front of the queue points to element 1 and the back points to element 3. Step B adds the first element to the list, placing the name Rachele into element 1. This makes the front of the list and the back of the list point to element 1. Step C adds another name to the list. Now the front of the list stays unchanged at 1 but the end of the line is now after element 2. The queue is filled to capacity in step D so no further names can be added to the list until one has been removed.

Step E asks for an item from the front of the list. Referring to the front variable, it takes element 1 from the list and points the new front of the list to element 2. When a circular queue reaches the maximum size of the list it loops back to the beginning to look for an available spot. This is what happens in step F where the name Gallardo is added to the list in element 1. This now becomes the back of the queue so the value for the front now equals 2 and the value for the back equals 1. This is the reason that the number of elements in the queue must be maintained separately. The operations required for the queue structure are to add a value and remove a value, checking to see if it is full or empty, respectively, and querying the list to find or set the insertion location. Similar to the project that was designed for the stack, we will build a small unit that supports the queue abstract data type.

Figure 10-9: The queue structure

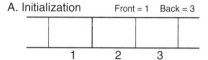

A. Initialization Front = 1 Back = 3

B. Add Rachele Front = 1 Back = 1

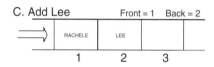

C. Add Lee Front = 1 Back = 2

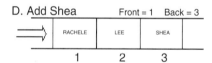

D. Add Shea Front = 1 Back = 3

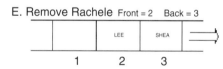

E. Remove Rachele Front = 2 Back = 3

F. Add Gallardo Front = 2 Back = 1

Customer Service is Job One!

Many call center applications utilize a queue to manage their incoming calls, if only to generate the message that all calls will be answered in the order in which they received! This ensures that everyone will be serviced in turn and it is not possible for someone to cut to the head of the line. Using the unit QueueUp, the application under development here is designed to manage the call activity of the center. There are only two functions available to the user. They can either add a call to the queue or accept one from the front of the list.

The structure for the record that encapsulates the queue is:

```
type

   queue = record
      front    : integer;
      back     : integer;
      el_count : integer;
      elements : array[1..MAXSIZE] of string[15];
   end;
```

We will still use an array to contain the elements of the list, in this case strings that represent the name of the caller. The record also contains component variables that hold the values that point to the front and the back of the list as well as the number of elements currently in the queue.

The first operation is to add a name to the queue. After initialization the component variable front will have a value of 1 and the variable back will have a value of 3. Before an element can be added we have to determine where the back of the list is. Though there is a value there already, we don't want to use the initialization value for an insertion. Instead, the procedure add calls the function insert_loc to determine where to place the element. Insert_loc takes as a parameter the current value for the back of the list, in this case 3. The equation in insert_loc makes the loop around effect work:

```
insert_loc := (in_back MOD MAXSIZE) + 1;


insert_loc = (3 MOD 3) + 1
insert_loc = (0) + 1
```

This sets the insert location to element 1. Using this value the procedure add assigns the data value to this component variable.

```
procedure add( var in_queue: queue; in_elem : string15);
begin
  if not full(in_queue) then
  begin
    with in_queue do
    begin
      back := insert_loc(back);
      elements[back] := in_elem;
      in_queue.el_count := in_queue.el_count + 1;

      {- comment out for production - }
      writeln('Front ',front);
```

```
          writeln('Back   ',back);
        end;
      end
      else
        writeln('Queue full. Cannot add item.');
    end;
```

After the assignment statement the final operation is to increment the number of elements.

Removing an element from the queue requires that we simply look at the variable containing the pointer to the front of the list and go get that element. Using function insert_loc again we reset the front of the line after the element has been removed from the queue. Listing 10-3 shows the complete listing for the QueueUp abstract data type unit.

─────────

Listing 10-3

```
unit queueup;
{ --------------------------------------------------- }
{ UNIT QueueUp - ADT for Queue structure            }
{ PUBLIC                                             }
{    Add                                             }
{    Remove                                          }
{    Init_Queue                                      }
{ PRIVATE                                            }
{    Full                                            }
{    Empty                                           }
{    insert_loc                                      }
{ --------------------------------------------------- }

INTERFACE
  const
    MAXSIZE = 3;

  type

    queue = record
      front    : integer;
      back     : integer;
      el_count : integer;
      elements : array[1..MAXSIZE] of string[15];
    end;

    string15 = string[15];

  procedure add( var in_queue: queue; in_elem : string15 );
```

```
{ ---------------------------------------------------------- }
{ proc push - add  an element onto the queue               }
{ Param: in_queue = queue record                           }
{        in_elem = string to be added                      }
{ ---------------------------------------------------------- }

procedure remove( var in_queue: queue; var out_elem : string15 );
{ ---------------------------------------------------------- }
{ proc pop - remove the next element from the queue        }
{ Param: in_queue = queue record                           }
{        out_elem = the element removed from the queue     }
{ ---------------------------------------------------------- }

procedure init_queue( var in_queue : queue );
{ ---------------------------------------------------------- }
{ proc init_queue - initialize the queue record            }
{ param: in_queue - queue record                           }
{ ---------------------------------------------------------- }
```

IMPLEMENTATION

```
function full( var in_queue : queue ): boolean;
{ ========================================================= }
{ func full - determine if the queue if full              }
{ param : in_queue - queue record type                    }
{ return: true if full, false otherwise                   }
{                                                         }
{ ========================================================= }
begin
    full := (in_queue.el_count = MAXSIZE);
end;

function empty( var in_queue : queue ) : boolean;
{ ========================================================= }
{ func: empty - determine if the queue is empty           }
{ param: in_queue - queue record type                     }
{ return: boolean - true if empty, false if members       }
{                                                         }
{ ========================================================= }
begin
    empty := (in_queue.el_count = 0);
end;

function insert_loc( in_back : integer ): integer;
{ ========================================================= }
{ func: insert_loc - determines the insertion location    }
```

```
{                     for a circular queue            }
{ param: in_back - back of the line                   }
{ return: integer - new insertion location            }
{                                                      }
{ ==================================================== }
begin
  insert_loc := (in_back MOD MAXSIZE) + 1;
end;


procedure add( var in_queue: queue; in_elem : string15);
{ ==================================================== }
{ proc: add - add operation for queue structure        }
{ param: in_queue = queue record                       }
{        in_elem  = element to be added                }
{ return: N/A                                          }
{ NOTE: calls func full to determine if filled         }
{       calls insert_loc for add location              }
{ ==================================================== }
begin
   if not full(in_queue) then
   begin
     with in_queue do
     begin
      back := insert_loc(back);
      elements[back] := in_elem;
      in_queue.el_count := in_queue.el_count + 1;

      {- comment out for production - }
      writeln('Front ',front);
      writeln('Back  ',back);
     end;
   end
   else
     writeln('Queue full. Cannot add item.');
end;


procedure remove( var in_queue: queue; var out_elem :
  string15 );
{ ==================================================== }
{ proc: pop - get next item in the queue               }
{ param: in_queue = queue record                       }
{        out_element = returned element from queue      }
{ return: N/A                                          }
{ NOTE: uses func empty to determine no elements        }
{       uses insert_loc to determine tail of list      }
{ ==================================================== }
```

```
      begin
         if not empty( in_queue ) then
         begin
           with in_queue do
           begin
             out_elem := elements[front];
             elements[front] := ' ';
             front := insert_loc(front);
             el_count := el_count - 1;

             {- comment out for production -}
             writeln('Front ',front);
             writeln('Back  ',back);
           end;
         end
         else
           writeln('Queue empty .. no more items.');
      end;

      procedure init_queue( var in_queue : queue );
      { ======================================================= }
      { proc: init_queue - initialize queue components          }
      { param: in_queue - queue record                          }
      { return: N/A                                             }
      {                                                         }
      { ======================================================= }
      var
         count       : integer;
      begin
         with in_queue do
         begin
           front := 1;
           back  := MAXSIZE;
           el_count := 0;
           for count := 1 to MAXSIZE  do
             elements[count] := ' ';
         end;
      end;

      end.
```

The following *calllist* program contains the call center program that is used to exercise the unit. Making liberal use of constants and typedefs can make these units much more flexible and easier to use for the programmers using your unit.

```
program calllist;
uses
  QueueUp;

var
  line_up     : queue;
  x           : integer;
  ans         : char;
  name        : string[15];

begin

  init_queue( line_up );

  ans := ' ';
  while not ( ans in ['Q','q']) do
  begin
    write('(A)dd Caller, (N)ext Caller, (Q)uit : ');
    readln(ans);

    case upcase(ans) of
      'A' :
        begin
         write('Add a caller to the customer service queue ) ');
          readln( name );
          add( line_up, name );
        end;

      'N' :
        begin
          remove( line_up, name);
          writeln('Next caller is : ', name );
        end;

      'L' :

        begin
          for x := 1 to MAXSIZE  do
             writeln( line_up.elements[x] );
        end;
      'Q' :

    else
      writeln('Invalid menu choice');
```

```
        end;
      end;
    end.
```

Figure 10-10 shows the program being used in the manner described in Figure 10-9.

Figure 10-10

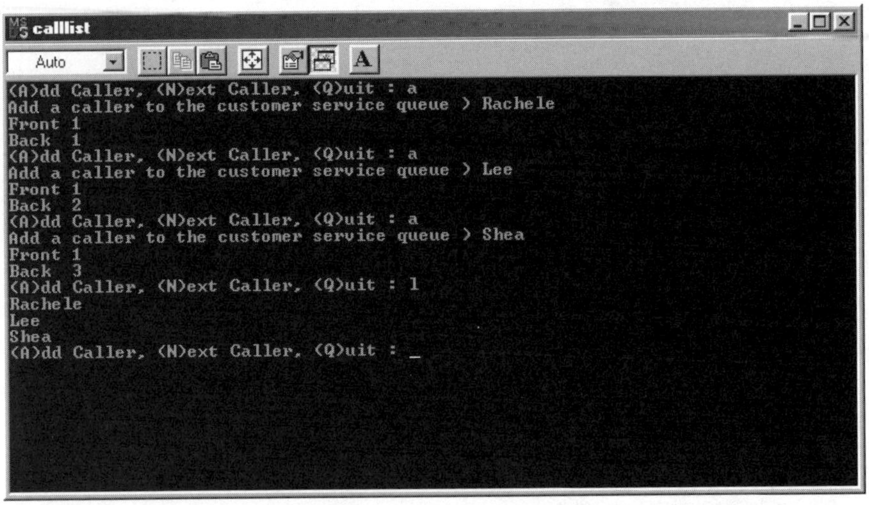

Three members are added to the queue and then the debugging tool (L) is used to display the members of the queue. Now the oldest caller, Rachele, is removed from the queue and Gallardo is added to the back of the queue in Figure 10-11.

Figure 10-11

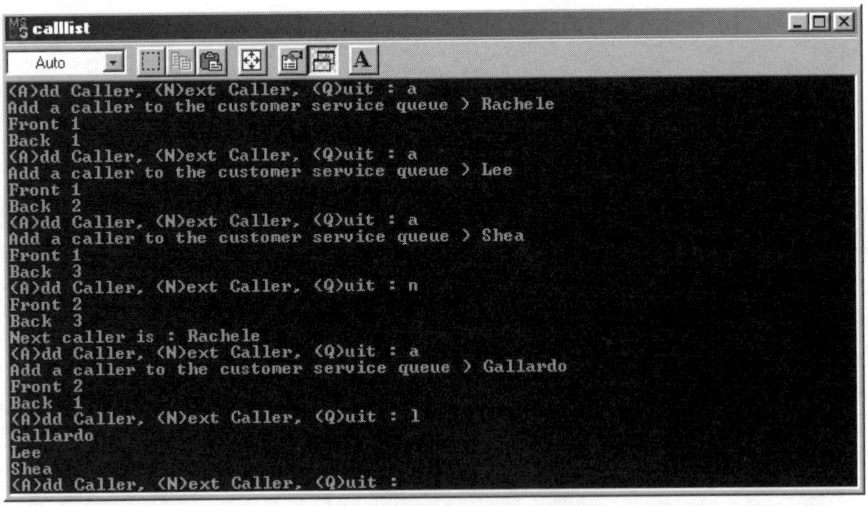

QUICK CHECK

1. What is the difference between the stack and the queue data structures?

2. Is the stack a First In Last Out structure?

Is the stack a Last In First Out structure?

Is the queue a First In Last Out structure?

Is the queue a First In First Out structure?

Summary

Modeling real life is the goal of programming. All software that is written models some task or object and, to fully describe it, the programmer needs to be able to make full use of all available data types. The Object Pascal record serves the purpose of encapsulating multiple, diverse data types into a single data object. These discrete objects can be used on their own or collected together in an array or some other collection. We learned in this chapter about the two varieties of records, the fixed and the variant record.

This chapter used the record structure to describe and build two fundamental data structures, the queue and the stack. The stack is a LIFO structure in which data elements are pushed onto the stack and popped off of the stack. We looked at both of those operations and built a unit to support this abstract data type. The same exercises followed for the queue. This structure is a FIFO structure in which data elements enter from the back of the line and are only accessible again when they reach the front of the line. The unit we built supported a special kind of a queue called a circular queue.

TEST YOUR KNOWLEDGE

1. Modify the student records program developed earlier in this chapter to support the following requirements. The grading for each student should be modified to support the following grading criteria:

   a. There are five quizzes, each worth ten points.

   b. There will be a midterm exam, a final exam, and a term paper due. Each of these assignments is worth 100 points.

   c. The final grade will be based on the percentage of total points earned. 90-100% will be awarded an A, 80-89 a B, 70-79 a C, 60-69 a D, and anything below 60 will be an F.

   The program should print out a grade report that displays, in a single row, the student last name, each of the grades earned (including any 0's assigned), the final total, the percentage earned, and a letter grade assigned for the class.

2. Write a stack-based program that plays Blackjack using a single 52-card deck. There is no need to represent the suits of the cards; your only task will be to ensure that the correct number of each card is randomly placed in a stack. The dealer (the program) should issue two cards to the player and two cards to the house. The player should be able to ask for a number of cards which will be

dealt from the top of the desk as expected. The user may hold on their own or will be stopped by the program if the cards total over 21.

The Aces represent a unique case that needs to be accommodated. When first dealt the Ace is assumed to equal 11. If the total, including the 11-valued Ace, is less than 21 it will be left as 11. If the user is going to go over 21, the Ace should automatically be revalued to 1 and the user's hand total should reflect it. Play should continue until the user terminates the program or the deck is used up. (Once you have this working you might want to try and implement this using a queue so that the dealt cards can be replaced on the bottom of the deck to continue playing.)

Introduction to Object-Oriented Programming with Object Pascal

Key Concepts

- ⚷— What is object-oriented programming?
- ⚷— The concepts of encapsulation, inheritance, and polymorphism
- ⚷— Using the OOP extensions in Object Pascal
- ⚷— Creating and using your first class

Introduction

All right, pardner, get ready to change horses in mid-stream. Get ready to change tactics on the beach. Prepare to switch from zone to man to man. Okay, enough cliches—prepare to change your viewpoint on how programs are constructed. Within the pages of this chapter, we are going to be looking at a method of program development that is significantly different from anything we have done up to this point. Why now and not in Chapter 1? The coding examples that have been used to demonstrate the Object Pascal language concepts thus far stayed with traditional structured programming techniques because they were so short and the overhead of developing the objects would have detracted from the point of the exercises. The intention of the sample programs was to demonstrate a specific programming construct and, because of that, I did not want to add anything mysterious that would obfuscate the point. Following our exploration of the record, however, we are more than ready to make the jump into object-oriented programming.

Once you learn OOP and have a little experience, you will discover that OOP can be one of the most efficient methods of software development yet conceived, with lots of advantages and very little downside. In fact, it is what makes environments such as Delphi possible. Unfortunately, a programmer's initial forays into this methodology can sometimes be so fraught with frustration that the previous sentences will seem to be anything but true. Have faith and stick with it. In becoming a Delphi programmer, the OOP model is going to be the whole world, and developing an understanding of the tenets of object-oriented programming is going to be very important to your ability to capitalize on the efficiency of the environment.

This chapter is going to take a step-by-step approach to the topic. Object-oriented programming will be covered in the abstract first since the conceptual underpinnings must be understood before the implementation is explored. Once the basics have been established in your mind, the Object Pascal extensions that implement OOP will be examined and explained. Finally, the creation and use of classes will round out the chapter. Coverage of the topic will include:

- The first item for discussion will be establishing what object-oriented programming is and how it differs from the traditional structured programming approach.
- There are three fundamental philosophies to object-oriented programming that serve to separate it from structured programming efforts: encapsulation, inheritance, and polymorphism. Each concept in turn will be defined and explained.
- Object Pascal is an object-oriented extension to standard Pascal. We will look at the extensions to the language that enable this programming methodology.
- This chapter will round out your exploration of OOP by demonstrating the creation and use of classes within an Object Pascal program.

At this point in the development of your Object Pascal programming skills you are able to write a wide variety of programs to solve numerous types of problems. Don't be put off if this sudden paradigm shift in the development methodology seems to arrest that advance. The concepts are approached in a simple, easy to understand method meant specifically not to swamp you. As important as what this chapter covers is, it is equally important to establish what it is not. This single chapter in a book about Object Pascal is not intended to be a treatise on OOP. Entire books are written on this abstract subject alone, with or without a code base, so this is certainly not meant to be the most thorough treatment of the topic available. To satiate that burning desire, I would recommend any of the numerous object-oriented programming and design books available on the market.

TwhatIsAnObject = Object

Object-oriented programming is a design and development methodology that emphasizes modularity and code reuse. It is an evolutionary jump from the structured programming methods that many are comfortable using and learning—and that jump is a big one. In order to successfully immerse yourself in this methodology you must put aside the programming methods that you have learned and be willing to change your thinking and perception about a program's structure. In addition to the implementation specifics, there are three fundamental ideas behind OOP that you will need to learn: inheritance, polymorphism, and encapsulation. We will discuss each of these in detail but before we do, we have to establish what this object is that we're working with.

The basis for all object-oriented programming is a data element called an object. What is this mysterious thing, this object? Well, it is simply everything around you on which you model your programs. Computer programs are models of real-life things that you encounter every day and these things have two sets of characteristics that describe them: what they look, feel, smell, etc., like and the things that they can do. Structured programming (and worse) have required that these characteristics be made mutually exclusive of one another, forcing the model of reality to assume an unnatural method of doing things. OOP takes a more natural approach to software development, packaging the characteristics and behaviors together into a single data element, the object. The word that describes this is encapsulation, a concept we will explore in more detail shortly. This bundling protects the integrity of the programming by encapsulating nearly all of the activity, hiding things that you have no business seeing, and enforcing good programming practices.

An *object* is a data structure that wraps data and code together into a single item. The technical description of an object is that it is an instance of a class. The *class* is a structure consisting of fields, methods, and properties; it is the blueprint from which the object is built, or *instantiated*. It bundles together the three elements mentioned earlier, the first being the fields. *Fields* are data variables that are defined as a part of an object. What makes an object's fields different from the variables that we have declared up to now is that we are going to be able to manage multiple copies of an object within a program and that each one of those instances will carry these variables within it. This means that multiple copies of the same variable are going to comfortably coexist within the executing software. Because the data is encapsulated within the object, the programmer is not required to manage it—the object will.

A *method* is a function or procedure that is a part of the same class definition. The method defines the behaviors that the object can perform and it can only be referenced via the object itself. This ensures that the method is acting on the correct data since both the methods and the data they act upon are encapsulated within the object. The methods can also act independently of other methods of the same name since each object is a discrete data structure. The third piece of the class definition is the property. *Properties* also describe the characteristics of the object and can have default values, unlike the variables we have used. What truly separates the properties from the fields is that your program cannot directly modify the contents of the property. All reading and writing must go through specified functions and procedures before the object will let the changes in or out. If the program does not follow the rules set by the specifiers, the shot will be denied.

The data structure of an object is often likened to a Pascal record, a structure that we have explored in great detail. One of the records that we created represented a student and it was defined something similar to:

```
type
  student = record
    lastname  : string;
    firstname : string;
    gpa       : real;
  end;
```

Object Pascal builds on your knowledge of this structured data. The class definition appears almost identical:

```
type
  Tstudent = class
    lastname  : string;
    firstname : string;
    gpa       : real;

    procedure Add;
    procedure Modify;
  end;
```

Notice the difference? It's actually very subtle. The class definition replaces the word `record` with the `class` reserved word to describe the type of structure that follows. Included within this class definition are the operations necessary for the TStudent data type. The two procedures that are declared in the class are later defined in the implementation section of the unit that defines this class, just as you would expect. The important point is that the structure you have created encapsulates the code and the data into the same structure. Binding the two together like this causes the code to work with its own data rather than blithely modifying a wide open list of variables.

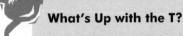

Fundamentals in Focus

What's Up with the T?

By convention, Delphi object-oriented notation prefaces the identifier of every data structure of the object type with a capital T. This helps to differentiate classes from other data structures throughout your program. There is no Object Pascal rule that requires this but if you read through the Delphi classes or others you will find that this notation is nearly universal. Have a good reason if you are going to be different.

Using a Class

A class is merely the definition of the object's structure. Only when it is put to use does it become an object. To use a class you perform a process called *instantiation* which results in you creating an instance of the class, or an object. To do this you must define a variable of the class type:

```
Stud1 : Tstudent;
```

and then call the constructor for the class:

```
Stud1 := Tstudent.create;
```

The *constructor* is a routine, specific to the class, that is responsible for setting up the resources needed by the class when it is put into use. We will be covering the process from development to use later on in this chapter. Before we do that we need to develop a further understanding of the troika of OOP: inheritance, encapsulation, and polymorphism.

Inheritance

As important as the structure of the object is, more important is its ability to inherit properties, methods, and fields from those objects that come before it. This ability to inherit makes Object Pascal the extensible language that it is. Once a base class definition has been established, the programmer is free to extend it to best suit the task at hand. She is released from the need to redefine all of the basic characteristics of the object, say a dialog box, and merely needs to add the new features required to match her specification.

To set the foundation for a discussion of the OOP concept of inheritance, consider a non-computer oriented example shown in Figure 11-1.

Nearly everyone can define the characteristics of the base object in the diagram, the motor vehicle. It has an engine, four wheels and tires, a steering mechanism, and some method of stopping its forward movement. As far as actions go, the vehicle will either be moving or stopped. The properties and methods provide enough information for someone to get a pretty good idea of what this object is or does. Looking

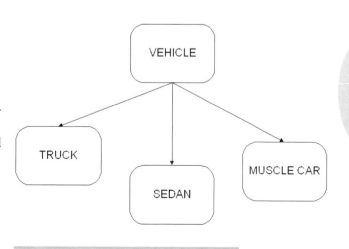

Figure 11-1: The concept of inheritance

at the definitions that descend from it, you will notice that each of them inherits these common characteristics from the base object, or class.

The first *child* class that descends from the vehicle class is the sedan. Since it is a direct *descendant* of the vehicle *parent* class, it inherits all of the characteristics from it. This means that it does not have to re-create the engine, wheels, etc., or devise some method of moving or stopping. The only things that the sedan class is responsible for are the exceptions, those things that make it different from the base class. In development parlance, this is known as programming by exception. The advantages of not having to "re-create the wheel(s)" are more obvious in the other pair of child classes. In the case of the muscle car class, the designer was able to improve the suspension, the traction, and the horsepower because he was not bogged down with having to reinvent the basic pieces each time a new car was wanted. Think Lime-Green Plymouth Superbird with its 3-foot airfoil and you'll get the picture. It still has all of the basic features of a Road Runner under the paint.

A further benefit accrues when it comes time to maintain the basic design. When maintenance is required to the inherited characteristics it need only be performed one time, to the base class. When the change is made, all of the classes that descend from it will automatically have the modifications propagated to their definitions. In Delphi, all objects automatically descend from the mother of all objects, the TObject class. In fact, our earlier class definition could have been written as:

```
type
  TStudent = class(TObject)
    lastname  : string;
    firstname : string;
    gpa       : real;

    procedure Add;
    procedure Modify;
  end;
```

When a class is descended from the TObject class, Delphi includes all of the functionality included with the base class including constructor and destructor routines. (Even if you were to leave out the specific class in the class() definition, Delphi automatically descends everything from TObject.)

Encapsulation

Though it was mentioned earlier, the concept of *encapsulation* means that data and the routines that manipulate that data are bound together, or encapsulated, into a single object. Just as we saw in the unit, there are public declarations and private declarations. To access the data elements of the object they must be exposed in the public declarations and accessed through the public methods. If a field, property, or method is not defined as a part of the interface section then it will be hidden from the user of the class. The hidden methods, fields, and properties are not accessible anywhere but inside of the object.

One of the big advantages of encapsulation in OOP is that data not only can be hidden from other classes but it is protected as well. Data that is privately held within the object cannot be inadvertently modified by the code of other objects. The only way that another object has access to the data encapsulated within an object is through the public methods. This protection adds to Object Pascal's already strong scoping and typing abilities.

Polymorphism

The scariest sounding of the three basic concepts, polymorphism is really quite common. In fact, within the pages of this book you can find numerous examples of the practice. Loosely translated from the Greek definition it means "many shapes." Within this book you can find several instances in which I have used the same word to mean a number of different things. The meaning attached to the word is entirely dependent on its context. Take the word "execute," for example. In terms of the programs that we have written here it means to run them. If you find yourself in a very small room with bars for a door that word could take on an entirely different and much more unpleasant meaning. In the world of objects, *polymorphism* refers to the ability to define a routine in the base class that acts a little bit differently in each descendant.

Consider an object hierarchy that starts with a base class called `shapes`. From that class there are three child classes descended from it called `square`, `circle`, and `triangle`. In the base class we are going to define a method called `draw`; its job will be to display the shape on the screen. In the basic class `shapes` it doesn't need to do much except place a point on the screen. Things get a little different, on the other hand, when we approach the class `square`. Just like its parent, this class has the ability to draw itself on the screen; it's just the way that it does it that is different. The same applies to `triangle` and `circle`. Polymorphism states that each of the classes shares the ability to do some action—display the figure on the screen—but the way that the task is performed is different depending on the particular context in which it is executed.

Virtual Versus Static Methods

Static methods are the same as the static variables that have been declared in the programs developed so far. The compiler resolved all of these references at compile time. Virtual methods are a different animal altogether; their references are resolved later in the context of the object from which they are called. This is the tool of polymorphism that supports the generalization abilities we just discussed. In the shapes example, the method `draw` is a virtual method defined in the `shapes` class. Each of the child objects that is descended from it can have their own implementation of the `draw` method. The reference to the method is resolved at run time, an action known as *late binding*. If this method were bound at compile time, then its actions would be fixed to that in the base definition. What we want to occur is that the decision as to what version of the `draw` method to be executed is dependent on the particular shape that is to be drawn.

1. What is the difference between a class and an object?
2. Explain the concepts of polymorphism, encapsulation, and inheritance. Give non-programming examples to support your answers if possible.

Your First Class

To put these concepts into action we're going to define and build a class. To ease the transition from the structured programming demonstrations that we have been using to our new OOP paradigm, we are going to do away with the design process at first and simply convert an existing project to an OOP based program. For the conversion I have selected the work we did on the queue structure so that we can concentrate more on the OOP side of things rather than the actual problem solving. If you skipped over that section in the last chapter, I would recommend that you go back and familiarize yourself with the project so that developing the class will be your primary focus, not the code required to make the queue structure work.

Define the Class

The first step in the process is to combine data and code to create the object that we want. This means that the data that is used for the queue itself, the variables for front and back, the element count, and the array that contains the elements will be defined together with the actions that manage and manipulate it. To implement the queue structure the program will need to initialize itself, add elements, and remove elements. The class definition that defines all of this is:

```
type

  string15 = string[15];

  TQueue = class(TObject)
     front     : integer;
     back      : integer;
     el_count  : integer;
     elements  : array[1..MAXSIZE] of string[15];

     procedure init_queue;
     procedure addelem( in_elem : string15 );
     procedure remove( var out_elem : string15 );

  end;
```

Notice that the class definition descends from the TObject class. By doing this we are going to inherit the functionality encapsulated in that fundamental Delphi class, including the Create constructor needed to instantiate the object. Far different from the record definition used in the other project, the procedures that define the tasks for the queue are now encapsulated within the class. Do you notice anything different about the procedure headers?

To facilitate our experimentation with the class the project will be built step by step. This is going to require that we build the skeleton of the unit as shown below and then go back and edit it as we progress.

```
unit QueueCls;
{ --------------------------------------------- }
{ UNIT QueueCls - defines the class TQueue      }
{ --------------------------------------------- }

INTERFACE
  const
    MAXSIZE = 3;

  type
      string15 = string[15];

    TQueue = class(TObject)
      front    : integer;
      back     : integer;
      el_count : integer;
      elements : array[1..MAXSIZE] of string[15];

      procedure init_queue;
      procedure addelem( in_elem : string15 );
      procedure remove( var out_elem : string15 );
    end;

IMPLEMENTATION

  procedure TQueue.AddElem( in_elem : string15);
  begin
     writeln('stub');
  end;

  procedure TQueue.remove( var out_elem : string15 );
  begin
     writeln('stub');
  end;

  procedure TQueue.init_queue;
```

```
    var
      count      : integer;
    begin
      front := 1;
      back  := MAXSIZE;
      el_count := 0;
      for count := 1 to MAXSIZE  do
        elements[count] := ' ';

    end;
  end.
```

The first task that needs to be accomplished is to initialize the structure. (Some things <u>never</u> change.) This action is performed by the init_queue procedure shown above. Sharp eyes will notice an important difference between this definition and the old structured definition. Notice that parameters aren't being passed to the procedure anymore. This change continues into the internals of the procedure. You will not find a WITH .. DO construct in the code, nor any explicit reference to the TQueue object. The scope of the object removes the requirement to explicitly reference the object since the methods and the variables are all within the same scope. The data fields are openly available to any of the methods defined within the same scope.

Fundamentals in Focus

Initialization

Delphi automatically initializes the data elements of an object when it is instantiated. You can safely assume that all numeric variables are set to zero and all strings will be empty. The reason that we initialize the TQueue structure is the front and back components need to point to specific elements within the array.

None of the field references in init_queue need to be qualified because they all belong to the object already. There is an implied with myself do statement processed anytime a member method is called. This is accomplished behind the scenes through the passing of an invisible parameter called Self. This pointer to the object itself removes the qualifying requirement as well as the need to pass the structure itself back and forth. If you'll refer back to the Queue unit, every function and procedure required that we pass the queue record back and forth through the parameters in order to process the elements internally. OOP has already simplified things by doing away with this requirement.

A short program file is all that is necessary to test the new class.

```
program QueueTest;

uses
```

```
    QueueCls;

var
  Queue1     : TQueue;

begin

  {- Instantiate the TQueue object -}
  Queue1 := TQueue.create;
  Queue1.init_queue;

end.
```

Add the QueueCls unit to the uses statement to link the unit into the program. Defining the variable Queue1 does not create an object; there is no object in memory until it is instantiated. Every object is required to have a method called the *constructor*. Its job is to allocate memory for the object and create a pointer back to the instance of the object in memory. The TQueue class has no constructor because we inherited one from the TObject class, the ancestor object that TQueue derived from. When the program needs to create an instance of TQueue it calls the inherited create method. Once the instantiation process is complete the fields and methods of TQueue become accessible.

The initialization of the queue is performed through a call to the TQueue object's init_queue method. Calling the method of an object from an external statement requires qualification and, similar to the calls to components of a record, you use dot notation to create this reference. The call:

```
    Queue1.init_queue;
```

specifies the use of the init_queue method of the Queue1 object. The WITH .. DO construct can replace the need for these explicit references as we will see as the program develops.

Add the Methods

In the previous listing for TQueue's unit the other methods were "stubbed" in so that the compiler would not return an error message. The next step in refining the class definition is to finish adding the procedures and functions. Listing 11-1 shows the complete listing for the QueueCls unit.

Listing 11-1

```
unit QueueCls;
{ ---------------------------------------------- }
{ UNIT QueueCls - defines the class TQueue       }
{ ---------------------------------------------- }

INTERFACE
```

Chapter 11

```
const
  MAXSIZE = 3;

type

  string15 = string[15];

  TQueue = class(TObject)
     front    : integer;
     back     : integer;
     el_count : integer;
     elements : array[1..MAXSIZE] of string[15];

     procedure init_queue;
     procedure addelem( in_elem : string15 );
     procedure remove( var out_elem : string15 );

  end;

IMPLEMENTATION

  function full(in_elems : integer) : boolean;
  { ======================================================== }
  { func full - determine if the queue is full              }
  { param : in_elems - number of elements in queue          }
  { return: true if full, false otherwise                   }
  { ======================================================== }
  begin
     full := (in_elems = MAXSIZE);
  end;

  function empty(in_elems : integer) : boolean;
  { ======================================================== }
  { func: empty - determine if the queue is empty           }
  { param: in_elems - number of elements in queue           }
  { return: boolean - true if empty, false if members       }
  { ======================================================== }
  begin
     empty := (in_elems = 0);
  end;

  function insert_loc( in_back : integer ): integer;
  { ======================================================== }
  { func: insert_loc - determines the insertion location    }
  {                    for a circular queue                 }
  { param: in_back - back of the line                       }
```

```
{ return: integer - new insertion location             }
{ ===================================================== }
begin
  insert_loc := (in_back MOD MAXSIZE) + 1;  end;

procedure TQueue.AddElem( in_elem : string15);
{ ===================================================== }
{ proc: AddElem - add operation for queue structure     }
{ param: in_elem  = element to be added                 }
{ NOTE: calls func full to determine if filled          }
{       calls insert_loc for add location               }
{ ===================================================== }
begin
  if not full(el_count) then
   begin
     back := insert_loc(back);
     elements[back] := in_elem;
     el_count := el_count + 1;

     writeln('Front ',front);
     writeln('Back  ',back);
   end
   else
     writeln('Queue full. Cannot add item.');
end;

procedure TQueue.remove( var out_elem : string15 );
{ ===================================================== }
{ proc: Remove - get next item in the queue             }
{ param: out_element = returned element from queue       }
{ NOTE: uses func empty to determine no elements         }
{       uses insert_loc to determine tail of list        }
{ ===================================================== }
begin
   if not empty( el_count ) then
   begin
     out_elem := elements[front];
     elements[front] := ' ';
     front := insert_loc(front);
     el_count := el_count - 1;

     writeln('Front ',front);
     writeln('Back  ',back);

   end
   else
```

```
            writeln('Queue empty .. no more items.');
        end;

        procedure TQueue.init_queue;
        { ========================================================= }
        { proc: init_queue - initialize queue components            }
        { param: none                                               }
        { ========================================================= }
        var
            count       : integer;
        begin
            front := 1;
            back   := MAXSIZE;
            el_count := 0;
            for count := 1 to MAXSIZE  do
              elements[count] := ' ';

        end;

    end.
```

Notice that the procedures and functions that are members of the class must be quali-fied in the implementation section of the unit. The non-member functions do not have this requirement. The first task procedure added is the `AddElem` procedure:

```
    procedure TQueue.AddElem( in_elem : string15);
      begin
        if not full(el_count) then
          begin
            back := insert_loc(back);
            elements[back] := in_elem;
            el_count := el_count + 1;

            writeln('Front ',front);
            writeln('Back  ',back);
          end
          else
            writeln('Queue full. Cannot add item.');
      end;
```

Once again relying on the implied WITH .. DO construct, none of the field or class ref-erences requires qualification. It is also no longer necessary to pass the queue structure as a parameter because of the tight binding between the code and the data.

Listed below is the *QueueTest* program that exercises your new class definition. It works exactly the same as it did in the non-object form.

```
    program QueueTest;
```

```
uses
  QueueCls;

var
  Queue1     : TQueue;

  x          : integer;
  ans        : char;
  name       : string[15];

begin
  {- Instantiate the TQueue object -}
  Queue1 := TQueue.create;

  with Queue1 do
  begin
    init_queue;

    ans := ' ';
    while not ( ans in ['Q','q']) do
    begin
      write('(A)dd Caller, (N)ext Caller, (Q)uit : ');
      readln(ans);

      case upcase(ans) of
        'A' :
          begin
           write('Add a caller to the customer service queue ) ');
            readln( name );
            AddElem( name );
          end;

        'N' :
          begin
            remove( name);
            writeln('Next caller is : ', name );
          end;

        'L' :

          begin
            for x := 1 to MAXSIZE  do
              writeln( elements[x] );
          end;
        'Q' :
```

```
      else
        writeln('Invalid menu choice');
      end;
    end;
  end;
end.
```

Take a few moments and compare the code listings for the two forms of the unit and program. You will find the OOP forms much more appealing in terms of their simplicity of use. Think of this as a payoff for all of the work that it takes to learn this new form of programming.

Properties

Sound OOP design includes more than encapsulation and inheritance; it also includes access control. *Access control* is the concept of protecting the internal data from the users of the class. One of the methods used to implement this control over the values that go into and out of the class variables are properties. Rather than allowing direct access to fields of the class, a property can specify methods for reading and writing to the data element. For example, you might want to validate data before it is assigned to the internal variable and used by your class. The write access specifier method can check the data, raise an exception if necessary, and then apply the validated data to the hidden data element.

When a property is defined, the declaration specifies the name and type of the property, the action that is associated with reading the contents of the property, and the action that is associated with writing a value to the property. As a simple example of a property we will modify the Queue class with a property definition.

```
type

  string15 = string[15];

  TQueue = class(TObject)

    private
      front   : integer;
      back    : integer;
      el_count: integer;
      in_name : string15;
      function GetFindName : string15;
      procedure SetFindName( value : string15);

    public
      elements : array[1 .. MAXSIZE] of string[15];
```

```
        procedure init_queue;
        procedure addelem( in_elem : string15 );
        procedure remove( var out_elem : string15 );
        function FindCaller : integer;

        property FindName:string15 read GetFindName write
           SetFindName;

   end;
```

The private and public visibility specifiers will be discussed in a moment. The property FindName is defined as a string data type with read and write access specifiers.

When you attempt to modify the property findname as in

```
findname := tempname;
```

you will actually be calling a procedure called SetFindName. This intermediate action gives your class the ability to filter or manipulate the value before it reaches the internals in your class. In this case, the procedure does nothing; it is simply for demonstration purposes. The value parameter is simply assigned to the hidden internal field in_name. This field cannot be accessed directly by the user of the class; the field in_name is only used in the FindCaller procedure to find a caller's position in the list.

```
function TQueue.GetFindName : string15;
begin
  GetFindName := in_name;
end;

procedure TQueue.SetFindName( value : string15 );
begin
  in_name := value;
end;

function TQueue.FindCaller:integer;
var
  x   : integer;
  found : integer;
begin
      found := 0;
  x := 1;

  repeat
    if elements[x] = in_name then
      found := x;
    x := x + 1;
  until (found <> 0) or (x > MAXSIZE);
```

```
     FindCaller := found;
   end;
```

Visibility Specifiers

Even further control can be exercised over the accessibility of the data and code in a class by using Object Pascal's visibility attributes. There are five possible visibility specifiers: published, public, protected, private, and automated. The components listed below the specifier will have that span and type of control assigned to them.

Published

The components in this section have the same visibility as in the public section but they also generate Runtime Type Information. An application can use this RTTI to query the fields and properties to gain additional information about them.

Public

The components listed in this section have no specific restrictions and are accessible throughout the application that uses the class.

Private

Components in the private section are only visible within the unit that contains the class's definition. None of these components can be seen by the user of the class.

Protected

The protected components are visible to descendants of the class definition. This hides the implementation details from the user but allows for maximum flexibility to descendants of the object.

Automated

This is an obsolete attribute and is only included for backward compatibility.

Listing 11-2 shows lists the modified QueueCls unit so that you can view the changes in context.

Listing 11-2

```
unit QueueCls;
{ --------------------------------------------- }
{ UNIT QueueCls - defines the class TQueue      }
{ --------------------------------------------- }

INTERFACE

  const
    MAXSIZE = 3;

    type
```

```
       string15 = string[15];

   TQueue = class(TObject)

     private
       front   : integer;
       back    : integer;
       el_count: integer;
       in_name : string15;
       function GetFindName : string15;
       procedure SetFindName( value : string15);

     public
       elements : array[1 .. MAXSIZE] of string[15];

       procedure init_queue;
       procedure addelem( in_elem : string15 );
       procedure remove( var out_elem : string15 );
       function FindCaller : integer;

       property FindName:string15 read GetFindName write
         SetFindName;

   end;

IMPLEMENTATION

  function TQueue.GetFindName : string15;
  { ======================================================= }
  { func GetFindName - access method for findname property }
  { ======================================================= }
  begin
     GetFindName := in_name;
  end;

  procedure TQueue.SetFindName( value : string15 );
  { ======================================================= }
  { proc SetFindName - access method for findname property }
  { ======================================================= }
  begin
     in_name := value;
  end;

  function TQueue.FindCaller:integer;
  { ======================================================= }
  { func FindCaller - locate a name in the queue           }
```

```
{ param : none                                              }
{ return: element # if match, 0 if not                      }
{ ========================================================= }
var
 x   : integer;
 found : integer;
begin

  found := 0;
  x := 1;

  repeat
    if elements[x] = in_name then
      found := x;
    x := x + 1;
  until (found  0) or (x  MAXSIZE);

  FindCaller := found;
end;

function full(in_elems : integer) : boolean;
{ ========================================================= }
{ func full - determine if the queue is full                }
{ param : in_elems - number of elements in queue            }
{ return: true if full, false otherwise                     }
{ ========================================================= }
begin
    full := (in_elems = MAXSIZE);
end;

function empty(in_elems : integer) : boolean;

{ ========================================================= }
{ func: empty - determine if the queue is empty             }
{ param: in_elems - number of elements in queue             }
{ return: boolean - true if empty, false if members         }
{ ========================================================= }
begin
    empty := (in_elems = 0);
end;

function insert_loc( in_back : integer ): integer;
{ ========================================================= }
{ func: insert_loc - determines the insertion location      }
{                       for a circular queue                }
{ param: in_back - back of the line                         }
```

```
{ return: integer - new insertion location              }
{ ======================================================= }
begin
  insert_loc := (in_back MOD MAXSIZE) + 1;
end;

procedure TQueue.AddElem( in_elem : string15);
{ ======================================================= }
{ proc: AddElem - add operation for queue structure       }
{ param: in_elem  = element to be added                   }
{ NOTE: calls func full to determine if filled            }
{       calls insert_loc for add location                 }
{ ======================================================= }
begin
  if not full(el_count) then
   begin
     back := insert_loc(back);
     elements[back] := in_elem;
     el_count := el_count + 1;

     writeln('Front ',front);
     writeln('Back  ',back);
   end
   else
     writeln('Queue full. Cannot add item.');
end;

procedure TQueue.remove( var out_elem : string15 );
{ ======================================================= }
{ proc: Remove - get next item in the queue               }
{ param: out_element = returned element from queue        }
{ NOTE: uses func empty to determine no elements          }
{       uses insert_loc to determine tail of list         }
{ ======================================================= }
begin
  if not empty( el_count ) then
   begin
     out_elem := elements[front];
     elements[front] := ' ';
     front := insert_loc(front);
     el_count := el_count - 1;

     writeln('Front ',front);
     writeln('Back  ',back);

   end
```

```
      else
        writeln('Queue empty .. no more items.');
   end;

   procedure TQueue.init_queue;
   { ======================================================= }
   { proc: init_queue - initialize queue components          }
   { param: none                                             }
   { ======================================================= }
   var
      count      : integer;
   begin
      front := 1;
      back  := MAXSIZE;
      el_count := 0;
      for count := 1 to MAXSIZE  do
        elements[count] := ' ';

   end;

end.
```

The modifications to the test program are listed below.

```
program QueueTest;

uses
  QueueCls;

var
  Queue1      : TQueue;
  x           : integer;
  ans         : char;
  tempname    : string15;
  name        : string[15];

begin

  {- Instantiate the TQueue object -}
  Queue1 := TQueue.create;

  with Queue1 do
  begin
    init_queue;
```

```
ans := ' ';
while not ( ans in ['Q','q']) do
begin
  write('(A)dd Caller, (N)ext Caller, (F)ind Caller, (Q)uit : ');
  readln(ans);

  case upcase(ans) of
    'A' :
      begin
      write('Add a caller to the customer service queue ) ');
        readln( name );
        AddElem( name );
      end;

    'F'  :
      begin
        write('Who shall I find : ');
        readln( tempname );
        findname := tempname;

        if FindCaller = 0 then
           writeln('No caller by that name.')
        else
           writeln('Caller is ', findcaller);
      end;
    'N' :
      begin
        remove( name);
        writeln('Next caller is : ', name );
      end;

    'L' :

      begin
        for x := 1 to MAXSIZE  do
          writeln( elements[x] );
      end;
    'Q' :

  else
    writeln('Invalid menu choice');
  end;
end;
end;
end.
```

Extending Objects

Though we have put this into practice in the earlier example program, the practice of extending objects deserves a closer look. Properly designed class definitions provide for the ability of your Object Pascal programs to take a base class definition, inherit all of the properties and methods, and then extend the object to make it better fit a particular programming solution. The alternative to this would be to make a full copy of all of the code written to support the original class, rename it, and then use the copied version. Besides having twice the amount of code, anytime that you would want to maintain the class you will have to apply the changes to both sets of code. Remember that object inheritance allows you to make modifications to the lowest point in the class hierarchy in which the code is defined and have the changes automatically propagated throughout all of the descendants.

As an example of this hierarchy we will look briefly at an example. This sample hierarchy models a Boy Scout troop volunteer corps, the adults who make things run behind the scenes for the boys. The model starts with the most common attributes of all of the adults—they are all volunteers. This is modeled as the class definition:

```
type
   TVolunteer = class(TObject)
       name        : string[25];
       apponfile   : boolean;
       years       : integer;

       procedure init;
       function GetName;
       function GetAppOnFile;
       function GetYears;
   end;
```

Since every adult is a volunteer, this definition contains data fields that are common to each and the methods that handle access to those fields. One level up in the troop are those adults who hold leadership positions. The same questions and criteria will be required for these adults; i.e., their name, the number of years they have been with the troop, and whether they have a current application on file. Since they are already volunteers in addition to being leaders it won't be necessary to repeat these fields in their new class. The second tier class will inherit these attributes from the base class.

The leaders are modeled by deriving from the object TVolunteer. The class definition only needs to add those items specific to the leaders:

```
TLeader = class(TVolunteer)
      position   : string[15];
      volunteers : integer;

      procedure DivideResponsibility( in_vols: integer );
end;
```

The TLeader class inherits the name, app, etc., fields and methods from TVolunteer. To this base class it adds the fields position and volunteers and a method that divides up the responsibility for the volunteer corps among the leaders.

Finally, the class at the top of the defined hierarchy is the TScoutmaster class, which derives everything before it including TObject, way back at the beginning. In addition to all of the attributes of the volunteer and the responsibilities of the leader, the scoutmaster is responsible for the boys and their organizational units, the patrols. This is reflected in the class definition:

```
TScoutMaster = class(TLeader);
       patrols    : integer;
       boys       : integer;

       function GetPatrols;
       function DivideResponsibility( in_Boys: integer );
    end;
```

Though this has been simplistic in nature, it was intended to provide the flavor and a framework from which you can design your own classes and hierarchies. The unit definition showing how all these classes were all defined, one after the other, is shown below:

```
unit volclass;

interface

  type
    TVolunteer = class(TObject)
        name       : string[25];
        apponfile  : boolean;
        years      : integer;

        procedure init;
        function GetName;
        function GetAppOnFile;
        function GetYears;
    end;

    TLeader = class(TVolunteer)
        position   : string[15];
        volunteers : integer;

        procedure DivideResponsibility( in_vols: integer );

    end;
```

```
TScoutMaster = class(TLeader);
    patrols     : integer;
    boys        : integer;

    function GetPatrols;
    function DivideResponsibility( in_Boys: integer );
end;

implementation
....
```

Fundamentals in Focus

Inheritance

One of the points of contention that people often raise regarding the ongoing battle of Object Pascal versus C++ or other OOP comparisons is the issue of single versus multiple inheritance. In Object Pascal a class definition may only have a single ancestor. (The same as Java.) C++ usually allows multiple inheritance or the ability to descend simultaneously from two parent classes. Analysis of the problem often reveals, however, that multiple inheritance often causes more problems than it solves through the complexities it introduces into your classes. Single inheritance might be limiting in some cases but the direct line of lineage for any class, all the way to TObject is straightforward and easy to understand.

Summary

You are probably experiencing one of two feelings at the conclusion of this chapter; you are either overwhelmed by the 180 degree turn we took in program development or you are feeling let down that it ended so soon. Both of these feelings are easily understood with this topic. Object-oriented programming and its implementation through Object Pascal could be the subject for a couple of hundred pages or even an entire book. The presentation in this chapter was meant solely as a primer to introduce the topic and demonstrate how Object Pascal implements the concept. There are numerous, more advanced OOP topics that did not get covered within these pages simply because a beginning coder is better off concentrating on the fundamental data and logic structures. With a rich environment like Delphi with its VCL and class library it could be years before you find something in a project that requires you to write your own classes. Much of what you will want to accomplish will have already been defined and written for you and placed at your disposal, a mere click away.

You will learn a lot about the Delphi object model as you expand your development efforts and delve deeper into Delphi, so use this chapter to understand the basic tenets of OOP. We discussed what object-oriented programming is and how it differs from the traditional structured approach. The trio of characteristics that define OOP are encapsulation, inheritance, and polymorphism. Once the conceptual side of things was discussed we put some of the Object Pascal object-oriented extensions to work. The conversion and creation of the new class TQueue reinforced the concepts by putting them into action. The class was expanded with properties to see how these aid in data hiding abilities innate to OOP.

Don't stop here. Borland has always provided one of the most outstanding OOP resources in its product documentation. One of the clearest explanations that I have ever read on the topic comes from the Turbo Pascal 5.5 manual dated 1988. Object Pascal provides one of the cleanest and most understandable implementations of OOP and through the years the manuals and help files that ship with the Delphi product have done an outstanding job of explaining the concepts and practices to many, many users.

TEST YOUR KNOWLEDGE

1. Modify the Stack unit and test program from the previous chapter. Perform the same steps that we took to convert the Queue record and supporting procedures and functions into the TQueue class. Remember to hide as much of the implementation as possible.

2. Write a unit that defines the base class People which has the following attributes: name, social security number, years with the company. From this base class derive two other classes, Programmer and Manager. For the programmer add the following fields: Object Pascal, a Boolean that states whether the programmer has experience in this language; Manager, the name of the programmer's manager; and an array called Projects that contains the programmer's current projects. The manager class should have additional fields for the name of the department she manages and an array that contains the names of the programmers reporting to her. The manager class should also have a method called Reorganize that empties the programmer array and refills it with new names.

3. Using the unit and classes written in the above project, write a program that allows a manager to display all of the programmers reporting to her and their projects. Add the ability to then display all of the projects and the programmers assigned to them.

File Handling and Pointers in Object Pascal

Key Concepts

- File handling in Object Pascal
- Beginning text file handling
- Reading and writing text files
- Working with non-text files
- Pointers

Introduction

This chapter returns to the basics from our foray into the wild world of object-oriented programming on the preceding pages. One thing that has probably frustrated you most about the programs that we have developed in the prior pages is the fact that you must constantly re-enter all of the data with each iteration of the program. For example, we've worked with the queue structure in a couple of different formats and yet each time we make a modification or fix to the program, all of the data had to be entered again because we had no way of saving it and simply reloading it. One task that is required of nearly every meaningful piece of software is the ability to save the user's work to a disk file either so that it can be reloaded the next time the program is started or simply for archival purposes. File handling, the ability to read and write data to and from a disk file, is a fundamental skill.

Object Pascal supports both text and typed files so your program will not be artificially limited as to what kinds of data files they can work with. The only limitations that you will discover with the file tools are your own imagination and design skills. The text file will be our first exploration in the area of file handling since these are among the simplest and most common of the file types. There are five steps that are common to any file read or write operation, and we are going to look at the Object Pascal implementation of the commands needed for each step. Non-text, or typed, files will be examined and demonstrated so that your programs will be free from the constraints of strictly using text files as the storage tool. Finally, the chapter is going to close out with a discussion of pointers and dynamic data structures. In many Object Pascal contexts, pointers have become invisible to the programmer but that does not preclude us from having to develop the knowledge of how they work and how to work with them. The approach to the chapter is:

- The text file will be defined so that you are familiar with the structure that we are discussing.
- The five steps of Object Pascal file handling will be enumerated and the specific statements that match them will be put to use. Practical experience is the best teacher.
- The `read`, `readln`, `write`, and `writeln` commands will demonstrate their overloaded nature in reading and writing to and from the file.
- We are going to look at exception handling in this chapter. Once learned, it is applicable throughout your programming.
- Once we have established what a text file contains and have developed some dexterity with reading and writing to them, we will take our knowledge to the non-text file. The processes will be basically the same, only the data access abilities will be significantly different.
- Finally, we will wrap up the chapter with a discussion and demonstration of pointers in Object Pascal.

After completing this chapter you will have a well-rounded education in the Object Pascal language and its usage. Continue to work on the example programs and expand them in any way that interests you. Playing with a programming language and testing the outer limits of its capabilities is always much less stressful when you are not trying to meet a deadline or fix a client problem. When you work in the Delphi IDE now, you will have a new respect for the internals of that program, the amount of very good work that goes into creating such a strong visual development tool. Your Delphi programs will take on an entirely new depth as well, since you will no longer be constrained to simply dropping the components onto a form and setting a few properties. Instead of relying on the default actions, you will be able to actually program the software and make it sing.

This is Going into Your Permanent File

Who knows what happened to all of our permanent records that we were beaten down with in school? Did this threatening folder prevent anybody from achieving what they wanted to do? Probably not, since that permanent record was most likely the first thing to hit the principal's trash can after we graduated from high school. Computer users, on the other hand, have an expectation that they will be able to save their work to secondary storage and then be able to retrieve it in perpetuity. While we may not be able to guarantee that a file will exist forever, a software user should be able to rely on the fact that whatever data is expected to be stored is actually what is written to the file.

A file is another named collection of data, this one stored in non-volatile secondary storage. What makes the file important is that users can create a data set that can be saved and loaded for use in another session or by another user. A text file is the easiest type of file to work with and to understand. These files consist of character data only that is stored in conceptual lines within the file. These lines are separated by CR/LF (carriage return/line feed) character pairs. Figure 12-1 shows this concept.

Line 1	This is a line of text.[CR/LF]
Line 2	Each line in a text file ends[CR/LF]
Line 3	with a carriage return and a line feed.
Line 4	[CR/LF]
Line 5	The line above would print [CR/LF]
Line 6	out as a blank line.[CR/LF]

Figure 12-1: The text file

If you were to use the DOS TYPE command with a text file it would print out on the screen in a readable fashion, unlike the binary file (such as an .exe file) that would fill your screen with nonsense characters and squawking. If you TYPE a text file you will find that you do not see the CR/LF characters, only their actions. These are non-printing characters and are used to signal the computer to perform a type formatting operation.

The Five Steps of File Handling

Object Pascal has a regimented series of five steps that must be followed when using a text file. Each step has a specific purpose, separate from the others, and it must be accomplished or the reading and writing of files will not occur.

Create a Variable

Creating a variable is step one. In order to work with any data in Object Pascal you know that you have to create a variable to contain that data, and the text file is no exception. The data type that you will assign to the identifier is `text` and it is declared as all of our variables have been:

```
var
   file1 : text;
```

This type of variable differs slightly from the others we have worked with. It cannot appear on the left-hand side of an assignment statement nor can it be used in most of the other contexts that we have used variables for in the preceding chapters. The `text` variable has a set of operations all its own and statements within this operating range are all that it recognizes.

Assign the Filename

Object Pascal adds a sometimes confusing twist to the simplicity of working with files when the discussion turns to filenames. Object Pascal uses two different names to identify the file, the internal variable name and the external operating system name. The second step in text file usage is to use the `assignfile` procedure to assign the DOS name to the Object Pascal variable name. The DOS name is likely to be something the user can easily remember and will be followed by a three-letter extension. The file that the sample program will be using is called TEST.TXT. "TXT" is the extension that most programmers use to indicate the text contents of the file but you are free to use anything that you want as long as it is not associated with some other program. You will only use the DOS name once in a program, in the assignment statement.

```
assignfile( file1, 'TEST.TXT');
```

Any reference to the file throughout the rest of the program must now be made through the variable, in this case `file1`.

The DOS name does not have to be a constant string as shown in the example. It can be a string or a string expression that evaluates to a filename. For instance, the lines

```
write('What is the file name : ');
readln( in_file );
assignfile( file1, in_file );
```

would give the user the opportunity to specify the filename that the program should work with.

Open the File

Before any action can occur on the contents of a text file it must be opened. Object Pascal supports opening text files for either read or write access but not both simultaneously. There are three commands used to open text files in Object Pascal. Table 12-1 lists them and their actions. For this exercise we will use the `rewrite` procedure. `Rewrite` opens a new, empty text file, destroying any text that was in the file from a previous write operation. If the filename provided does not exist, `rewrite` will create a new file with that name. The statement uses the file variable as its only parameter:

```
rewrite( file1 );
```

Table 12-1: The Object Pascal text file opening commands

Command	Results
rewrite	Opens a file for write access. Creates an empty file with the filename assigned in the assign statement and places the file pointer at the zero byte position.
append	Opens a file for write access. Adds data to an existing file by placing the file pointer at the end of the existing file.

Table 12-1 (cont.): The Object Pascal text file opening commands

Command	Results
reset	Opens a file for read-only access. The file pointer is placed at the zero byte position in preparation for the read operation.

The program now has an empty, open file to work with.

Write Data to the File

Writing the data to a text file is exactly the same as writing data to the screen as you are going to use the `write` or `writeln` procedures. The formatting of the statement is slightly different as you must provide the file variable in addition to the text to be written to the file. The statement

```
writeln( file1, 'Get Up Kids' );
```

will write the string 'Get Up Kids' to the text file linked to the variable `file1`. The difference between the `write` and `writeln` commands is the same as it would be on the screen. `Write` will not add the CR/LF pair after the text, so the next text that is added to the file will abut the text immediately before it.

The `write` and `writeln` statements used in this context can sometimes be confusing. We have learned to this point that anything put in the parameter list of these procedures is destined to be printed out. This is no longer true when these procedures are used in the context of file handling. Deep down inside of Delphi, in the compiler, is a filter that parses the parameter lists to determine what data type each of them is and then process them appropriately. If the first parameter of the `write` or `writeln` procedure is of type `file` the data will be written to the file variable instead of to the screen. Another thing to remember about the `write` or `writeln` statements is that numerical data is converted to character data within the file. This means that the data will not be immediately usable for any type of computation when it is read back from the file; it will need to be either typecast or converted.

Close the File

The final, and very important, step in handling text files is that the file must be closed. When the file is closed the file handle is released back to the operating system. If you do not close the file, it will be invisible to you and your program until the operating system terminates. One of the last acts of the operating system is to clean up and close any open file handles. Many, many students have spent hours trying to debug this situation, looking in vain for their text files that do not exist at first but magically reappear the next time that they work on the program. The `closefile` procedure is used for this operation.

```
closefile( file1 );
```

Those were the five steps: create a variable, assign the filename, open the file, write the data, and close the file. The following listing places these steps into a complete, working program:

```
program textfile;
var
  { - STEP 1 - create a text file variable - }
  file1      : text;
  in_file    : string;

begin
  write('What is the file name : ');
  readln( in_file );

  { - STEP 2 - Assign the DOS name to the file variable - }
  assignfile( file1, in_file );

  { - STEP 3 - Open the file for write access - }
  rewrite( file1 );

  { - STEP 4 - write the text - }
  writeln( file1, 'GET SOME GO AGAIN');

  { - STEP 5 - Close the file - }
  closefile( file1 );
end.
```

Run the program but don't be surprised when nothing spectacular happens. To view the results of your masterpiece, use the editor to view the contents of the file or simply type it from the DOS prompt as shown in Figure 12-2.

Figure 12-2

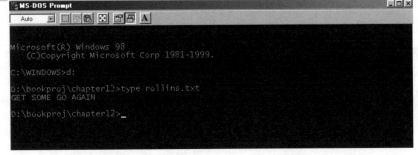

Non-Destructive Writing to a File

Often you will not want to delete the contents of a text file when you open it. Instead, you will want to be able to add new text to the existing contents of a file. For this task you use the append procedure to open the file. This procedure functions exactly the same as the rewrite procedure except that it does not delete the contents of the file that it opens; rather, it moves the file pointer to the end of the file in preparation for the addition of new text lines. The statement usage is exactly the same:

```
append( file1 );
```

Try this new version of the *textfile* program to see the effect of this new statement:

```
program textfil2;
var
  file1 : text;
  in_file    : string;
  more       : char;
  title : string;

begin
  more := 'Y';

  write('What is the file name : ');
  readln( in_file );

  assignfile( file1, in_file );

  { - NOTE THE CHANGE HERE - }
  append( file1 );

  while more in['Y','y'] do
  begin
    write('Type a CD title : ');
    readln( title );

    writeln( file1, title );

    write('Any more ? Y/N : ');
    readln( more );
  end;

  closefile( file1 );
end.
```

When you run this program, be sure that you use the filename that you used in the previous exercise. The `append` procedure requires that the file already exist when you try to open it; a run-time error will occur otherwise. Append will not create a new file for you. Figure 12-3 shows the results of running this version of the program a few times. You see that the additional titles of the Rollins Band CDs have been appended to the file rather than overwriting one another.

Figure 12-3

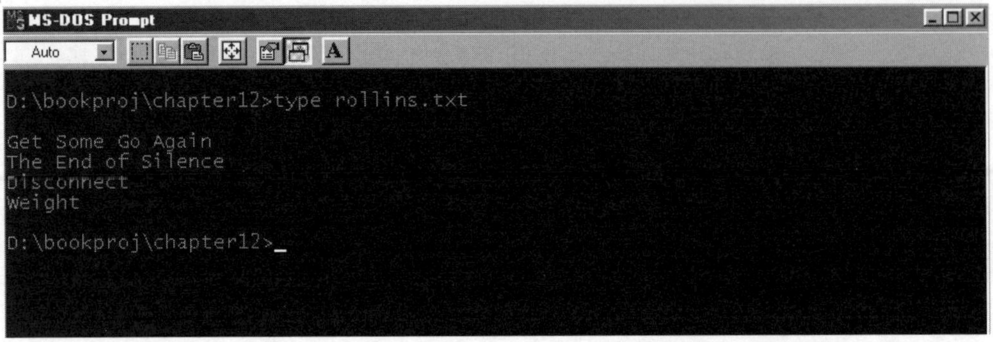

Reading a Text File

All of the steps shown for writing a file are required for reading a file as well. The file variable must be declared, the DOS filename must be assigned to the file variable, and the file must be opened. The `reset` procedure is used to open a file for read access. This statement takes the form:

```
reset( f1 );
```

Once the file is opened, you are able to use the `readln` procedure to extract the data from the file. For example, if we wanted to read the first line of the file created in the previous exercise, we could use the following program:

```
program readfile;
var
  f1      : text;
  fname   : string;
  in_char : string;

begin
  write('What is the name of the file : ');
  readln( fname );

  assignfile( f1, fname );
  reset( f1 );

  readln( f1, in_char );
  writeln( in_char );

  closefile( f1 );
end.
```

The results of running the program are shown in Figure 12-4.

Figure 12-4

Just like the `writeln` procedure, the first parameter used in the `readln` statement must be of the type `file` for the procedure to be pointed to the file. Leaving this parameter out is a common error, so pay close attention. You will notice in the output that only the first line of the file has been displayed on screen. How would you modify this program to read all of the lines?

Error Handling

Both the `reset` and the `append` procedures require that the file pointed to by the file variable exist prior to any attempt to open it. If the file does not exist, an IOError is generated. When using either of these two procedures in a program, it is imperative that you add error handling code to your software. Properly designed, error handling code will allow your program to gracefully recover from abend situations that would otherwise crash the software. There are two methods that we are going to examine for introducing error handling code into your file handling procedures: the old style of manually handling the error and the Delphi exception method.

IOResult

The old Pascal style of handling I/O errors is to test for them using compiler directives and then examine the results via the function `IOResult`. `IOResult` returns zero or non-zero depending on the success of the input-output operation. To use this function you must turn on and off the IO checking directive switches, {$I-} and {$I+}, around the I/O operations as shown in the following program:

```
program iocheck;
var
   f1    : text;
   fname : string;

begin
   fname := 'testfile.txt';

   assignfile( f1, fname );
```

Chapter 12

```
      {$I-}
      reset( f1 );
      {$I+}

      if IOResult <> 0 then
      begin
        writeln( 'Cannot find file, ', fname );
        halt;
      end;
   end.
```

The IO checking switch {$I+} or the longer form {IOCHECKS ON} tells the compiler to generate code used for checking the results of an Input-Output call such as the file open command. If this switch is off, as in {$I-} or {IOCHECKS OFF}, then you may check for errors on the preceding operating with IOResult after turning IO checking back on.

Exceptions

Using exceptions in your programming is the modern way of handling errors that is well supported by Delphi. Exceptions add significantly to your programs by allowing them to recover gracefully from an error condition that normally would have crashed the program. Exception handling is the practice of writing the appropriate code to either shut down quietly without damage to the user's data or, ideally, to correct the error. To implement this you must use the TRY .. EXCEPT or TRY .. FINALLY constructs to surround the code that you want to fall under the control of the exception handler. The try reserved word marks the top of the protected block and the end that follows except marks the end. It is the code within the construct that is of interest to the exception handler. Let's look at an example:

```
program excptfil;
uses
   sysutils;

var
   f          : text;
   fname      : string;
   in_string  : string;

procedure handleIO;
begin
   writeln('Unable to locate ', fname);

   try
     write('Enter new filename : ');
     readln( fname );
     assignfile( f, fname );
     reset( f );
```

```
      except
        on EInOutError do HandleIO;
      end;
    end;

  begin
    fname := 'xxxxx.txt';
    assignfile( f, fname );

    try
      reset( f );
    except
      on EInOutError do HandleIO;
    end;

    readln( f, in_string );
    writeln( in_string );

        closefile( f );
    end.
```

The first time through the program, the TRY .. EXCEPT block encloses the reset statement so that if there is an error opening the file an exception will be raised. Such is the case with the sample program as there should be no file on my system named xxxxx.txt.

Figure 12-5

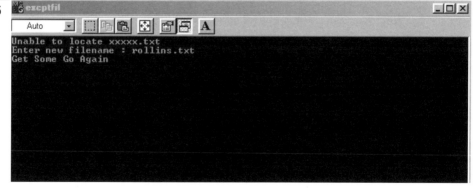

When an exception is raised, the exception handler for that class is called using the ON .. DO statement. In the sample code we see that if an IO error occurs, the procedure HandleIO will be called. In the case of HandleIO, it seeks to correct the error by asking the user to provide an alternative filename. Your design would likely give the user the option of quitting the program as well. Error handling is a sign of a quality program and your software should implement it everywhere necessary to improve the robustness. You can choose between the two methods shown

Chapter 12

here for IO errors, but for other operational problems you will want to spend more time studying the exception handling tools in Delphi.

Fundamentals in Focus

Recursion

You probably noticed that the procedure `HandleIO` calls itself repeatedly until a valid filename is entered. This process is called **recursion**. Discussions of recursion can take many pages while arguing the most efficient way to implement this logical practice, so consider this merely an introduction. More of a problem solving technique than a programming skill, recursion comes from circular definitions in mathematics that are called recursive definitions.

Object Pascal has no restrictions on how recursion functions are implemented in the language. The greatest challenge facing the programmer in utilizing this tool is to ensure that it terminates at some point. From this perspective, the example given above is a poor sample as it has the potential to run forever if the user continues to enter bogus filenames. On the other hand, she could simply press the CTRL-BREAK keys and halt the processing. The termination arrangement becomes much more of an issue in mathematical functions where the user does not have access to the processing within the function.

QUICK CHECK

1. What is the difference between `reset`, `rewrite`, and `append`?
2. What are the steps necessary in any program that uses external files as input or output?

EOF and EOLN

Two functions are used quite often when reading text files, each of which indicates whether or not the file pointer has reached a specific place in the file. EOF returns a Boolean true if the file pointer has passed the last character in a file or if a file is empty. EOLN returns a Boolean true if the end of a text line has been reached, the point where the CR/LF pair is. Using these functions you can loop through the entire file reading every element. The program below will loop through the source code of the *readfile.dpr* file and list it out to the screen. It uses EOF to determine when the loop is to be terminated.

```
program charfile;
var
  f        : text;
  fname    : string;
  in_char  : char;
```

```
begin
  fname := 'readfile.dpr';
  assignfile( f, fname );

  reset( f );

  while not eof( f ) do
  begin
    read( f, in_char );
    write( in_char );
  end;

  closefile( f );
end.
```

The program uses a `while` loop controlled by the EOF function to repeat the read process until the end of the file is reached. Notice that the NOT operator is used to control the loop by ensuring that the character at the file pointer is not the EOF character. If the NOT is left out, the loop will never run unless the file is empty, causing the EOF character to be the only thing found.

Translation, Please

The project that follows will build a code framework that is useful in a number of situations. In this program, characters from a file are read and trapped until a complete word is formed. The assembled word is compared to a list of keywords in an array. If a match is found, the word is replaced with an alternative language form of the keyword and written to a target file. This is a form of a filter program, a piece of software that reads and then manipulates the contents of a text file before writing it out to a second file. This process has many uses such as beautifying source files or changing the case of members of a file.

The reserved words are loaded from an external file into an array in memory. This file is called *xlatsorc.txt* and its format is very specific. Each reserved word is followed by a common delimiter and then the translated word.

```
and,warand;
array,wararray;
asm,warasm;
begin,warbegin;
case,warcase;
const,warconst;
constructor,warconstructor;
destructor,wardestructor;
div,wardiv;
do,wardo;
downto,wardownto;
```

```
   else,warelse;
 . . . .
```

You can see that the translation in this project simply places the author's initials in front of the keyword as the alternative language form of the new word. You could just as easily translate the reserved words into Spanish or some other language. The procedure that loads this file, `loadwords`, simply loops through the entire file until it reaches the `EOF`. When each text line is read it is internally parsed and broken into the needed segments.

```
procedure LoadWords;
var
   xlatin       : text;
   xlincount    : integer;
   target       : string;
   source       : string;
   dc           : integer;

begin
   assign(xlatin, 'xlatxorc.txt');
   {$I-}
   reset(xlatin);
   {$I+}

   if ioresult <> 0 then
   begin
     writeln('Unable to open translation source');
     halt;
   end
   else
   begin
     writeln;
     write('Loading translation file');
     xlincount := 1;

     dc := 1;
     while not eof(xlatin) do
     begin
       readln(xlatin, source);
       target := copy(source, 1, (pos(',',source)-1) );
       xlatarray[1,xlincount] := target;
       delete(source, 1, length(target)+1 );

       target := copy(source, 1, (pos(';',source)-1) );
       xlatarray[2,xlincount] := target;
```

```
      xlincount := xlincount + 1;
      write('.');
      dc := dc + 1;
      if dc > 30 then
      begin
         dc := 1;
         writeln;
      end;
   end;
   close(xlatin);

   writeln;
   numwords := xlincount;
   writeln('Successfully loaded ',numwords:0,'
      source/translastion words.');
   writeln;
  end;
end;
```

The `readln` procedure will read an entire text line in a single operation by combining the read operation with an unsized string variable. In the *xlatsorc.txt* file each of the text lines is ended with a CR/LF pair to facilitate this. The source file is no longer needed after the words have been read in so the source file is closed.

Most of the heavy lifting in this program is done by the `translate` procedure. Within this procedure the program is going to manage two separate files simultaneously, one for input and the other for output. As the input file is read character by character, whole words are assembled based on the occurrence of *word delimiters*. These delimiters are anything within the file that would indicate that the end of a word had been reached such as a space, a semicolon, or a period. When these delimiters are reached, all of the characters read in prior to that point should be considered a word and compared against the array to determine if the word you have assembled is a reserved word.

```
procedure Translate;
var
   infile      : text;
   outfile     : text;
   ifilename   : filestring;
   ofilename   : filestring;
   inchar      : char;
   commentflag : boolean;
   tempword    : string;
   xlated      : string;

begin
   GetSourceFile(ifilename);
   GetTargetFile(ofilename);
```

```
assign(infile, ifilename);
assign(outfile, ofilename);

reset(infile);
rewrite(outfile);

commentflag := false;
tempword := '';
while not eof(infile) do
begin
  while not eoln(infile) do
  begin
    read(infile,inchar);

    if inchar = '{' then
      commentflag := true;

    if inchar = '}' then
      commentflag := false;

      if inchar in [' ',';','.','(','}',chr(10),chr(13)] then
      begin
        if not commentflag then
        begin
          xlated := Xlate(tempword) + inchar;
          write(outfile,xlated);
          tempword := '';
        end
        else
        begin
        if inchar = chr(10) then
          writeln('got one');

          write(outfile,tempword + inchar);
          tempword := '';
        end;

      end
      else
      begin

        tempword := tempword + inchar;

      end;

  end;
```

```
     readln(infile);
     writeln(outfile);
   end;

   close(infile);
   close(outfile);

end;
```

Notice that the procedure uses both EOF and EOLN nested one within the other. This is necessary so that the CR/LF pairs at the end of each line are handled and the pair does not throw off the delimiter handling. Listing 12-1 shows the entire program, which includes the supporting functions for properly handling the files used by the program. The *xlatsorc.txt* file continues in the same fashion shown above but includes all of the reserved words.

Listing 12-1

```
program xlator;
{ ---------------------------------------------------------- }
{ Author: Warren Rachele                                     }
{ ---------------------------------------------------------- }
type
   xarray = array [1..2,1..55] of string;
   filestring = string[79];

var
   xlatarray   : xarray;
   numwords    : integer;

function FileExists(FileName: filestring): Boolean;
{-------------------------------------------------- }
{ Boolean function that returns True if the file }
{ exists; otherwise, it returns False. Closes the}
{ file if it exists.                             }
{ -------------------------------------------------- }
var
 F: file;
begin
 {$I-}
 Assign(F, FileName);
 FileMode := 0;
 Reset(F);
 Close(F);
 {$I+}
 FileExists := (IOResult = 0) and (FileName    '');
end;   { FileExists }
```

```pascal
procedure LoadWords;
{ ----------------------------------------------- }
{ PROCEDURE LoadWords                             }
{ Load words and their translation from an ext    }
{ source file.                                    }
{ PARAMETERS: none                                }
{ RETURNS: none                                   }
{ ----------------------------------------------- }
var
  xlatin      : text;
  xlincount   : integer;
  target      : string;
  source      : string;
  dc          : integer;

begin
  assign(xlatin, 'xlatsorc.txt');
  {$I-}
  reset(xlatin);
  {$I+}

  if ioresult  0 then
  begin
    writeln('Unable to open translation source');
    halt;
  end
  else
  begin
    writeln;
    write('Loading translation file');
    xlincount := 1;

    dc := 1;
    while not eof(xlatin) do
    begin
      readln(xlatin, source);
      target := copy(source, 1, (pos(',',source)-1) );
      xlatarray[1,xlincount] := target;
      delete(source, 1, length(target)+1 );

      target := copy(source, 1, (pos(';',source)-1) );
      xlatarray[2,xlincount] := target;

      xlincount := xlincount + 1;
      write('.');
```

```
        dc := dc + 1;
        if dc > 30 then
        begin
          dc := 1;
          writeln;
        end;
      end;
    close(xlatin);

    writeln;
    numwords := xlincount;
    writeln('Successfully loaded ',numwords:0,'
      source/translation words.');
    writeln;
  end;
end;

procedure GetSourceFile(var filename:filestring);
{ --------------------------------------------- }
{ PROC: GetSourceFile                           }
{ Gets the source filename and validates it     }
{ PARAMETERS: variable filename - passes name   }
{ RETURNS: none                                 }
{ --------------------------------------------- }
var
  tempstr     : filestring;

begin

  write('Source file name: ');
  readln(tempstr);
  while not FileExists(tempstr) do
  begin
    write(chr(7));
    writeln('ERROR: File not found.');
    write('Source file name: ');
    readln(tempstr);
  end;

  filename := tempstr;
end;

procedure GetTargetFile(var filename:filestring);
{ --------------------------------------------- }
{ PROC: GetTargetFile                           }
{ Gets the target filename and validates it     }
```

```
{ PARAMETERS: variable filename - passes name    }
{ RETURNS: none                                   }
{ -------------------------------------------- }
var
  tempstr      : filestring;
  ch           : char;

begin
  write('Target file name: ');
  readln(tempstr);
  if FileExists(tempstr) then
  begin
    write(chr(7));
    writeln('WARNING: Filename already exists.');
    write('Do you want to overwrite it? (y/n) ');
    readln(ch);
    if ch in ['Y','y'] then
      filename := tempstr
    else
      GetTargetFile(tempstr);
  end
  else
    filename := tempstr;
end;


function xlate( inword:string ): string;
{ -------------------------------------------- }
{ PROC: xlate                                  }
{ takes the word and returns a translated word }
{ PARAMETERS: inword - the word to be xlated   }
{ RETURNS: xlated word/original word           }
{ -------------------------------------------- }
var
  counter      : integer;
begin
  for counter := 1 to numwords do
  begin
    if xlatarray[1,counter] = inword then
    begin
      xlate := xlatarray[2,counter];
      break;
    end
    else
      xlate := inword;
  end;
end;
```

```pascal
procedure Translate;
{ --------------------------------------------- }
{ PROC: Translate                               }
{ spins through the input file and performs the }
{ search for delimiters and calls the xlate proc}
{ PARAMETERS: none                              }
{ RETURNS: none                                 }
{ --------------------------------------------- }
var
   infile      : text;
   outfile     : text;
   ifilename   : filestring;
   ofilename   : filestring;
   inchar      : char;
   commentflag : boolean;
   tempword    : string;
   xlated      : string;

begin

   GetSourceFile(ifilename);
   GetTargetFile(ofilename);
   assign(infile, ifilename);
   assign(outfile, ofilename);

   reset(infile);
   rewrite(outfile);

   commentflag := false;
   tempword := '';
   while not eof(infile) do
   begin
     while not eoln(infile) do
     begin
       read(infile,inchar);

       if inchar = '{' then
         commentflag := true;

       if inchar = '}' then
         commentflag := false;

         if inchar in [' ',';','.','(','}',chr(10),chr(13)] then
         begin
           if not commentflag then
           begin
```

```
                    xlated := Xlate(tempword) + inchar;
                    write(outfile,xlated);
                    tempword := '';
                  end
                  else
                  begin
                  if inchar = chr(10) then
                    writeln('got one');

                    write(outfile,tempword + inchar);
                    tempword := '';
                  end;

              end
              else
              begin

                  tempword := tempword + inchar;

              end;
            end;
            readln(infile);
            writeln(outfile);
          end;

          close(infile);
          close(outfile);

      end;

      begin

          LoadWords;
        Translate;

      end.
```

As always, a copy is included on the CD-ROM if you don't want to type. Note that it only includes the reserved words and not the common procedures and functions that we have become accustomed to seeing.

The handling of text files is not a complicated process as long as you are sure to follow the necessary steps and select the reading or writing mechanism that is most appropriate to your needs. Text files are not the only type of file that Object Pascal can handle and in the next section we will look at some of the other types of files you can create.

Non-Text Files

Text files are an easy introduction to the concept of files and the associated routines. They are made up of characters only so they can be viewed in any editor or other program that can read a character file. On the downside, text files must be accessed sequentially starting at the beginning and going to the end because they have no structure to them. Text files do not allow you to zero in on a specific character or word in a file and then go directly there to access it; in other words, once you have set the file pointer in motion it cannot be backed up to reread or modify something that has been passed.

Non-text or typed files are made up of components. The components can be simple data types or structured data types but they will have the properties within the file of having a specific size and a specific, numbered location within the file. This characteristic often causes typed files to be referred to as random access files since Object Pascal has the ability to move the file pointer to a specified location within the file. The declaration for a typed file is an expansion of what we used for the text file. The type definition starts in the type section with the two reserved words `file of`:

```
type
   IntFile = file of integer
```

The components of a typed file can be either a simple data type or a complex data structure. The definition:

```
type
  student = record
    name     : string;
    gpa      : real;
    id_num   : integer;
  end;

  stdfile = file of student;
```

establishes a record type of `student` and then declares a file of these records.

Reading and Writing Typed Files

Each of the steps that were established for reading and writing text files apply to typed files as well. You must continue to declare a variable of the appropriate data type and then assign the DOS name to the file variable using the `assignfile` procedure. When it comes to opening the file, however, things are a little different. The procedures `reset` and `rewrite` are used to open typed files with a slight twist. Typed files allow simultaneous read and write access initiated by either of these statements. You will use `reset` when the file already exists in secondary storage and use `rewrite` when you want to open a new file or clear the contents of an existing file. `Rewrite` has the same caveat as it did with the text files; it always creates a new empty file when it is used, so exercise caution and make sure

Chapter 12

that your program's users know what to expect. The append procedure is not used with typed files. Back to the file handling steps, the final step is to always close the file using the closefile procedure.

There is a slightly different usage for the read and write commands when used with typed files. The following program shows an example.

```
program typefile;
type
   intfile = file of integer;

var
   f1: intfile;
   x  : integer;
   y  : integer;

begin
   assignfile( f1, 'intgrfil.bin' );
   rewrite( f1 );

   x := 9;
   y := 11;

   write( f1, x, y );

   closefile( f1 );
end.
```

When reading or writing the typed file, the transfer of data must be made through variables passed as the parameters to the read or write procedures. This means that the following statements:

```
write( f1, 8, 77 );
write( f1, x+1, 22 mod 3 );
```

would cause an error to be generated.

Random Access

Read and write operations can be mixed in the same block of statements when working with typed files. For this to work effectively it is often necessary to specifically position the file pointer. This operation is performed using the seek statement. Similar to an array, each component in a typed file is in a numbered position that can be directly accessed by providing this offset. Seek takes two parameters, the file variable and the numeric offset that points to the component that you want to access:

```
seek( f1, 3 );
```

This statement will result in the file pointer being moved to the third component of the file which you can access immediately. The following program demonstrates this by modifying the program we have already outlined:

```
program typefil2;
type
  intfile = file of integer;

var
  f1: intfile;
  x : integer;
  y : integer;

begin
  assignfile( f1, 'intgrfil.bin' );
  rewrite( f1 );

  for x := 1 to 10 do
       write( f1, x );

  y := 0;
      while y < 10 do
  begin
       seek( f1, y );
    read( f1, x );
    writeln('Position ',y:0,' Value ',x:0);
    y := y + 2;
  end;
  closefile( f1 );
end.
```

Figure 12-6 shows the results of this program. Is this what you were expecting?

You must exercise caution not to write or allow a `seek` statement offset that is more than one component count past the current end of the file. Object Pascal allows the file pointer to be placed one step past the end of file for the purposes of adding a record. Any further than that will result in a run-time error. The function filesize returns this end of file position. The call to the statement is:

```
x := filesize( f1 );
```

To simply add a new component to the end of the file, the statement:

```
seek( f1, filesize( f1 ) );
```

would place the file pointer just past the end of the file in position for a component to be added. Does the math work on this? It does because the file pointer starts numbering at zero, not one.

The Students File

The demonstration programs so far have worked with the integer simple data type, but using a more complex, structured type is equally as easy. We will create the file of the student record type we defined earlier and then put it through its paces. The entire listing of the program is shown below:

```
program stdtfile;

type
   Student = record
name      : string[15];
gpa       : real;
id_num    : integer;
   end;

   StdFile = file of student;

var
   F1          : StdFile;
   y           : integer;
   choice      : char;
   in_stud     : Student;

begin
   assignfile( f1, 'studfile.bin');

   rewrite( f1 );

   choice := ' ';
   while not (choice in ['Q','q'] )do
   begin
      write('(A)dd record, (L)ist, (Q)uit ');
      readln( choice );

      case upcase(choice) of
```

```
      'A':
        begin
          with in_stud do
          begin
            write('Name : ');
            readln( name );
            write('GPA  : ');
            readln( gpa );
            write('ID : ');
            readln( id_num );
          end;

          seek( F1, filesize( F1 ));
          write( F1, in_stud );

        end;

      'L':
        begin
          y := 0;
          while y < filesize( F1 ) do
          begin
            seek( F1, y );
            read( f1, in_stud );
            with in_stud do
            begin

              writeln('Record ', y );
              writeln( name );
              writeln( GPA:0:2);
              writeln( id_num:0 );
              writeln;
            end;
            y := y + 1;
          end;

        end;

      'Q':
    else
      writeln('Invalid menu choice.');
    end;

  end;
end.
```

The program asks for the data and adds a record to the end of the file. The `list` function loops from the 0 record through the end of the file and lists the contents of the records.

QUICK CHECK

1. When working with typed files, what is the proper usage for the `rewrite`, `reset`, and `append` procedures?

2. What will the outcome be when a file of integers is read with the following set of statements?

```
for x := 1 to 10 do
   read( f1, x );
```

Will there be any missing data? If so, where?

Pointers

There is nothing better to round out this book than a quick discussion of pointers. Pointers sometime send shivers through even the most experienced programmers simply because they never took the time to understand the relatively simple concepts. By learning how to best use pointers in our programs we can get away from relying solely on the static data structures we have used thus far. A static data structure is one that is completely defined at compile time. A dynamic data structure, on the other hand, is one that can be defined during run time and lets our programs avoid the boundaries inherent in the static structures.

Simply put, a *pointer* is a data element that holds the memory address of another variable. The variable pointed to can be of the data types we have discussed. Refer back to Chapter 4 for a refresher on the basics of the pointer. Working hand in hand with the pointer is a special class of variable in Object Pascal called dynamic variables. Dynamic variables are intended to act as nodes in dynamic structures, though they can be used alone. In usage, these variables are exactly the same as static variables. They can be written to and read from, they have a type, they can be assigned to one another, etc. The only limitation that they have is that they cannot be of the type `file`. These variables are created and destroyed by your program during run time. For this reason, they are not declared and they are not named. You access these nodes via a pointer variable.

Pointer Variables

Pointer variables are declared and they are named. The pointer variable has a type associated with it which correlates to the node that will be created. For example, the structure `student` is defined as:

```
type
  student = record
```

```
    name : string[20];
       testscore : integer;
  end;
```

The nodes will be created of this data type. When the pointer variable is declared it is written as:

```
var
   ptr          :^Student;
```

The ^ (caret) character is very important in this definition and it is known as the dereferencing character. You will use this character in nearly every pointer reference. One thing you must remember is that once a pointer variable has been declared it is not all-purpose; it continues the Object Pascal tradition of being strongly typed and it can only contain pointer to nodes of type student.

Creating the Dynamic Variable

The pointer has no value until a dynamic variable is placed into memory. To do that, the procedure new is used. When the following statement is executed

```
new( ptr );
```

the memory location of the student record is placed into the variable ptr. In order to reference that memory location now, all access must go through ptr. The caret moves to the other side of the expression and becomes the *referencing* character. For example, to assign a name to the dynamic variable the statement

```
ptr^.name := 'Henry Rollins';
```

would be used. This reads as "assign the value Henry Rollins to the structure pointed to by ptr."

The following program demonstrates the dynamic creation of two variables and the writing of data to them. The data is also simply retrieved and displayed.

```
program prtfile;
type
 student = record
    name   : string[20];
       testscore : integer;
  end;

var
   ptr1          :^student;
   prt2          :^student;

begin
  new( ptr1 );
  prt1^.name := 'Rachele';
  ptr1^.testscore := 99;
```

```
       new ( ptr2 );
       ptr2^.name := 'Lee';
       ptr2^.testscore := 100;

       writeln (ptr1^.name, ' ',ptr1^.testscore);
       writeln (ptr2^.name,' ', ptr2^.testscore);
   end.
```

The Linked List

The program above doesn't really give you a good idea of the use of pointers in your program since we artificially limited the number of instances by declaring two pointer variables. It is much more likely that pointers to structured data are going to be used to build dynamic collections of data in memory. The last project that we are going to build is a linked list, another of the fundamental data structures that all programmers should know. A *linked list* is a set of dynamic nodes linked to one another through the use of pointers. The list has a top and a bottom and pointer variables that point to these locations.

The first thing that must be defined is a new record structure. This new structure definition is a two-part process since a part of the record structure is going to contain a pointer.

```
type
  stptr = ^student;

  student = record
    name :string[20];
    next : stptr;
  end;
```

The first thing we need to do is define a type that points to the student record and that will be stptr. Next, define the record that will contain the data in memory. This record is composed of the student's name plus a pointer variable that will point to the next item in the list.

A singly-linked list uses at least three control pointers: one to point to the top of the list, one to point to the current record, and one that points to the previous record. We'll define these as

```
var
  top          : stptr;
  current      : stptr;
  prev         : stptr;
```

What makes the linked list structure work is the careful management of these pointers. You should be able to traverse the list from top to bottom by starting at the top pointer and following the pointer links until one is reached that equals nil.

The creation of the list begins by setting the pointer `top` to nil. This also has the effect of emptying and destroying the list since once you have lost the value of the pointer you cannot get it back. Next we begin adding records to the list. In this list, without any ordering to it, it is a chain of records. The procedure `newrecord` takes care of this:

```
procedure newrecord;
{ ------------------------------------------------ }
{ newrecord - adds a new record to the llist      }
{ ------------------------------------------------ }
var
   in_name   : string[20];

begin
   {- check to see if this is the first record -}
   if top = nil then
   begin
     new( current );
     with current^ do
     begin
       write('Enter name : ');
       readln( in_name );
       name := in_name;
     end;

     top := current;
     current^.next := nil
   end
   else
   {- not the first record -}
   begin
     next := current;
     new( current );
     with current^ do
     begin
       write('Enter name : ');
       readln( in_name );
       name := in_name;
     end;
     next^.next := current;
     current^.next := nil
   end;
end;
```

There are only two conditions that need to be handled in this list. Either the record being added is the first record, which is tested by the statement

```
if top = nil then
```

or it is an additional record being added to the end of the list. The pointer variable current points to the newly created record in both cases; once it has been created we can assign the name value to it. If this is the first record in the list we copy the value in current to top. Also very important is that the pointer in the new data structure is set to a nil pointer so that it becomes the bottom of the list as well.

If this is an additional record the fundamental processes are the same, but the management of the pointer is different. First we must place the value of the pointer current on hold before we create a new current. This is done so that the new pointer for the new structure can be passed back to the previous link in the list. Following this step is setting the new record's next pointer to nil to represent the bottom of the list.

Listing 12-2 contains the complete listing for the singly-linked list program.

Listing 12-2

```pascal
program linklist;

type
     stptr = ^student;

  Student = record
      name : string[20];
      next : stptr;
  end;

var
  top      : stptr;
  current  : stptr;
  next     : stptr;
  choice   : char;

procedure newrecord;
{ ------------------------------------------------ }
{ newrecord - adds a new record to the llist       }
{ ------------------------------------------------ }
var
  in_name    : string[20];

begin
   {- check to see if this is the first record -}
   if top = nil then
   begin
     new( current );
     with current^ do
     begin
```

```
      write('Enter name : ');
      readln( in_name );
      name := in_name;
    end;

    top := current;
    current^.next := nil
  end
  else
  {- not the first record -}
  begin
    next := current;
    new( current );
    with current^ do
    begin
      write('Enter name : ');
      readln( in_name );
      name := in_name;
    end;
    next^.next := current;
    current^.next := nil
  end;
end;

procedure list;
{ ------------------------------------------------ }
{ list - list the contents of the linked list    }
{ ------------------------------------------------ }
var
  temp     : stptr;

begin
  temp := top;
  while temp  nil do
  begin
    writeln( temp^.name );
    temp := temp^.next;
  end;
end;

begin
  { - init top of list -}
  top := nil;

  choice := ' ';
  while not (choice in ['Q','q'] )do
```

```
begin
  write('(A)dd record, (L)ist, (Q)uit ');
  readln( choice );

  case upcase(choice) of
    'A': newrecord;

    'L': list;

    'Q':

  else
    writeln('Invalid menu choice.');
  end;

end;

end.
```

There are extensive modifications that could be made to this program very easily. For one, you could insert the records in alphabetical or numerical order; aside from the additional coding it would not be very difficult to accomplish. You could also build a doubly-linked list, a list where each record points to the previous and the next record in the list. This type of list can be traversed forward and backward as necessary.

Summary

File handling is a very important addition to any piece of software. Users are going to expect that they will be able to save their work at any point during the execution of the program and that the file created will be there when they return. Text files are unstructured files that contain lines of text. These files can generally be manipulated, not only by your program but by other software as well. Object Pascal handles these sequential data stores quite easily as long as the five fundamental steps are followed consistently. These steps are number one, declare a variable of type `text` and two, assign the DOS filename to this variable. The third step is to open the file using the procedure that implements the type of access most appropriate to your task. Step four is to read from or write to the file using `read` or `readln`, or `write` or `writeln`. Step five is closing the file.

Typed files are structured files that are designed to contain either simple data types or structured data and are usually only accessible by your program. These files have random access capabilities because each of the components of the file is in a specific, numbered position within the file. Differing from the text files, these files can be opened for simultaneous read and write access. Unlike the text file which must be read from beginning to end and does not allow access to a specific point, the typed file can seek out a numbered location and move the file pointer directly to it.

A brief discussion of pointers rounded out this chapter. Pointers are a device that provides indirect access to structures that are stored in memory and are known to the program only by their memory location. Using pointers is a matter of understanding the concept of referencing and dereferencing. To demonstrate the benefits of the dynamic data structure we built a simple example of the fundamental data structure, the singly-linked list.

TEST YOUR KNOWLEDGE

1. Modify the linked list program to insert records in alphabetical order within the list.

2. Write a program that combines the linked list and the typed file. After creating a linked list in memory, give the user the option of saving the records in order to disk. Once the file has been saved to disk the user should be able to reload the linked list from this disk file.

3. Modify the program written in number 2 to allow you to manipulate the disk file. Add several records to the end of the file and then load them into a linked list in alphabetical order. Once this has been accomplished you should save the linked list back to the disk file. Print the records from the disk file. This will demonstrate a rudimentary form of sorting.

4. Modify the *Queue* program written in an earlier chapter to save the records to a disk file.

5. Modify the *Queue* program to use a dynamic data structure instead of the static definitions currently in use.

Reserved Words

Any computer language has a set of identifiers that make up the working core of the language, and Object Pascal is no exception. The following pages briefly list the reserved words for the most current implementation of the language. Because these words are a part of the syntax of the language, any attempt to redefine them or use one of them as an identifier will be greeted with an error message generated by the compiler.

In addition to the listed words, certain other identifiers will be considered reserved within the context of specific situations. `Private`, `protected`, `public`, `published`, and `automated` act as reserved words within class type declarations; in other contexts within your programs they will be considered to be directives. Special meanings are also attached to the words `at` and `on`.

Definitions

Though many of these words can be located interspersed throughout the text of the preceding chapters, definitions for all of the keywords have been included below. This will make the learning process easier since you will also be able to associate the words with those nearby.

AND

The AND reserved word is used in logical operations, both in Boolean and bitwise operations. Logical AND requires that the operands on both sides of the operator evaluate to true in order for the entire statement to evaluate to true.

```
x := 10
if (x > 1) and (x < 20) then
  writeln('Evaluates to True');
```

ARRAY

An array structure is a collection of similar data elements recognized within the program by a single identifier. It is defined through the use of the `array` keyword, as in the statement:

```
array[1..10] of integer;
```

AS

The AS operator is used as a part of a typecasting operation. The operator will return a reference to an object cast as a different class type.

ASM

ASM is the reserved word used to write inline assembler statements in some dialects of Object Pascal. The rules that apply to these statements are defined by the specific implementation.

BEGIN

The begin reserved word denotes the beginning of a code block in an Object Pascal program. Begin is matched with an offsetting end statement in the program's structure and tells the compiler to treat all of the statements surrounded by these delimiters as a compound statement. The statements themselves may be simple or other compound statements and are separated by the terminating semicolons.

```
begin
  writeln('First statement');
  writeln('Second statement');
end;
```

CASE

A CASE structure is used to provide an alternative method for performing a series of nested IF statements. The reserved word case defines the structure as follows:

```
case menuchoice of
'A':
...
'B':
...
end;
```

CLASS

The reserved word class is used in declarations of class methods. It casts the definition that follows as that type of an object within Object Pascal.

CONST

Const is used to declare an identifier as a constant.

CONSTRUCTOR

The constructor reserved word identifies a special method that is used to create and initialize objects.

DESTRUCTOR

Similar to the `constructor` keyword, the `destructor` reserved word declares a method that releases resources when an object is destroyed. When called, this method destroys the declared object and deallocates the memory used by the object.

DISPINTERFACE

Dispatch interface types define the methods and properties that an automation object implements through IDispatch.

DIV

One of the integer division operators. `Div` returns the number of times operand B goes into operand A.

```
x := 17 div 5
```

In this case `x` will have a value of three.

DO

The reserved word `do` is only used in conjunction with the loop control structures. It indicates the transition point between the control of the loop and the processing that the loop must do.

```
for x := 1 to 10 do
...

while x <= 25 do
...
```

DOWNTO

`Downto` is used only with a FOR .. DO loop to facilitate counting down the loop iterations in reverse order. Instead of incrementing the control variable, it is decremented at each iteration.

```
for x := 10 downto 1 do
...
```

ELSE

The `else` reserved word is found only as a part of an IF .. THEN control structure. The code block that follows this word is processed only if the IF .. THEN expression evaluates to false.

```
if x < 21 then
begin
  no_means_no(x);
end
else
```

```
begin
  writlen('Welcome to adulthood');
  approve_id;
end;
```

In this snippet, if the value assigned to x indicates that the patron is over 21, the x < 21 statement will evaluate to false. If an else reserved word is present in the IF .. THEN structure, processing will transfer to this block. If it is not present, processing is transferred to the statement immediately following the closing semicolon.

END

End is a very common reserved word. It denotes the end of a code block, the end of a CASE structure, the end of a record definition, or the end of unit or program.

EXCEPT

The reserved word except will be found in a TRY .. EXCEPT block. This structure is used for exception handling.

```
try
  mathematical_op(x);
except
  on EmathError do MathHandler;
end;
```

If the statement(s) following the try reserved word processes without a problem, then the statements following the except keyword are ignored. If an exception is raised by the call to mathematical_op, the exception handler is called in the except block.

EXPORTS

The exports clause lists the name and index value of the procedures or functions that are exported as a part of a DLL.

FILE

The reserved word file in Object Pascal is a data type that represents a data set stored on disk.

FINALIZATION

Finalization is a reserved word used in a unit exclusively that indicates the section of code that is processed upon termination of the unit. This is used as cleanup code to free any resources used by the unit that are no longer needed.

FINALLY

The reserved word finally is a part of the TRY .. FINALLY block. This statement is used to ensure that specific statements, namely those that follow the finally keyword, are always processed regardless of the success of the operations in the try section. A good example of this is a file resource that is opened and an operation attempted upon it. Even if the operation fails, the file resource must be released. The statement to close the file can be placed in the `finally` section, ensuring that it will get processed.

FOR

The `for` reserved word is a part of the FOR .. DO loop structure.

FUNCTION

The reserved word `function` declares the block of code that follows the identifier to be a function. A function is a programming construct that automatically returns a result value when it is executed.

```
function squared( in_num : integer ): integer;
begin
  squared := in_num * in_num;
end;
```

The Object Pascal function structure uses assignment of the result value to the identifier of the function in order to return the value. In the case of the code above, the product of the `in_num * in_num` equation is assigned to the function name `squared`. Through this portal the value is passed back to the calling statement:

```
x := squared(3);
```

GOTO

The rarely used `goto` keyword transfers processing to a label identified by the statement.

```
while x <= 100 do
begin
  writeln('Enter guess: ');
  readln(guess);

  if guess = 50 then
    goto EndProg;

end;

. . .
LABEL EndProg;
. . .
```

IF

`If` is used in the IF .. THEN control structure immediately before the evaluation expression.

IMPLEMENTATION

The reserved word `implementation` is used in a class or unit to identify the beginning of the implementation section. This section contains the definitions of any routines defined in the interface section and any private declarations used by the class or unit.

IN

`In` is a reserved word that tests for inclusion in a set.

INHERITED

The reserved word `inherited` is used to implement polymorphic behavior by calling the immediate ancestor of that method.

INITIALIZATION

The keyword `initialization` will be found in a class or unit. It defines a block of code that will be processed when the class or unit is first called. The code is used to initialize any resources needed by the object. (See finalization.)

INLINE

The reserved word `inline` (obsolete in some implementations but maintained for backward compatibility) tells the compiler that the code that follows should be processed as machine-language instructions.

INTERFACE

Used in class or unit definitions, the reserved word `interface` identifies the public data objects and routines to the caller of the class or unit. The routines declared are later defined in the implementation section.

IS

The `is` keyword is an operator that performs dynamic type checking to verify the runtime class of an object.

```
if ActiveControl is Tedit then ...
```

LABEL

See GOTO.

LIBRARY

The reserved word `library` identifies the file as a DLL. The structure of the DLL is identical to the program file with the exception that it begins with `library` instead of `program`.

MOD

Mod is an integer division operator. It returns the remainder from the division operation.

```
x := 10 mod 3;
```

This statement would result in a value of 1 being assigned to variable x.

NIL

Nil is used in comparison with a pointer to determine if the pointer contains a valid value. This value may be assigned to any pointer variable.

NOT

The reserved word NOT is an operator that reverses the result of a Boolean expression. This means that NOT true equals false.

```
x := 10;
if not (x = 10) then
  writeln('Not Ten')
else
  writeln('Ten');

The result of this snippet would be 'Ten';
```

OBJECT

An object is an instance of a class.

OF

The reserved word of is used in a couple of different places in an Object Pascal program. Its general usage is to identify the type or contents of another data object such as an array or set or in a CASE statement to identify the variable type to be compared.

OR

OR is a Boolean operator used for building compound expressions. In the case of the statement

```
if ( x < 10 ) or ( y > 20 ) then
```

if either of the two expressions evaluates to true, then the entire statement is considered to be true.

OUT

Out is a reserved word used to modify a parameter declaration. Out parameters are variable parameters where the initial value of the referenced variable is discarded by the routine it is being passed to; it is for output only. Out parameters are used frequently with distributed-object models such as COM or CORBA.

PACKED

`Packed` is a modifier that is applied when declaring a structured data type. It overrides the compiler's default practice of aligning data on word or double-word boundaries and stores it in a compressed format. This results in slower data access and possible incompatibility.

PROCEDURE

The reserved word `procedure` identifies the code block that follows as being a procedure object, a defined routine that can be called from other parts of the program.

PROGRAM

`Program` is the reserved word that identifies the code block as a program file to the compiler. It is followed by an identifier that names the program.

```
program MyProgram;
```

PROPERTY

The reserved word `property` identifies a data declaration as being a property within a class. The declaration of a property specifies a name and a data type and at least one access identifier.

```
property ColorCode: integer read Ccode;
```

The property is defined first by a valid identifier, in this case `ColorCode`, followed by its data type. Every property declaration requires a minimum of one read or write specifier. The specifier `read` is a parameterless function that will return a type of `integer`, the property's type.

RAISE

`Raise` is used to raise an exception creating an exception object. The word is followed by the identifier of the exception class and a call to its constructor.

```
raise EColorError.create;
```

This call creates an object of type `EColorError` and passes control to the error handler.

RECORD

The reserved word `record` defines a structured data type that can include multiple simple and structured data types.

```
type
  CubScout = record
    Name    : string[20];
    rank    : string[10];
    years   : integer;
  end;
```

The example defines a data object called `CubScout` that is composed of two strings and an integer. All of these elements can be referenced together as the single data type but also dereferenced to use the individual fields.

REPEAT

`Repeat` is used in the REPEAT .. UNTIL loop structure. The unique characteristic of this type of loop is that it will always be executed at least one time since the evaluation expression is not encountered until the processing reaches the bottom of the structure.

```
x := 0;
repeat
  writeln( x );
  x := x + 1;
until x > 10;
```

RESOURCESTRING

The reserved word `resourcestring` is similar to the word `const` because it defines a type of constant. Resource strings are stored as resources and then linked to an executable program. The external resource file can then be modified without recompiling the program. This is often used to provide messages to a program, sometimes in a variety of languages.

```
resourcestring
  LanguageId = 'English';
  ResourceFile = 'Engres';
  ...
```

SET

`Set` defines a set variable or data type. A set is a collection of ordinal types with no meaningful order. The `in` operator is used to test for inclusion in the set.

SHL

The reserved word `shl` shifts the bits in a byte or integer one position to the left and sets the rightmost bit to zero.

SHR

Similar to `shl`, `shr` shifts the bits in a byte or integer one position to the right and sets the leftmost bit to zero.

STRING

The reserved word `string` defines a string data type. You must verify which string type is declared by this simple declaration in the Object Pascal implementation that you are using.

THEN

Then is a part of the IF .. THEN statement. (See if.)

THREADVAR

Threadvar declares a variable that is thread-local. These are similar to global variables except that each executing thread gets its own private copy of the variable. Each of these copies is protected from the other threads. Thread-local variables are declared using threadvar instead of var.

```
threadvar x : char;
```

TO

The reserved word to is used in FOR .. DO loops to clarify whether the control variable is incremented or decremented. (See downto.)

TRY

The reserved word try is found in the code blocks TRY .. EXCEPT and TRY .. FINALLY. (See except and finally.)

TYPE

The heading type tells the compiler that user-defined data type declarations follow.

UNIT

The reserved word unit tells the compiler that the file that follows is an Object Pascal unit file.

UNTIL

Until is a part of the REPEAT .. UNTIL control structure. It defines the evaluation expression for the loop.

USES

The reserved word uses tells the compiler which external units need to be compiled into the program to provide the declarations for called functions or procedures.

```
uses
   crt, mylibrary;
```

VAR

Var defines variables or variable parameters to the program. This reserved word is followed by the variable definitions themselves.

WHILE

The reserved word `while` is a part of the WHILE .. DO loop structure. This loop's control expression is evaluated before any processing is done which could result in the statements within the loop never being executed.

```
x := 11;
while x <= 10 do
   writeln(x);
   . . .
```

In the example, when the statement x <= 10 is evaluated it returns false and skips to the next statement after the end of the loop. In this case, the end of the loop is the semicolon after the `writeln` statement.

WITH

`With` is a shorthand way of referencing the fields of a record or the properties or methods of an object. By using `with`, your program is not required to reference the fields by using dot notation.

```
var
    Cubs       : CubScout;

with Cubs do
   name   := '';
   rank   := 'Tiger';
   years := 0;
```

is the equivalent of

```
Cubs.name   := '';
Cubs.rank   := 'Tiger';
Cubs.years := 0;
```

XOR

The reserved word XOR represents the Boolean operator exclusive-or. The truth table for this expression states that either of the two sub-expressions may be true, making the entire compound statement evaluate to true. If both of the sub-expressions evaluate to true, however, the entire compound statement evaluates to false.

Index

Index

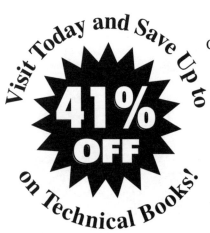

Delphi
INFORMANT MAGAZINE

GET 3 FREE ISSUES

FEATURING articles written by respected trainers, speakers, fellow professional developers, and members of the Delphi development team, the award-winning *Delphi Informant Magazine* provides the world's most extensive coverage of Delphi. Each monthly issue is packed with technical articles that will make you a more productive Delphi developer, keep you informed, and keep your skills sharp.

TRY three issues of *Delphi Informant Magazine* without obligation! If *Delphi Informant Magazine* delivers the information that helps you learn Delphi development, you can subscribe by simply paying $49.95 for 12 additional monthly issues (15 in all). Plus, you'll get a full membership to the DelphiZine.com Web site. *If for any reason you are not satisfied, simply write "cancel" on the invoice and owe nothing.* The three free issues are yours to keep.

SIGN UP TODAY!

WEB **www.DelphiZine.com/3free**
Enter Offer Code WWP301

TELEPHONE **(800) 884-6367** option 4
Mention Offer Code WWP301
Outside the US call +1 (916) 686-6610 option 4

I don't have time for learning curves.

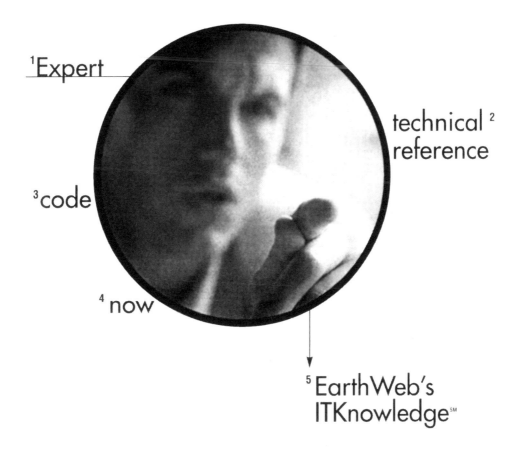

¹Expert

technical ²
reference

³code

⁴ now

⁵ EarthWeb's
ITKnowledge℠

They rely on you to be the ❶ expert on tough development challenges. There's no time for learning curves, so you go online for ❷ technical references from the experts who wrote the books. Find answers fast simply by clicking on our search engine. Access hundreds of online books, tutorials and even source ❸ code samples ❹ now. Go to ❺ EarthWeb's ITKnowledge, get immediate answers, and get down to it.

Get your FREE ITKnowledge trial subscription today at itkgo.com.
Use code number 026.

EARTHWEB
Go further *faster*

About the CD

The CD-ROM that accompanies this book contains the source files for all of the projects in each chapter, trial software provided by Greg Lief and Unlimited Intelligence Limited, and Delphi 5 Standard Edition.

Delphi 5 will auto-run when you insert the CD in your disk drive. Click on Delphi to start the setup, and follow the on-screen instructions.

Use Windows Explorer to access the Source, Uil, and Glad folders.

The source code for each chapter's projects is located in a like-numbered folder in the Source folder. You may copy all of the folders at once by dragging the entire Source folder to your hard drive or you can pick and choose which projects to work with by selecting them from their folders. Remember that all of the files on the disk will have a read-only attribute, so when you copy them you will need to turn this flag off prior to working with the source code. You are free to modify and utilize these files in any way that you find suitable.

Installation instructions for the trial run software are included in a readme.txt file found in each product folder. Greg Lief has provided trial versions of his GLAD components for both Delphi 4 and Delphi 5. Unlimited Intelligence Limited has also provided a trial version of the UIL Security System. Using the readme.txt files, locate the appropriate setup file for each product and install them using the included instructions. The vendors' URLs are also included if further support is necessary.

For more information about the CD, see the BOOK-README. txt file.

Warning:

Opening the CD package makes this book non-returnable.

CD/Source Code Usage License Agreement

Please read the following CD/Source Code usage license agreement before opening the CD and using the contents therein:

1. By opening the accompanying software package, you are indicating that you have read and agree to be bound by all terms and conditions of this CD/Source Code usage license agreement.

2. The compilation of code and utilities contained on the CD and in the book are copyrighted and protected by both U.S. copyright law and international copyright treaties, and is owned by Wordware Publishing, Inc. Individual source code, example programs, help files, freeware, shareware, utilities, and evaluation packages, including their copyrights, are owned by the respective authors.

3. No part of the enclosed CD or this book, including all source code, help files, shareware, freeware, utilities, example programs, or evaluation programs, may be made available on a public forum (such as a World Wide Web page, FTP site, bulletin board, or Internet news group) without the express written permission of Wordware Publishing, Inc. or the author of the respective source code, help files, shareware, freeware, utilities, example programs, or evaluation programs.

4. You may not decompile, reverse engineer, disassemble, create a derivative work, or otherwise use the enclosed programs, help files, freeware, shareware, utilities, or evaluation programs except as stated in this agreement.

5. The software, contained on the CD and/or as source code in this book, is sold without warranty of any kind. Wordware Publishing, Inc. and the authors specifically disclaim all other warranties, express or implied, including but not limited to implied warranties of merchantability and fitness for a particular purpose with respect to defects in the disk, the program, source code, sample files, help files, freeware, shareware, utilities, and evaluation programs contained therein, and/or the techniques described in the book and implemented in the example programs. In no event shall Wordware Publishing, Inc., its dealers, its distributors, or the authors be liable or held responsible for any loss of profit or any other alleged or actual private or commercial damage, including but not limited to special, incidental, consequential, or other damages.

6. One (1) copy of the CD or any source code therein may be created for backup purposes. The CD and all accompanying source code, sample files, help files, freeware, shareware, utilities, and evaluation programs may be copied to your hard drive. With the exception of freeware and shareware programs, at no time can any part of the contents of this CD reside on more than one computer at one time. The contents of the CD can be copied to another computer, as long as the contents of the CD contained on the original computer are deleted.

7. You may not include any part of the CD contents, including all source code, example programs, shareware, freeware, help files, utilities, or evaluation programs in any compilation of source code, utilities, help files, example programs, freeware, shareware, or evaluation programs on any media, including but not limited to CD, disk, or Internet distribution, without the express written permission of Wordware Publishing, Inc. or the owner of the individual source code, utilities, help files, example programs, freeware, shareware, or evaluation programs.

8. You may use the source code, techniques, and example programs in your own commercial or private applications unless otherwise noted by additional usage agreements as found on the CD.